Text Knowledge and Object Knowledge

COMMUNICATION IN ARTIFICIAL INTELLIGENCE SERIES

Artificial Intelligence (AI) is a central aspect of Fifth Generation computing, and it is now increasingly recognized that a particularly important element of AI is communication. This series addresses current issues, emphasizing generation as well as comprehension in the AI communication. It covers communication of three types: at the human–computer interface; in computer–computer communication that simulates human interaction; and in the use of computers for machine translation to assist human–human communication. The series also gives a place to research that extends beyond language to consider other systems of communication that humans employ such as pointing, and even in due course, facial expression, body posture, etc.

Communication in Artificial Intelligence Series Editors:
Robin P. Fawcett, Computational Linguistics Unit, University of Wales College of Cardiff
Erich H. Steiner, IAI EUROTRA-D and University of the Saarland

From Syntax to Semantics: Insights from Machine Translation, eds: Erich Steiner, Paul Schmidt and Cornelia Zelinsky-Wibbelt

Advances in Natural Language Generation: An Interdisciplinary Perspective, 2 volumes, eds: Michael Zock and Gerard Sabah

Text Generation and Systemic-Functional Linguistics: Experiences from English and Japanese, Christian M.I.M. Matthiessen and John A. Bateman

Expressibility and the Problem of Efficient Text Planning, Marie W. Meteer

Linguistics Issues in Machine Translation, ed.: Frank Van Eynde

New Concepts in Natural Language Generation: Planning, Realization and Systems, eds: Helmut Horacek and Michael Zock.

User Modelling in Text Generation, Cecile L. Paris

Text Knowledge and Object Knowledge, Annely Rothkegel

Text Knowledge and Object Knowledge

Annely Rothkegel

Pinter Publishers, London and New York

*Distributed in the United States and Canada
by St. Martin's Press*

Pinter Publishers Ltd
25 Floral Street, Covent Garden, London WC2E 9DS, United Kingdom

First published in 1993

Distributed exclusively in the USA and Canada by St. Martin's Press, Inc., Room 400, 175 Fifth Avenue, New York, NY 10010, USA

Annely Rothkegel is hereby identified as the author of this work as provided under Section 77 of the Copyright, Designs and Patents Act, 1988.

British Library Cataloguing in Publication Data
A CIP catalogue record for this book is available from the British Library

ISBN 0 86187 136 7

Library of Congress Cataloging in Publication Data
Rothkegel, Annely.
    Text knowledge and object knowledge / Annely Rothkegel.
       p.   cm. — (Communication in artificial intelligence series)
    Includes bibliographical references and index.
    ISBN 0–86187–136–7
    1. Knowledge representation (Information theory) 2. Computational linguistics. I. Title II. Series: Communication in artificial intelligence.
    Q387.R68   1993
    006.3'5—dc20   92–44023
                                                                                    CIP

Translation by Janet Wheeler
Graphics by Monika Weissgerber

Typeset by Koinonia Limited
Printed and bound in Great Britain by Biddles Ltd., Guildford and King's Lynn

Contents

1. Introduction   1
    1.1 Assumptions   1
    1.2 Procedure and goal   3
    1.3 Sections   4
    1.4 The organisation of the book   6

2. What is meant by text knowledge?   8
    2.1 Definition   8
    2.2 Text production   11
    2.3 Text topic (text semantics)   14
    2.4 Text function (text pragmatics)   20
    2.5 Text connectivity (text syntax)   25
    2.6 Properties of the text type   29
       2.6.1 Book announcements as a text type   29
       2.6.2 Orientation towards the goal structure   31
       2.6.3 Empirical basis   32
    2.7 Principles of computational modelling   33

3. Text generation   35
    3.1 Definition   35
    3.2 Object knowledge, linguistic knowledge, text knowledge   37
    3.3 Static and dynamic aspects   40
    3.4 Text structure and processes of choice   42
    3.5 Rhetorical structures   43
       3.5.1 Schema and hierarchy   43
       3.5.2 Text structure as schema   44
       3.5.3 Hierarchical text structure   45
    3.6 Text planning in machine translation   47
    3.7 Text structure as structure of action   48
    3.8 Summary   49

4. Text actions   52
   4.0 Introduction   52
   4.1 Intention and change of context   53
   4.2 Text actions and text production   58
   4.3 Structure and process of text production   59
   4.4 Internal structure of text actions   62
       4.4.1 The ILL component (illocution)   62
       4.4.2 The PRO component (propositional content)   66
       4.4.3 The LOC component (locution)   67
   4.5 Complex text actions   67
   4.6 Text action schema (TAS)   69

5. Text grammar I: Selections   71
   5.0 Overview   71
   5.1 Units of the object construction   72
       5.1.1 Semantic representations   72
       5.1.2 Schema knowledge and reference frame   75
       5.1.3 Object model   80
       5.1.4 Thematic text questions   85
       5.1.5 Text role configurations (TROC)   87
   5.2 Interactional knowledge   92
       5.2.1 Interaction model   92
       5.2.2 DESCRIBING   96
       5.2.3 ASSERTING   101
       5.2.4 EVALUATING   103
       5.2.5 Clusters of predicates (CLUST)   106
   5.3 Text grammar and lexicalisation   107

6. Text grammar II.1: Principles of composition   111
   6.0 Overview   111
   6.1 Principles of sequencing   112
       6.1.1 Coherence formation and expansions   112
       6.1.2 Local coherence relations   114
       6.1.3 Global coherence relations   117
       6.1.4 Expansions of ILL and PRO   118
   6.2 Directionality as a dynamic principle of text forming   120
   6.3 Text connectivity patterns   124
       6.3.1 The concept of connectivity   124
       6.3.2 Representation of connectivity   126
       6.3.3 Connectivity scope   130
       6.3.4 Connectivity markers   130
   6.4 Strategies of composition   131

7. Text grammar II.2: Sequencing operations 136
  7.0 Overview 136
  7.1. Operation: FRAMING 137
      7.1.1 Framing conditions 137
      7.1.2 Framing of illocutions (EX-FRAM/ILL) 137
      7.1.3 Framing of thematic structure (EX-FRAM/THEM) 140
  7.2 Operation: CHAINING 142
      7.2.1 Chaining conditions 142
      7.2.2 Chaining through enumeration 143
      7.2.3 Chaining through domain-specific enumeration 144
      7.2.4 Chaining through position indication 145
  7.3 Operation: PAIRING 147
      7.3.1 Pairing conditions 147
      7.3.2 Operation: COPYING 148
      7.3.3 Operation: SPECIFYING 150
      7.3.4 Operation: ALTERNATING 154
  7.4 Series of PAIRINGs 155
  7.5 Connectivity forms (CONFO) 157
      7.5.1 General remarks 157
      7.5.2 CONFO: EX-ILL/FRAM 161
      7.5.3 CONFO: EX-THEM/FRAM 162
      7.5.4 CONFO: EX-THEM/CHAIN 162
      7.5.5 CONFO: EX-THEM/PAIR 163
      7.5.6 CONFOs and text action grammar 164

8. Integrated view of the text grammar 165
  8.1 The idea of text grammar 165
  8.2 Design of text production 167
      8.2.1 The several components 167
      8.2.2 A two-way model: text grammar and text space 167
      8.2.3 Construing the text row (TR) 169
      8.2.4 Construing the text list (TL) 170
  8.3 Summary 170

References 174

Index 192

1 Introduction

1.1 Assumptions

When we produce a text, we employ a certain knowledge about what a text is. The question is, how can this knowledge be described and reconstructed in a computational model.

The writing of texts belongs to the cultural skills that on the one hand have developed within the social context, and on the other are tied up with cognitive preconditions for linguistic processes. The present study is an attempt to relate the two within the framework of 'social cognition' (Winograd & Flores 1986). In this sense, the question *What does a program do?* or *How does it do it?* is replaced by *What do we do with the computer?* Central to this is an interpretation of language in which the action character is in the foreground. 'Language is a form of human social action directed towards the reaction of what Maturna calls "mutual orientation". This orientation is not grounded in a correspondence between language and the world, but exists as a consensual domain – as interlinked patterns of activity. The shift from language as description to language as action is the basis of speech act theory, which emphasizes the act of language rather than its representational role' (Winograd & Flores, 1986, p. 76). The approach presented here points out consequences that result from such an understanding of language for the development of a computational model of text production. In concrete terms, this concerns the representation of conditions of written text production which play a role in the conveying of information through the medium text. We are concerned in particular with linguistic techniques of the presentation of an object, especially with the presentation of new books as communicative objects. Book announcements, as offered by publishing houses and magazines, are the text type chosen to illustrate this.

Text as a medium implies on the one hand communicative standards, on the other hand standards of linearisation. Correspondingly, the development of a text syntax which takes account of the pragmatic conditions of the medium is in the foreground. We believe that a pragmatic perspective most readily corresponds to the real situation of conveying information through texts. Text writers do something when they impart information. They do it in a communicative context, i.e. related to readers, standards of knowledge about objects and evaluation norms, as well as standards of textual presentation forms that are applicable for certain communicative situations and certain social groups. They do it equally within the conditions of a cognitive apparatus. In our model, we consider the relations mentioned above with respect to this apparatus. For this, we shall assume the following:

• Conveying information about an object is to be understood as a symbolic construction of this object. This construction first and foremost serves the orientation of the communication partners. This means, for example, that a book announcement is not merely concerned with a presentation of what is authentically to be found in the respective book. What is important is an organisation of information in the sense of an object construction. This determines what the new book is regarded as and can be integrated in various presentation modes. That means that apart from principles of the object construction, principles of the presentation must also be taken into account. We consider the former within the framework of a text-thematic structuring, the latter as an interactional structure in which the object is considered as the object of a specified interaction. Both are combined in the concept of text action. In this context, we restrict ourselves to text actions of describing, evaluating and asserting.

• Text production is understood as a communicative event and can be described as a 'constructive action' with the object construction as goal. This concerns constructions on the part of the writers, which provide the point of departure for object constructions by the readers. Although in this analysis only the first group is discussed, text readers are implicitly integrated in the model. This is apparent from the fact that text production is seen interactively as an answer (reaction) to questions (text questions). In addition, there are expectations with respect to structural norms according to which the conveying of information takes place and which are reflected in a linguistically describable text structure. We proceed from the assumption that the connectivity structure in the text reflects such expectation structures.

• The computational modelling is a suitable instrument for the presentation of text production processes in the above sense. It permits the formal representation of defined relations with regard to selection and composition processes in the construction of texts.

1.2 Procedure and goal

The goal of this study is the development of a theory of text writing in which strategies of structure formation in the text are in the foreground. The assumption is that text structure formation can be explained by means of two simple formal principles. Text is understood as an independent linguistic form, which is explained as the result of two opposing strategies. Under consideration are 'higher-level' processes at the text topic and text function level. They are combined with formal sequencing strategies. In this way they can be described as global 'left–right' and local 'right–left' directed strategies, which control the development of the text topic and text function in the linearisation and which are reflected in the linguistically manifested connectivity structure of the text.

In order to represent these strategies, the concept of the text action as a text-producing action is introduced. As representation forms text action schemata are developed, which provide the link between the overall text structure and the sentence level. The assumptions on text production in the sense of the establishment of a text structure are re-examined by attempting to reconstruct corresponding text actions on the basis of analyses of available authentic texts. With respect to a machine-aided system for text production, their modelling is to be seen as a specific methodical access, which on the one hand opens up a superordinated frame, on the other hand, by virtue of this frame and the limits inherent in the method, is restricted. What is required of the modelling is that it should deal with 'higher-level' phenomena of the communicative context in the text and at the same time permit links to semantic-syntactic sentence representations. In the present text production model an attempt is made at an integrating approach, which is grounded in text linguistic findings and computational models of text generation. The questions considered are to be seen within the framework of

- a linguistic-conceptual modelling of text production on a linguistic-action-theoretical basis as a description and
- a computational linguistic modelling with formal methods of representation.

It is the goal of this study to develop a framework for the integrated examination of text production phenomena. It should be sufficiently general to take into consideration as many areas of application for text production as possible. It should also be sufficiently open to allow further processes, such as revision processes in text writing, to be integrated. On the other hand, it should be sufficiently specific to take account of the linguis-

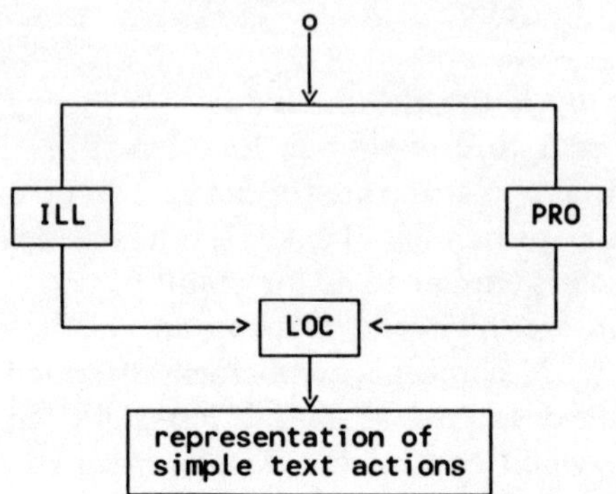

Figure 1.1 Correlation of selection components

tic aspects that are relevant for the textual conveying of information. It should also be possible to consider texts in their entirety as structures.

1.3 Sections

Text knowledge is understood in a dynamic sense. At the focus of attention are processes of selection and composition. It is intended to formulate them as a grammar and thus make them accessible for processing in a program system for text production. Selection refers to the choice of the text-building units, composition concerns their sequencing according to text-oriented patterns.

As text-building units we consider the three components of the linguistic action:

* illocution (ILL)
* propositional content (PRO) and
* the linguistic means, which we subsume under locution (LOC).

The illocution indicates the presentation mode for contents. The propositional content represents the object construction and is in this sense determined by the domain and the text topic. The domain is understood as a reference frame, the text topic as text-thematic question. The locution, finally, indicates possibilities for linguistic realisation.

The idea is that the combination of ILL and PRO determines lexical preferences, which can be listed in inventories. In this way, the process of lexicalisation can be reconstructed on the basis of text-related constraints of ILL and PRO. We restrict ourselves to the definition of inventories of text-related verbal expressions, in particular collocations (verb-noun-

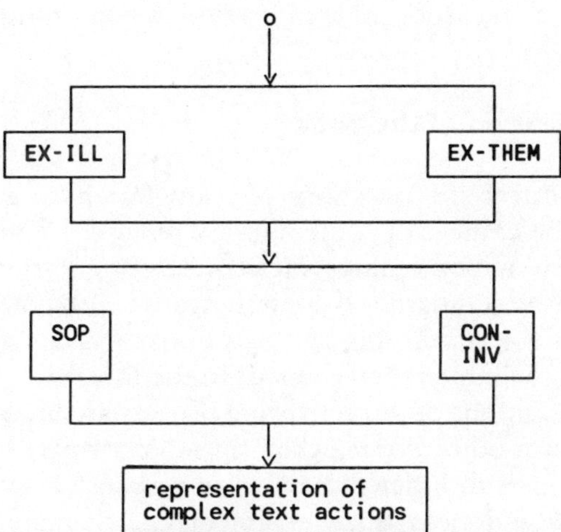

Figure 1.2 Correlation of composition components

preferences). Selection is in this context modelled in the form of relating the components of simple text actions to one another (see Figure 1.1).

Text composition is concerned with the sequencing of simple text actions according to specific sequencing strategies. The combination of four components results in the structure of complex text actions:

- expansions of the illocutions (EX-ILL)
- expansions of the thematic-propositional component (EX-THEM)
- sequencing operations (SOP)
- connectivity inventories (CON-INV)

The expansion of illocutions corresponds to the development of the presentation mode, e.g. in descriptive, narrative or even in an argumentative manner. The thematic development is to be seen as a linking of propositions which give answers to the thematic question. The sequencing operations organise the illocutionary and thematic development according to formal principles of text organisation. As the three fundamental operation types we consider FRAMING, CHAINING and PAIRING. The application of different sequencing strategies is reflected in the connectivity structure in the text. Connectivity inventories in turn contain lexical preferences with respect to the type of the respective attachment. The three components of the linguistic action schema ILL, PRO and LOC find their correspondence in the complex structure as follows: EX-ILL is the complex form of ILL, EX-THEM corresponds to PRO and the combination of SOP and CON-INV is analogous to LOC. Figure 1.2 shows the sections that cover the aspect of composition in text production.

1.4 The organisation of the book

Chapter 2 introduces the questions relevant for the present model and places them in the context of contemporary research. The point of departure for the determination of linguistically relevant questions is a genuinely occurring, relatively standardised communicative situation, in which information about an object – in this case new books – is conveyed. Topic and communication goal are predetermined. In the foreground is the question as to how the conditions of the conveying process are linked to the linguistic conditions, or in other words, what must a text writer know about text-organising principles in order to be able to verbalise a specific content in text form in a situation-adequate manner. The thematic subject of text producing is developed on the basis of task-orientation; the theoretical access and principles of computational modelling are founded on this.

With reference to the questions developed in Chapter 2, Chapter 3 outlines important contemporary models of automatic text generation. This problem-oriented overview is intended to highlight similarities and differences to the present approach.

Chapter 4 is concerned with the concept of text actions (TA). It forms the basic unit for the text representation. The chapter discusses fundamental aspects of the concept of actions. The internal structure of text actions, as well as their epistemic-cognitive interpretation, form the basis for the definition and operationalisation of the illocution component. In accordance with the communicative task, we distinguish three text action types (DESCRIBING, EVALUATING, ASSERTING) that form complex text actions and are thus a suitable instrument for representing the text structure.

Chapter 5 deals with the conditions that are linked to the individual propositions. Here object and interactional knowledge of writer and reader within the framework of a communication-specific domain modelling play a role. The first section concentrates on the conception of an appropriate reference frame for the object class, its substantiation and its structural organisation as a basis for the organisation of a thematic structure in the text. A domain-specific object model (for the object book) is developed, which is related to a topic-structuring text question. The second section is concerned with the interactional component, in which the contribution that the illocutions make to lexicalisation is considered.

In Chapter 6 the theoretical basis for the representation of composition processes is developed. The emphasis is on principles of sequencing, which are defined with respect to content and form. Apart from the establishing of coherence, both globality and locality, as well as directionality and connectivity play a role. All of these aspects are integrated in the schema of the complex text action.

Chapter 7 applies the parameters developed in Chapter 6 to the decomposition of text examples. In an empirical analysis, the operability of this set of text-grammatical instruments is demonstrated. The sequencing types FRAMING, CHAINING and PAIRING are considered. This is followed by a suggestion for operationalisation, for which sub-sections of the text representation are isolated in the form of connectivity forms. This kind of division allows meaningful text relations within an assumed text space to be processed.

Chapter 8 summarises the possibilities offered by the developed text action grammar with respect to a computer system for text production. Of prime importance for this is the question of the consistency of the model. This is ensured because the concept of text action presents a homogeneous instrument for description that takes account of all the data processed in the system. Furthermore, the operational character of this instrument provides the possibility to develop (or further develop) a design in which the writing activities of system and writer can be synchronised. In conclusion, reference is made to the theoretical innovations that make it possible to bridge the gap between the concept of text-pragmatic action and computational modelling. This concerns above all the representation of higher-level processes of text production, with which socially determined linguistic actions are incorporated in a cognitively determined paradigm of symbolic processing. Furthermore, it also concerns the methodical contribution made towards the investigation of the still largely unresearched phenomenon of the sequence structure of texts.

2 What is meant by text knowledge?

2.1 Definition

Before moving on to discuss the main issues, we will outline the overall framework in which our modelling of text production is to be seen. This first of all concerns defining the text phenomena studied as well as the process-oriented approach taken. The overall view is subsumed under the concept of text knowledge (Keseling 1979, Sandig 1987, Koch 1991). Text knowledge is required for the description of text-producing processes. The concept of text knowledge points to two aspects:

- knowledge as an organised structure
- text structure as an autonomous linguistic structure.

As an organisation structure for text knowledge, we will develop a text action grammar in which simple and complex text actions are represented. The content of these representations is developed systematically. In this context a text structure will be regarded as an independent formal structure which goes beyond relating individual sentences to each other. Of interest to us is the global text structure and its implications for the sentence level. This perspective differs from approaches in which grammatical phenomena are related to contextual features. We will compare this kind of 'bottom-up' approach with our 'top-down' approach. This by no means implies 'communication-oriented' vs. 'transphrastic' (cf. difference in Kallmeyer et al., 1986, p. 221), since systemic grammar, for instance, postulates a communication-oriented, if bottom-up-oriented approach (cf. Halliday 1985, Halliday & Hasan 1976, Benson & Greaves 1985, Steiner & Veltman (eds) 1988). The 'top-down' approach aims at a consideration of the overall structure of the text. Similar global interpretations have been pursued in approaches such as Schmidt 1973, Petöfi (ed.) 1979, van Dijk 1980a, 1981, van Dijk & Kintsch 1983, de Beaugrande &

Dressler 1981, Kallmeyer et al. 1986.

The overall structure of the text also plays a role when the text is interpreted as the result of spoken actions. As a consequence, the description of the text structure is equated with the description of an action structure (cf. Hartung 1981, Sandig 1986, 1987, Gülich 1988, Motsch & Viehweger 1981, Motsch (ed.) 1986, Brandt et al. 1983, Brandt & Rosengren 1991a, 1991b). In the following, we are interested in those linguistic actions that realise a text structure. In this context, linguistic actions will be considered as text-constituting or text-producing actions. The text structure forms a kind of framework that supports selected information about an object (states of affairs, events, etc.). Insofar as the text structure represents a communicative structure, 'textualising' means 'making information available on a communicative level' by embedding it in an interaction between W (text writer) and R (text reader) and conditional upon this, realising it by linguistic means. In this sense, text knowledge represents an interface between object knowledge (knowledge of the world) and linguistic knowledge (Rothkegel 1989a). It connects object structurings with regard to communicative goals to linguistic structures of lexis and syntax. This connection is made in the text. In this respect, the text structure is assigned an independent status, the medium written text is regarded as a specific organisation form for the conveying of information. In the present study, we would like to examine what specific structuring possibilities the text offers and how these affect the choice of linguistic means. The theoretical basis for this will be provided by a text-related linguistic action theory. Of primary concern here is the structure formation in the text.

For our approach we will orient ourselves towards the three fundamental semiotic dimensions: reference to the world (text semantics), interactional reference (person reference, text pragmatics) and the innate structure of the text (text syntax). The reference to the world here is text-oriented. That means, it refers to the way in which an object is constructed in the text, not to the relation between words or sentences and reality. We describe the reference to the world as a relation between a knowledge base and text-thematic units. This concerns a structure of recurring text roles, which determine the predicate-argument structure of the individual propositions (see under section 2.3 Text topic). The interactional reference has to do with the embedding of information in communicative goals which link W (text writer) and R (text reader). It governs to a large extent the choice of lexical means (see below section 2.4 Text function). As the innate structure of the text we refer mainly to principles of successiveness, which express themselves in a linguistically marked connectivity structure (see below section 2.5 Text connection).

The theory of a text structure has a bearing above all on written functional texts (texts for everyday use). Here without doubt there are standards that are determined by standards for communicative purposes, thematic discussions as well as linguistic-textual organisation structures. Such standards by no means exclude flexibility in the actual realisations. Text grammars should therefore take both the standards and the organisational scope into consideration. Differences between spoken and written language have already been studied from a number of angles (Biber 1988, Chafe 1985, Vachek 1989). Brown & Yule (1984, p. 13) highlight the visual field of written language as compared to the acoustic field of spoken language. This, for example, has an effect on formal characteristics such as parallel structures in the text (cf. Lang 1987; on the issue of standard forming cf. also Ehlich 1989). Tannen (1986a) points out the stronger emphasis on lexical means for establishing coherence in written texts. This point will be discussed in sections 5.2 and 5.3.

We are aiming at an integrative method, in which the text-internal structure of the text organisation is related to the text-external structuring of states of affairs and interaction. As opposed to words or sentences, texts are genuinely characterised by a fixed context reference. This may already be determined by the choice of the text type. In the case of book announcement texts this is certainly true. The topic and communicative task are fixed. They can be roughly described as the conveying of information about a new object in the object class of books.

The central question arises from the assumption that the 'conveying of information' and 'generating a corresponding text' is not described in isolation, but can also be presented from a joint perspective of goal definition and realisation. For this we adopt two types of strategy: communicative and compositional strategies.

Communicative strategies refer to the development of a hierarchically determined content and interactional structure, compositional strategies are concerned with sequencing and establish a corresponding connectivity structure. The question arises as to how far these two strategies can be combined in one standard model. We are of the opinion that a speech-act-based model for text-producing processes can take account of both types of strategy.

Depending on the task, the reference to the world, person reference (interaction) and text reference can be combined within the framework of an action context. This is characterised as the conveying of information about an object via the medium 'written text' (see above). As an instrument for this kind of relation the text action is introduced as a production action. This permits text production to be described as a process in which a text structure is built up on the content, functional and linguistic level.

The regularities to be observed in this context are to be formulated in a corresponding text action grammar.

In our approach we proceed from the hypothesis that the linguistic realisation of text actions manifests itself in connectivity schemata. Connectivity schemata reflect the connection of textual units on the basis of complex text actions. We presuppose that the text structure is reflected in the transitions between the sections of the text and becomes clear in the form of limitation markers. Connectivity as a linking relation refers to both binary connections (two textual units) and sequence links (several textual units in a sequence). The markers can be lexical (e.g. collocation chains, enumeration adjectives, etc.) and/or syntactic (through connectors and/or position markers).

2.2 Text production

In the past few years, questions pertaining to text production have acquired increasing significance. This can be seen in interdisciplinary reviews (Antos & Krings (eds) 1989, Krings & Antos (eds) 1992) as well as in systematic-critical discussions of basic hypotheses (de Beaugrande 1984, 1989). In the field of text linguistics, previous approaches have discussed text understanding and text production as fundamental language-oriented questions (van Dijk 1980a, van Dijk & Kintsch 1983, Scherner 1984). Within the framework of computational linguistic and AI-oriented approaches, the first collections dealing with text processing in the sense of text analysis and text generation appeared around the beginning of the 1980s (Allén (ed.) 1982, Lehnert & Ringle (eds) 1982, Bara & Guida (eds) 1984). A systematic study of principles in the analysis and generation of texts in this context is given by von Hahn (1990). In the early discussions, the main focus was on the area of text understanding (Metzing (ed.) 1980, Joshi et al. (eds) 1981, Rollinger (ed.) 1984c, Rickheit & Strohner (eds) 1985, Brady & Berwick (eds) 1986, Herzog & Rollinger (eds) 1991). Only recently have problems concerning text generation aroused greater interest (Kempen (ed.) 1987, McDonald & Bolc (eds) 1988, Zock & Sabah (eds) 1988, Dale et al. (eds) 1990, Paris et al. (eds) 1991). From this it becomes apparent to just what extent theoretical prerequisites and goals differ and that a profile of questions is only now emerging.

In our model, the action-theory-based approach determines the understanding of the way in which text production is seen and what we can expect as output. Text production is understood here as the setting up of a text representation in the form of connectivity patterns within which the text units (e.g. propositions) are organised. Connectivity patterns give the type, sequence and connective relation of text units. Formally, this is a structured list with open propositions as basic units (in the sense of van Dijk, 1980b, p. 36). This forms the precondition for sentence formation. The generation of sentences will not be discussed here. For this, reference should be made to already existing sentence grammars and sentence generators. On the generation of sentences cf. a.o. Jacobs (PHRED 1985, KING 1987), as a link between the conceptual level and language surface, Danlos (1987), with respect to specific grammatical formalisms (Joshi 1987), Busemann (1988), De Smedt (1990), van Noord (1990), Uszkoreit (1991), Sigurd (1991), McKeown & Elhadad (1991). The PENMAN system (Mann & Thompson 1987) is grounded in a systemic grammar (NIGEL, Mann 1985).

The modelling of text production as the forming of structures on the basis of communicative and compositional strategies singles out certain focal points that differ from other modellings. We distinguish three lines of approach: text production as

- anticipation of text understanding
- translation of ideas into sentences
- establishing a text structure.

One of the lines of contemporary research considers text production as an anticipation of text understanding. The idea behind this is that when writing texts the writer assumes the role of reader. Writing constraints are determined by comprehension constraints. The approaches are logical-semantically-oriented or schema-oriented. Examples of logical-semantic modellings are a.o. LILOG (Bollinger et al. 1990, Geurts (ed.) 1991) and in the conceptions of LOKI (Binot et al. 1988). Schema-oriented approaches can be found a.o. in SEMTEX (Rösner 1987) and in Tonfoni (1990). As in the case of text understanding, implicit knowledge forms the basis for the process, and thus for the treatment of phenomena such as anaphora and ellipses. Considerable space is dedicated to inference processes (cf. 'reasoning' in Hobbs et al. 1987, 1988, Rickheit & Strohner (eds) 1985). Global connections are dealt with above all in the schema-oriented approaches. Here the emphasis is on phenomena relating to connectivity. The underlying text theories are as a rule derived from text understanding theories, which received attention in research earlier than text production theories (see collections above). The principal problems of text understanding lie in the area of identification of referents and the disambiguation of ambiguous lexemes. Reversing the methods developed for this to suit the purposes of text production is not without problems. They are in no way adequate for establishing a text structure, since text production is concerned with the verbalisation of explicit and not implicit knowledge.

A further basic concept is the understanding of text production as a translation. Cognitive contents are textually organised and brought into a lexical-grammatical form. This notion is to be found in AI-approaches with reference to expert systems (see below), in cognitive writing research (Flower & Hayes 1980, Nystrand (ed.) 1982) and finally also some approaches to machine translation (Defrise & Nirenburg 1990, Kittredge et al. 1991; cf. also Rothkegel 1986a, 1986b). What is meant by 'translation' is that a content structure can already be presupposed, which is then translated into a text form.

Text production within the framework of expert systems or text generation – as it is usually called – is motivated by the goal of generating responses in a question–answer system in the form of interconnected sentences (a.o. McKeown (TEXT, 1985), Paris & McKeown (RE-SEARCHER, 1987), Novak (NAOS, 1987), Reithinger (POPEL, 1991), Wahlster et al. (WIP, 1989), Horacek (WISBER, 1990)). In the 'translation' approach, a definite conceptual structure of the contents to be verbalised is presupposed. This structure is as a rule determined by the content structure of what is considered to be a predetermined knowledge base.

Our approach assumes that a new content structure is established that derives its terms of reference from conventional standards. Whilst the understanding approach is oriented towards problems of identification (e.g. ambiguous units and references) and interpretation (e.g. coherence relations), and these aspects are also in the foreground in the treatment of text production (creating explicit references, e.g. in anaphoric relations), and the translation approach concentrates on problems of 'coding' (surface-language possibilities for concepts), the problems in the case of the interpretation of text production as the establishing of a new structure primarily concern selection and composition. Hence de Beaugrande (1984, p. 36) also characterises text production as a system of 'selections'. The aspect of composition refers to such facets of text understanding that interpret comprehension not only as possibilities of inference, but as the establishing of a mental structure (e.g. in the sense of mental models (Johnson-Laird 1983) in Schnotz (1988)). This is concerned with the production of text representations that describe the coherence of the text (e.g. in networks such as in de Beaugrande & Dressler 1981, Hauenschild 1984, Vater 1992). In this sense, composition has to do with the construction of a text representation, for which – not a text and a knowledge base are necessary as in the case of text understanding – but a text planning component.

Text planning is a complex topic (for the overall plan of text production from the psycholinguistic point of view cf. Zammuner 1988; for the planning of action aspects Antos 1984, in the computational view Cohen & Perrault 1979, Appelt 1985; for text planning in text generation systems cf. above all Chapter 3). For such a text planning component we develop a grammar as a text action grammar (in Chapters 5, 6, and 7), which is founded on specific text production strategies. They are described as communicative (thematic-functional) and compositional (sequence-dependent) text production strategies. We place the emphasis on two dimensions:

- text levels, divided into:
  - a thematic text level
  - an interactional (functional) text level
  - a linguistic-formal text level (connectivity structure)
- principles, which are considered on the following axes:
  - structure and strategy
  - result orientation and development orientation
  - global and local references
  - hierarchies and sequences

2.3 Text topic
(reference to the world, text semantics)

The text content constitutes the text (= texts for everyday use). It stands in relation to text-external states of affairs, based on which the text – generally – is produced, and which are of interest to the readers. The linguistic organisation form, which makes a purposeful presentation of the content possible, does not interest the 'normal reader'. This constitutes the subject of text-linguistic studies. This distinction, which Noël (1990) points out with reference to the linguistic interest in text coherence, characterises the relation between the structure of states of affairs and text structure.

The predetermined coherence at the level of states of affairs may be used by the writer for the forming of structures on the text level. However, in this case, too, selections and decisions with respect to the order and types of connection are also made, for which the states of affairs context has no terms of reference, or which are not primarily employed by the writer of the text. Thus van Dijk (1980b, p. 36) generally distinguishes two possibilities for producing coherence:

- The coherence in the text is accounted for by the coherence at the level of states of affairs. It can be determined physically, logically-conceptually or conventionally. Physically and conceptually-based relations above all establish a connection between individual sentences (e.g. substantiations, explanations, causal and temporal sequences; cf. taxonomy in de Beaugrande & Dressler 1981). In contrast, conventional relations, e.g. on the basis of object, event and action schemata, also include whole texts.

• The coherence is accounted for by principles of text organisation. With respect to text content, these may be principles of text topic organisation.

Since for our goal text principles are in the foreground, we shall restrict ourselves primarily to text thematic constraints. These are to determine the way in which the semantic relations between topic and the level of states of affairs are defined. Before outlining the questions that arise in this context, we will attempt to distinguish the approach taken here from other methods. In the following, we will observe possible content structurings in relation to factual structurings and topic definitions (see overview of the concept of topic in Lötscher 1987). Roughly speaking, three main lines of approach can be recognised: structuring of the text content with respect to reference, inference and constituency.

Reference-oriented approaches aim at the identification of the thematised objects within the reference structure of the text. The recurrent reference to units (total or partial co-reference) forms a red thread which may run through the entire text (a.o. Fox 1987). In this context, studies of anaphoric and cataphoric relations in which co-reference constraints are used for the identification of the respective reference unit also play a role.

Inference-oriented approaches concentrate on contents that are inferrable on the basis of the text together with the knowledge of the communication participants. In the text generation system PAULINE (Hovy, 1988, p. 39), for example, inference rules are applied for the calculation of numeric values. These rules permit alternative linguistic realisations conditional upon a parameter labelled 'interest of the addressees'. If interest is assumed, then the exact values are given.

Constituency-oriented approaches have to do with text composition. Here, text grammar criteria are in the foreground. Our model fits into this category.

Structures of states of affairs in computational linguistics and AI have been modelled above all from the point of view of semantic knowledge and domain knowledge. In this context, knowledge about objects or states of affairs/events (world knowledge) is assumed to be mutual (or partially mutual) knowledge of the communication partners. The content in the text or sentence is determined by the content of the knowledge base.

Semantic knowledge and domain knowledge can be modelled separately (e.g. in KLEIST, Meier et al. 1988) or – as in the approach of 'naive semantics' (Dahlgren 1988, Palmer 1990) – treated as equivalent. A separation of both types of knowledge makes use of properties of word meanings that can be determined independently of a domain. However, this necessitates an explicit combination of both knowledge modules. Treating them as equivalent facilitates the process of inference and the assignment of linguistic units, requires, on the other hand, re-formulations of the overall knowledge for each new domain that is dealt with.

The topic in these approaches is in general sentence topic. This applies likewise to text representations in which the concepts (or lexemes) appearing in the text are linked together in a semantic network (cf. systems such as CONTRA (Hauenschild 1984), TOPIC (Kuhlen 1984, Reimer & Hahn 1990); also text-linguistic approaches such as de Beaugrande & Dressler 1981). 'Topic' is understood in a lexical-conceptual manner and finally means 'frequently recurring sentence topic', which is linguistically realised in nominal groups. The main problem is that of identification. In this context it is taken as true (has the truth value true), if an object or event can be identified in the referential network of a knowledge base or in a 'world model' (e.g. in discourse representation theory applied to temporal relations in Kamp & Rohrer 1983, to events with text deictic proforms such as *this, that, it* in Bäuerle 1988).

Even in dynamic approaches (principles in Viehweger 1987), which discuss the distribution of text information, a sentence-oriented concept of topic predominates. Respective classifications have been discussed under labels such as 'topic – comment', or theme – rheme' (Hajičová & Sgall 1988, Hajičová 1991) or 'focusing and defocusing' (Kallmeyer 1978, Erdmann 1990).

Operationalisations as focus mechanisms as developed for computational modelling (cf. Sidner 1986, Grosz & Sidner 1986, McKeown 1985), are concerned with operations which, however, only refer to one focus of the sentence. The focus as the centre of attention (generally realised as the subject) is either maintained in the sentence sequence (realised by pronominalisation) or shifted (realised by definite or indefinite nominal phrases; on the production of definite or indefinite nominal phrases see Dale (EPICURE system, 1990)). In this case, a unit from the preceding sentence or a unit from a sentence further back can become the focus. There is a certain amount of confusion with respect to the terminology. In an attempt at clarification, Hajičová (1986) pointed out that the psychologically determined 'focus' corresponds to the linguistically determined 'topic'. This means that what is highlighted as the focus of attention corresponds precisely to that part of the sentence which is considered as 'known' or already introduced, whereas the important (new) information is in the 'linguistic' focus or 'rheme', but not in the 'psychological' focus.

The dynamic consideration of the sequence of thematic elements has also been extended to the overall structure of the text. One example for this is the subdivision into text structure types known under the concept of 'thematic progression', which are distinguished according to hierarchically structured possibilities for the progression of thematic units (Daneš 1974a). This approach as well as studies concerning 'information flow' (in Chafe 1987) or the switch from foreground to background (Tomlin (ed.) 1987b) are interesting in our context in as far as larger text units are considered as units for the structuring of the text. For the structural organisation of a book announcement text, for example, it would be of little use to take the reference object book and observe the distribution of its occurrence in the text or determine its role in the generation. It would simply be established that 'book' occurs frequently with its corresponding pronominalised form. Such a method makes no contribution to text constituency in the sense of object construction. This requires the possibility to relate larger units to each other. The concept of text topic can serve us well here.

The relevance of the text topic and its distinction from the sentence topic was pointed out at a relatively early stage (Agricola 1976, Bayer 1980, Brinker 1980, Fries 1981). Brown & Yule (1984, p. 71) make a clear distinction between 'sentence topic' and 'discourse topic'. The treatment of the text topic presupposes that more complex units are taken into account. Although we intend to consider larger text units as the object of the description, nevertheless two requirements should be capable of being satisfied simultaneously:

- the relation to the sentence should be guaranteed and
- the relation to the overall text should be ascertainable.

These possibilities are, for example, given in a macrostructural approach. In this approach global structures of the text content are considered, which allow a hierarchically ordered structure of the overall text and at the same time reach back to the sentence level. Macrostructures in the sense of van Dijk are in addition topic structures (van Dijk 1980a, 1980b). Topic is understood here as a condensed form of propositionally represented content that is produced through macrorules (cf. on 'condensing' of the topic Greimas (1971, p. 65), Agricola (1979); the concept of condensing can also be found in computational modellings, e.g. TOPIC (Reimer & Hahn 1987)). What we adopt from this approach is not the notion of topic (cf. below topic as an expectation structure), but the formal structure of the propositional description, which on the one hand permits the description of individual sentences, and on the other of hierarchies and sequences in the text (for this see also Metzeltin & Jaksche 1983, Brinker 1992).

In our approach, factual structurings also play a role from the point of view of domain knowledge. At the same time, this view is conducive to macrostructural organisations of the text topic and a propositional representation in the form of predicates and text roles. These are the preconditions for a treatment of topic in which the newly established coherence of information in the text is in the foreground. The interest in coherence and the connectivity structure related to it aims at the modelling of relations which typify this new context. For this, a general form must be found which characterises the new context established in the text. Topic in this sense therefore does not refer to knowledge that is assumed (presuppositions), not to knowledge that is retrieved from a data base, not to the identification of reference, not to frequency and not to the shift or continuity of a sentence topic. Topic here means structure of a content coherence that is produced in the text and that manifests itself in the connectivity structure with its lexical-grammatical implications.

Aspects of this kind are best grasped in an understanding of topic as text question (Lötscher, 1987, pp. 135f). Considering the topic on the basis of a text question implies a dialogic-communicative basis for the thematic structuring of the text. A dialogic orientation seems to be adequate especially for informative texts, in which according to anticipated expectations (questions) a specific object is presented in the form of a response text. Corresponding to certain standards, expectations exist with respect to relevant information that is anticipated during the writing of the text (Rothkegel 1991b). This is interesting from a text-theoretical point of view in cases where text questions can be formulated in such a way that they also act as terms of reference for the structural organisation of the new coherence of information. The question approach is therefore especially suited for such texts that are characterised by a text topic in the sense of the establishing of a new coherence, i.e. whose text structure goes beyond an associative lining up of sentences. Questions as a thematic means of structuring also characterise the quaestio approach as pursued by Klein & von Stutterheim (1991), von Stutterheim (1992). This is concerned with the experimental examination of linguistic means of object description (e.g. 'how to put together an object x?') for the selection and sequencing of content units. It is considered a criterion for the use of specific means of reference and connectivity.

So how can the text question be formulated for our text type, book announcement? In order to decide this, we need two kinds of criteria. On the one hand the domain plays a role, on the other hand standards of object presentation specific to this text type. Questions concerning the domain have among other things been discussed in text-related computational modellings, in which the text is to solve a specific problem. This is the case, for example, with respect to the modelling of cooking instructions (cf. AUTOKOCH system in Koch 1988, 1991), of error messages for engines (cf. PROTEUS system in Grishman 1990), route descriptions (cf. the construction of a model town as 'mental map' in KLEIST (Meier et al. 1988), for a pulley domain in Palmer (1990)). Essential for domains is a situation-dependent structuring of objects (states of affairs, events, etc.), which are represented in formal models (e.g. 'feature types' and 'kind types' in Dahlgren (1988, pp. 98f.), 'types of entities' in Palmer (1990, p. 72), 'object classes' and 'verb classes' in Koch 1991)).

With respect to the modellings, two aspects can be distinguished: formal and content. Whereas the latter are considered an empirical problem, the former are assigned to theoretical questions. All the same, in our opinion the respective kind of knowledge on the basis of which a formal model is developed also plays a role. In this connection, accesses can be differentiated according to whether they refer to 'intuitive' (personal) knowledge of the model developer (e.g. Dahlgren 1988, Palmer 1990), to selective experiments (Meier et al. 1988, Klein & von Stutterheim 1991) or to text material (Koch 1991, Grishman 1990, Kittredge et al. 1991). The latter also applies for our approach. In task-oriented texts, such as book announcements, the new coherence of information to be established is related to such domain structurings. They form the actual reference frame (cf. also reference spaces in Grimes 1982), within which thematically relevant specifications are possible. In this respect there is, therefore, a close link between domain structuring and the thematical text question. Seen theoretically, the domain opens up the thematic frame and the text question restricts it again through the concretisation of certain aspects. Just what the domain and the text question actually look like is an empirical problem. For this reason, we analysed approximately 100 authentic book announcement texts and picked out one striking frequently occurring constellation for an exemplary demonstration. A central point here is the action perspective in which the individual object of the object class of book is presented. Similar procedures are known for text types such as route descriptions, which pursue the perspective of an 'imaginary pedestrian' (see above KLEIST) or for that of a 'vision tour' (von Stutterheim 1992).

The object book is a communicative object that originates and is operative in a communicative action context. It is presented as if it does, has done or will do something. The action is attributed to the book itself, the author or the reader. The action context relevant for books forms the basis both for the modelling of the domain as well as for the formulation of the thematic text question. Like this, the text topic and its sequential expansion can be specified with regard to the communicative task. These expansions are the object of text grammar rules, which produce the text-thematic structure.

Three focus points emerge for the concretisation:

- How is the domain structured as a reference frame?
  What problems result from the type of object and the type of target text?
  What does an object model 'book' that is suitable for the task of book announcements look like?
  To what extent does the frame theory propose a suitable basis for the development of an object model? (see section 5.1).

- How is the reference frame related to the thematic text question or its expansion?
  How does this relation affect the semantic structure of the sentences (predicate–argument structure)?
  Can a text-oriented structure of recurrent argument roles be produced in this way?
  What role does a thus derived semantic role structure play for lexicalisation?
  Are there specific criteria for the selection of verbs (which are not recorded in reference-oriented approaches)? (see section 5.2).

- In what way can text sequencing be presented on the basis of the expansion of the text question?
  What correlations are there with the interactional component?
  What are the combined effects with the text-specific linearisation strategies? (see Chapters 6 and 7).

2.4 Text function
(interactional relations, text pragmatics)

We consider the conveying of information in a real communication situation as being dialogically determined on the one hand, and interactionally determined on the other.

'Dialogic' is related to information and refers to the question–answer-connection. It is characterised by an expectation structure in the form of the text question. Its expansion characterises the text topic and its development in the text. The strategies operative here contribute to the object construction.

'Interactional' is related to persons and means distinctions with respect to the degree of involvement of the respective persons in the process of conveying information. This concerns W (text writer) and R (text reader). The strategies operative here contribute to the object presentation. We deal with three types of relation that occur frequently in book announcement texts and with which prototype structure formations can be presented.

(a) Object reference: the factual reference dominates; structures are formed by combining segments from the object model.
Example:

> *This book examines the adaptive Boundary Element Method for applications to 2-D elastostatics. The author first examines several problems using a commercial BEM package to compare it with the Finite Element Method. Next the adaptive BEM is developed to obtain accurate and reliable solutions.. . . Finally an adaptive strategy using p and h versions is proposed.*

(b) Writer reference: the impact of the information on W is dominant; structures are formed by combining segments from the object model with evaluative norms.
Example:

> *This is a fairly documented and coolly argued book whose moral stance and human warnings deserve the widest and most careful reading.*

(c) Reader reference: the impact of the information on R is dominant; structures are formed by combining segments from the object model with *PRO* or *CONTRA* convictions which provoke R into a reaction.
Example:

> *The subject-matter of the present monograph is paradigmatic structure, a not very 'à la mode' topic. This study takes the view that this neglect of the relationships between elements in absentia is highly unfortunate as far as word-structure is concerned. For, it claims that among morphological theories only those are fit to uncover the principles underlying . . . in which the paradigmatic dimension of word-structure is assigned a central position.*

This differentiation corresponds to the three sign functions introduced in Bühler's theory on language (1982 (1934)). They have become fundamental for functional text theories and have had a decisive impact on the discussion of text types (cf. Gülich & Raible 1977, Dimter 1981). The Bühler sign functions representation, expression and appeal have a correspondence in our model to object reference, writer reference and reader reference. We distinguish accordingly the text actions DESCRIBING,

EVALUATING and ASSERTING, whereby the latter is restricted to an argumentative text structure.

Our model proceeds from an action-oriented approach in which the text is considered as the result of linguistic actions. This raises the question as to what paradigm is best suited to the description of text production processes from a linguistic viewpoint. An action-oriented conception of language was reflected early on in systemic grammar (Halliday & Hasan 1976). In the 'systems' which provide alternative possibilities for realising grammatical phenomena, among other things parameters are used that characterise the respective context. This approach proceeds from the grammatical phenomena and relates them to superordinated action contexts (bottom-up approach). One example is the THEME system, which proceeds from argument roles (in the sense of case roles). This deals with the embedding of a message in the linguistic context and at the same time with the text constitution (cf. discussion in Lux, 1981, pp. 80ff.). Our approach is a top-down approach, which proceeds from a superordinated action context from which the descriptive units for grammatical phenomena are derived.

Action theories, which proceed from a general action model and have become relevant for linguistic contexts, are above all the psychologically developed activity theory (Wygotski 1972 (1934), Leont'ev 1971, Leont'ev et al. 1984), and the language-philosophically-developed speech act theory (Austin 1962, Searle 1969 (1971)). In addition to these, sociological theories (e.g. Garfinkel 1967) and action logics (e.g. von Wright 1968, 1977) also have an influence.

The consideration of language use in the sense of actions goes back to Wygotski (1972), who was the first to proceed from sign actions. These actions are classified under the central concept of activity, by means of which communicative and non-communicative utterances are psychologically examined. According to this, language use primarily has to do with processes of establishing meaning and not with formal structures. This assumption has also been elaborated in particular by A.A. Leont'ev (1971) with respect to its consequences for a linguistic theory and in this form has become the basis for unilingual studies. On these lines, respective 'communication processes' such as describing, reporting, reasoning, arguing, etc. (Schmidt (ed.) 1981, Michel (ed.) 1985) have been classified for the German language. Communication processes are specified by functional-communicative properties. These are oriented towards the two fundamental features of structurality and puposefulness, which define the concept of activity (Leont'ev, 1971, p. 31). The former refers respectively to parameters of the objects or events involved, the latter to context information. The feature description is suited to differentiating and typologising communication processes. However, an integration of this description in a text-related representation of sentences is not possible. The possiblity to represent specific structures such as hierarchies and sequences, which are necessary for the description of the text structure, is also lacking. The speech-act-theory approach – with relevant modifications – seems to be better suited for this.

Speech act theory is first and foremost also concerned with isolated single actions. Nevertheless, this approach, to which we refer with respect to the theoretical definition of the concept of text action, is interesting for our purposes for two reasons:

(a) With the isolation of the components of illocution as the action aspect, propositional content as the content aspect and locution as the form of expression, it offers the possibility of relating them to one another explicitly and definitely. Unlike, for example, in AI-oriented treatments of speech acts (Cohen & Perrault 1979, Ellman 1983), where the formal relation between content (proposition) and speaker/hearer-reference (illocution) are in the foreground, we are interested in the specific linguistic components, which is how we interpret the locution. The relating of all three components opens the possibility to combine action aspects and aspects of lexical selection. In this context we can profit from the fact that illocution is a suitable parameter for language use. In other words, linguistic realisations are distinguished according to whether they are descriptions, evaluations or assertions.

(b) The introduction of complex linguistic actions with the same internal structure as in (a), but with additional relations with respect to hierarchical and sequential orders permits a pragmatically-oriented description of the overall text structure.

The examination of complex speech acts has been promoted first of all within the framework of dialogue research (Kallmeyer (ed.) 1986, Hundsnurscher & Weigand (eds) 1986, 1989, Stati et al. (eds) 1991) and with a computer-oriented approach within the precincts of dialogue system developments (Metzing (ed.) 1981, von Hahn et al. 1980, Hoeppner & Morik 1983, Horacek 1990, Sitter & Stein 1990) or in modellings of communicative acts (Wachtel 1986, Airenti et al. 1984). Whereas the latter paid particular attention to sequencing (a question is followed by an answer, an answer by an enquiry, etc.), the former attempt to develop their own internal systematisation of linguistic actions in hierarchies and sequences (Wunderlich 1981, Franke 1983, Viehweger 1983). Of interest to us are such approaches which study hierarchical and sequential structures in written texts. In this context above all two description approaches play a role: text structures in the form of action patterns or action schemata (Zillig 1980, Gülich & Kotschi 1986, Gülich 1988, Sandig 1987) and text structures in the form of text illocution structures (Brandt et al. 1983, Brandt & Rosengren 1991a, 1991b, Viehweger 1991; cf. also Rothkegel 1984a, 1986c). In this context, there are two problems to be solved:

(i) Classifications within hierarchies and sequences require separate criteria. This question seems to us to be theoretically open (on the discussion of speech act classifications cf. Ballmer & Brennenstuhl 1981). It will also remain open in our approach. This is acceptable insofar as we are not concerned with classificatory or prototypical definitions of text actions. We simply distinguish the three sign-functional variants for the presentation of contents in the sense of Bühler (see above). Text actions are differentiated correspondingly as simple text actions (DESCRIBING, EVALUATING, ASSERTING), which are combined in complex text actions in order to ascertain the hierarchical and sequential structure of the overall text. From this, questions arise

- with respect to the internal structure of the simple text action and
- with respect to the structure of complex text actions in hierarchies and sequences.

(ii) The second point concerns the relation between action aspect and content aspect. This relation is also a topic that has been researched in the relevant literature. In Sandig (1987) the action structure is considered as a 'supporting structure for the content', in Brandt & Rosengren (1991b) content and text illocution are characterised as 'two sides of a coin'. Lötscher (1987) develops a systematic differentiation of topic concepts with the help of this relation. In rhetorical approaches, proceeding from the PENMAN system (Mann & Thompson 1987), which have recently been discussed increasingly within the framework of computer-oriented text generation systems, this relation also plays a role. Rhetorical approaches of this kind are distinguished by the fact that addressee-related description categories are made the basis for the text structure description. Asymmetrical relations between two text segments (nucleus–satellite relation) such as 'elaboration', 'enablement' as content-oriented relations on the one hand, and 'motivation', 'purpose', 'effect' as function-oriented relations on the other (Matthiessen & Thompson 1989) serve here as basic elements for the building of the overall text structure. These approaches, in which content and functional aspects are mixed, stand in contrast to semantic approaches (e.g. McKeown 1985), which refer solely to the content, and to pragmatic approaches (e.g. Hovy 1988, Defrise & Nirenburg 1990), which with individual pragmatic or rhetorical parameters organise the selection of linguistic alternatives for similar contents.

We argue in favour of a methodical separation of content and action aspects, which is predetermined in the structure of the speech act through the differentiation between illocution and propositional content. According to this, text function is to be analysed and described independently of the content aspects. Whereas the thematic aspect determines the role structure, the functional aspect governs the selection of linguistic means which realise the role structure. Structure from the functional point of view ensues as a result of the distinction between dominant and subsidiary functions of illocutions. With respect to the overall text, the respective dominant illocution determines the interaction type of the overall text and thus the type of sequencing. This in turn has an influence on the connectivity structure of the text. Corresponding to the expansion of the topic at the content text level, we can describe the functional text level as an expansion of the interaction type. Within the view chosen here, the following questions arise:

- What role does the interaction type play for the global structure of the text?
- What relations exist between the expansion of thematic text question and the expansion of the interaction type?
- How can the lexical selection be modelled on the basis of the interaction type?

2.5 Text connectivity
(text syntax)

One of the essential principles of text composition is the linking of text segments. We assume that structured texts display a specific connectivity structure. This is determined by the text principle of sequentiality and reflects global and local strategies of linearisation. Before taking a closer look at this, we should clarify what connectivity means with respect to the text structure.

Connection runs complementary to reference. Both are dominant principles of text formation (Kallmeyer et al. 1986). Whereas reference aims at text relations which characterise the relation of linguistic utterances to text-external objects or states of affairs, connectivity aims at relations between text segments and is specific for the text. Connections are produced in order to combine what is explicitly expressed in the text. Implicit connections, e.g. on the basis of context, can be used for this, but are of secondary importance. Structure of the states of affairs and structure of the text are thus not the same thing. A coherence is not produced as a duplicate of the coherence of the states of affairs, but rather as a result of 'what we say about them' (van Dijk, 1980b, p. 31).

Connectivity in the text belongs to the text constitutional features and has thus become the object of widely differing research approaches (cf. collections such as Petöfi & Sözer (eds) 1983, Heydrich & Petöfi (eds) 1986, Petöfi (ed.) 1988, Heydrich et al. (eds) 1989, Conte et al. (eds) 1989; on individual connectors cf. Abraham (ed.) 1991, especially for English Warner 1985). We can distinguish two procedures. In the one, the grammatical phenomena of subordination and coordination of sentences are re-examined from the point of view of their contribution to a superordinated text structure (Harweg 1988, Rudolph 1988, Haiman & Thompson (eds) 1989). This takes place, for example, within the framework of a rhetorical approach (e.g. in Thompson 1987, Matthiessen & Thompson 1989) or also with respect to underlying knowledge orientations (Meyer 1989, Tonfoni 1990, Fauconnier 1990). The other line of research proceeds from superordinated text or interactional structures and considers the connectivity of text units as a manifestation of these structures. This can refer to content text structures in the sense of a text grammar (van Dijk 1977a, Bajziková 1984, Biasci 1986), to structural signals that form or separate units in the text (Gülich 1970) or to indicators for speaker or hearer-oriented strategies, which are examined as 'discourse markers' (Levinson 1987 (1983), Schiffrin 1987, Fraser 1990, Redeker 1990, 1991) or as illocution markers (Roulet 1984, Lundquist 1989). In the field of text generation, processes of linking sentences or propositions (Danlos 1987, Brée & Smit 1986) and processes of selecting connectors (McKeown & Elhadad 1991) are above all of interest.

The dominant basis for the connection is generally considered to be the coherence in the text. Under the concept of 'coherence relation' quite different phenomena come together: anaphora, rhetorical relations, text thematically and/or text functionally determined relations, inferrential relations, relations based on the structure of the thematised states of affairs (cf. also Noël 1990). What is decisive in this context is a view that proceeds from the establishing of coherence as such and incorporates everything that constitutes a coherence in the text. Connectivity is, however, not to be equated with coherence (as in Samet & Schank 1984). Like Komlósi (1989) we distinguish coherence as implicit and interpretation-bound (dependent on person) and connectivity as explicit and conventionally or systematically coded relations (text-bound).

In our approach, we are interested in such connections that make it possible to recognise the successive organisation of the thematic-functional text structure in the linearisation. We consider the ensuing connectivity structure as a trace that makes certain linearisation processes in the text production visible. It is represented as series of propositions in the form of predicate-role-strucures.

Connectivity as it is understood here is based on two types of linearisation strategy which differ in perspective:

- 'left–right' and
- 'right–left'.

'Left–right' strategies are global. They refer to the whole text (or longer passages). The connectivity structure is formed by frames and chains, which link several propositions together. Similar global strategies aim at text features such as completion and delimitation. There is a result structure, which is recognisable as an overall structure and shows fixed positions such as beginning, middle and end.

'Right–left' strategies are local. They refer to neighbouring relations between propositions. Pair relations emerge as connectivity structures. They correspond to sequential relations between preceding and subsequent unit. Local strategies aim at the text feature of recurrence. They characterise a development of the information structure in the text, which can be described as a repetition of the same or contrast with the other (as compared to the preceding unit). This view differs from 'topic–focus' sequencings (Hajičová & Sgall 1988), in which content weighting leads to particular word orders, but also from focus mechanisms (McKeown 1985), in which one and the same concept can be in focus or not in focus. In our approach the repetition or contrast refers to text-related concept classes such as text roles. What is meant is that the role fillers attach to the preceding element in such a way that they either repeat or change the text role.

The connectivity model developed here is based on the application of both types of strategy as regards the expansion of the thematic text questions and the interaction type. From this, the following questions arise:

• It must first be clarified how linearisation is to be understood, temporally and/or spatially and what consequences this has (de Beaugrande 1984, Fleischman 1991).

• In addition, it must be examined in what way interaction type and text questions correlate with global and local strategies. Global expansions of the interaction type lead to different connection patterns, which determine the style of the object presentation. We show this with the help of examples of descriptive and argumentative presentations. The formalising of global strategies is here oriented towards schema-based approaches, without, however, adopting the description instruments (cf. systems such as SEMTEX (Rösner 1987), TEXT (McKeown 1985)). Local expansions

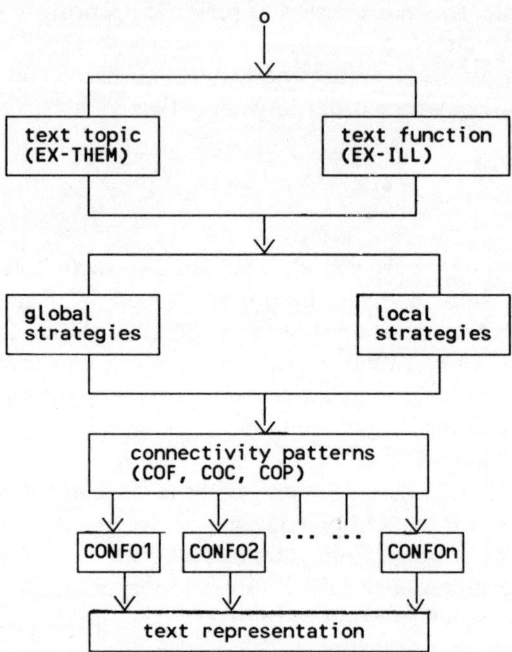

Figure 2.1 Correlation of internal components of text production

are structured in a binary manner and are similar to connection models organised on a binary basis (e.g. on a rhetorical basis the PENMAN system, Mann & Thompson (1987), on a frame basis Tonfoni (1990)).

• Finally the question arises as to the text grammar description. Here it is to be shown that different types of connectivity schemata can be included: connectivity frames (COF), connectivity chains (COC) and connectivity pairs (COP). Connectivity frames originate at the interactional level in the global sequence. Connectivity chains belong to the thematic level and are also determined globally. Connectivity pairs are determined locally and also characterise thematic relations. COF, COC and COP are formally represented as integrated parts of the text action description (for a graph-theoretical representation of connectivity cf. Grize 1989). They form the basis for the establishing of connectivity forms (CONFO) which represent the sequential structure of a text. The development of text syntactic connectivity forms with a global basic structure constitutes an approach that is complementary to local processes of 'right attachment' (Polyani 1988, Scha & Polyani 1988) and the principle of 'right frontier' (Webber 1989), which model the 'growth' of the text to the right – corresponding to the direction of writing (cf. also 'growing points' in Hovy

1991). Whereas that approach discusses the formal principle of the material lengthening of the text, we are concerned with structural principles of content-functional processes, which manifest themselves in the type of connection. Figure 2.1 gives an overview of the correlation of the questions.

2.6 Properties of the text type

2.6.1 Book announcements as a text type

The communicative integration of texts is the object of functional text or grammar theories. Research with respect to systematic differentiations, such as text classes, text types or registers (Dimter 1981, Lux 1981) is still incomplete. Nevertheless, at least two principal lines of research can be followed:

• The British register linguistics with early roots in the 1930s, which principally through Halliday became well known worldwide (cf. overview in Lux 1981);

• The Continental text pragmatic line of text linguistics since the 1970s (cf. van Dijk 1972, Gülich & Raible 1977, Heinemann & Viehweger 1991; cf. also the publications of the Lund Symposia 'Language and Pragmatics', edited by Rosengren (1981, 1983, 1984, 1986; continued in S&P reports, Lund)).

In both lines of research, the text is seen in a communicative context. With respect to text types, an attempt is made to classify texts according to text-external and/or text-internal factors.

Register linguistics concentrates grammatical phenomena which are associated with these contextual factors. This approach was strongly motivated by foreign language teaching, and thus helped the development of functional grammars. This is apparent in the systemic-functional grammar, which among other things is also a basis for a number of computational modellings (cf. the NIGEL grammar of the PENMAN system in Mann 1985, further Davey 1979, Patten 1988, Steiner & Veltman (eds) 1988, Steiner 1991, Matthiessen & Bateman 1992). The text pragmatic approaches are on the other hand characterised by language-philosophical, language-psychological or sociological research (from the point of view of sign theory in Bühler (1982), action logics in von Wright 1968, language philosophy in speech act theory (Austin 1962 (1975), Searle 1969 (1971)), sociology (ethnomethodology) in conversation analysis (Garfinkel 1967)).

What all approaches have in common is the principle that classifications are determined by text-external factors. To this extent, text types can be defined as sub-types of interaction types or communication types, whereby interaction types or communication types are in turn considered as being determined by certain speech acts or communication acts (Gvenzadse 1983, Isenberg 1984, Kallmeyer (ed.) 1986, Gülich 1986, Franke 1987). This approach contrasts with 'sublanguage' models (Kittredge & Lehrberger (eds) 1982, Grishman & Nhan 1984), which are defined text-internally, e.g. through the frequency of the occurrence of lexical or syntactic units.

The text types dealt with in text generation processes relate for the most part to descriptions. Here both stative objects and dynamic changes in the object play a role. However, the dynamism in the text is determined exclusively by the content of the text and not the text form and its progressive development as such. The following list shows certain preferences for descriptions:

- of objects:
  TEXT (ships; McKeown 1985);
- of functions of objects:
  RESEARCHER (loudspeakers; Paris & McKeown 1987);
  PROTEUS (engines; Grishman 1990);
  WIP (coffee machine; Wahlster et al. 1989);
- of events and/or actions:
  NAOS (mobile objects; Novak 1987);
  EPICURE (cooking instructions; Dale 1990);
  AUTOKOCH (cooking instructions; Koch 1991);
  KLEIST (route descriptions; Rickheit (ed.) 1991);
  SEMTEX (newspaper reports; Rösner 1987).

Book announcements are also concerned with an object, the object book. Why are book announcements as a text type of interest for our analysis? There are two reasons: the question of object knowledge and the aspect of two action levels.

We are concerned with object descriptions, whereby in this case the object is in turn a text. We speak here of communicative objects. Here, additional aspects are referred to in comparison with descriptions of physical objects, which are at the focus of attention in current text generation systems. This requires fundamental consideration with respect to the structuring of the object knowledge used in the text. Objects are often described as 'object in action'. This also applies to the communicative object book. At the content level the actions or interactions of the author of the book or the book itself are concerned. This action level is the object of the thematic-propositional description. This is assigned a language action

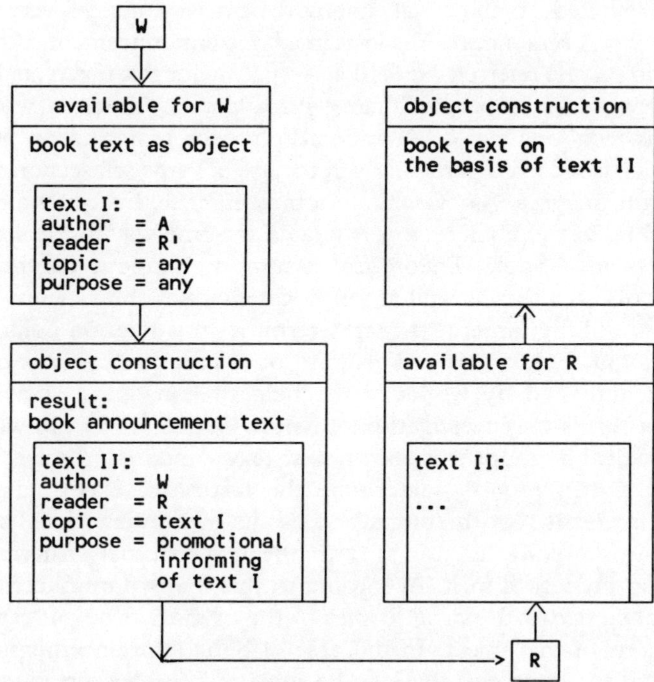

Figure 2.2 Relation between W, R, book text, and book announcement text

level, on which the writers of the text do something (text action level), i.e. describe, assert or evaluate. This action level is the object of the description of illocutions (see Figure 2.2).

2.6.2 *Orientation towards the goal structure*

As mentioned above, in the case of book announcements we have a situation where in two respects we are dealing with 'text'. On the content level: the object of the topic is a text, the book text. On the linguistic action level: the topic is embedded in an action schema and realised through connectivity patterns. The relation between object and book announcement text is outlined in Figure 2.2.

The participants in the communicative situation include the author of the new book, his/her potential readers (R'), the writer of the book announcement text and his/her potential readers (R), whereby R and R' at least form a sub-set. W's activities of conveying information are related to defined purposes and a fixed topic. The topic in this context encompasses all elements that are assigned to the book text. Further, W must also observe a restricted length (usually not more than 10 sentences, very often not more than 2 or 3 sentences). The lexis in a book announcement text is – with the exception of the referred expressions – specific for this text type. It reflects the fact that we are concerned here with a kind of 'reported writing' (cf. 'reported speech' in Ducrot 1984; cf. also 'speech reproduction' in Gülich 1978), which is reflected particularly in the use of verbs (cf. section 5.2).

We might imagine that a book announcement text is quasi a summary or an abstract of the book text or is related in some way to the source text of the respective book. Theoretical assumptions about communicative properties of text types as well as empirical analyses show clearly that it is the structure of the target text that determines this relation (Zillig 1982b, Wiegand 1983, Fluck 1988). This kind of orientation towards the target text is strengthened by works in the field of knowledge sociology. An example of this is the investigation of Knorr-Cetina (1986), in which with anthropological methods it is shown how text standards in scientific laboratories (e.g. test reports) determine the respective experiments themselves. This means that the target text has its own interactional structure, which only indirectly has to do with the text-external structure of the information processed in it. According to this, book announcement texts are not concerned with partial copies of the original text, but rather, new constructions of the object. In the case of book announcements, we can observe that the strategies that can be subsumed under various text types occur here equally. There are descriptions, reports, criticisms, which are realised in a descriptive, narrative or argumentative form. This can be interpreted in such a way that different strategies of communicative language use are used on principle for the promotional presentation of an object within the same text type.

2.6.3 *Empirical basis*

The basis for the construction of the production process in the model are text decompositions of prespecified (authentic) texts. The development of a theory is empirically integrated through reconstruction of the text structure in the data. These come from English book announcement texts (for the examination of German texts cf. Rothkegel 1991a). For the most part these are texts from publishing announcements from Cambridge University Press (Cambridge) and from 'Newsletter' published by Springer (Berlin). The text action-oriented approach itself is not text type-specific. Apart from book announcements as object descriptions, respective analyses have also been carried out for international agreements as regulatory texts (Rothkegel 1984a, 1986a), for instructive texts (Rothkegel 1986c) and for argumentative dialogue texts (Rothkegel 1988).

2.7 Principles of computational modelling

The modelling of a linguistic task with respect to a computer program is considered to be a methodical aid. The computational modelling characterises a possible kind of access to the solving of linguistic problems. This postulates a view according to which the following three dimensions characterise a text linguistic computational modelling: description, representation and construction.

The interpretation of the problem and task determines the choice of the method of description. Description refers to the designation of data from a selected object field according to the principles of a linguistic theory. In our model this concerns the speech-act-theoretical understanding of text actions as the module for the formation of structure in the text. They are modelled within the cognitive framework of the paradigm of information processing and provide the data structures that are required for purposes of representation and construction in the computational modelling.

The concept of representation originates in the field of cognitive psychology and refers there to internal processes of information processing in living beings. There is the hypothesis that the notion of 'environment' is represented in the memory and that these internal representations are relevant for the behaviour of individuals. This is the subject of theoretical models which are concerned with rule-derived operating with symbols, whereby specific representation systems are developed as a medium (e.g. 'mental symbols' in the sense of Johnson-Laird (1983)). The concept of information processing with the two related aspects of process and structure has been taken up in linguistics as a theoretical-methodical access to problems of language description (e.g. Bierwisch 1982, Ballmer & Wildgen (eds) 1987, Schnelle & Rickheit (eds) 1988, Schwarz 1992). In computational linguistics, possibilities for description which are oriented towards methods of information processing have become central. Here, formal representations produce a kind of interface between the presentation of the theoretical approach and the possibilities for implementation.

Construction means two things: modularity and functionality. The questions considered are to be seen within the framework of a system which in its single parts is oriented towards a coherence of these single parts among each other (modularity). From the point of view of text generation in particular, this is an important point, since here – as opposed to text analyses – a higher degree of complexity has to be considered (Koch, 1991, p. 6). Whereas with respect to problems of understanding or analysis individual phenomena can be treated in isolation, since a text is available as data input, this is not possible in the case of text generation. If here anything approaching even a simple structure is to be produced, then from the outset several partial components must be oriented towards each other. The difference can perhaps be characterised thus: in analysis we work in a structure, in generation a structure is worked out. The second point concerns the functionality of a system. The parts assembled here should at the same time in their coherence fulfil a task outside the system. This implies defining the parts of a system with regard to the envisaged task.

Computational modelling takes account of the process-orientation of the text knowledge in a specific manner. Metzing (1988) gives a differentiated systematic grid on the basis of the concepts structure, procedure and process on the one hand, specific research strategies on the other hand and selected object fields. They characterise types of linguistic theory and their relation to computational modellings. According to this, our approach could be classified as 'linguistic structure analysis related to process analysis' (Metzing, 1988, pp. 68f.).

In cognitive paradigms of information processing it is possible to model the process character of linguistic actions in the form of (programmable) instructions. This takes place above all through the development of representations for structures and processes, which document the constraints, process and result of the structure formation in the text. This approach follows a cognitive view of communicative actions, which is gaining in importance (Dahlgren 1985, Sperber & Wilson 1986, Dietrich & Graumann (eds) 1989, Kasher (ed.) 1989). In computational linguistics and AI this development is programmatically reflected in the term of 'social cognition' (Winograd & Flores 1986).

With respect to computational modelling, we develop a representation schemata for simple and complex text actions, which correspond to predicate-logical notations and which are formalised as list structures. In this context we proceed from the assumption that list structures are adequate for the representation of the sequence structure of texts and thus take account of the linguistic states of affairs. We also satisfy the requirement of choosing a method of presentation that is as uncomplicated as possible, and that is also relatively easy to implement (e.g in the list-processing programming language LISP).

Questions concerning the construction aim at the modularisation of the overall process and the components involved. From this general standpoint we are interested in questions with respect to the role of text actions in text planning. The model developed here should be able to be integrated into a modelling of human text production and is therefore action-oriented. It is divided into such components as can be separated in working processes of text writing (cf. Chapter 8).

3 Text generation

3.1 Definition

The term 'text generation' is commonly used in computer-oriented literature exclusively to refer to automatic text production (cf. Kempen (ed.)
1987, Zock & Sabah (eds) 1988, Dale et al. (eds) 1990, Paris et al. (eds)
1991). In this chapter we shall use the term in this sense.

Automatic text generation embraces various fields of research belonging
to a number of different disciplines, for example computational linguistics,
research of artificial intelligence, linguistics – especially text linguistics,
psychology, rhetorics, writing research. Computer models for text generation have their origins in these various schools of thought, with the result
that a certain heterogeneity with respect to the different approaches and
goals is inevitable. Hence in this continually expanding field, with a growing trend towards specialisation, it is not possible to isolate one continuous
line of research. Nevertheless, with the help of one central concept, namely
text structure, we would like to attempt to discuss some of the more
important questions that have arisen in connection with recent developments in text generation systems.

We shall disregard problems which arise from individual aspects with
regard to the effect of text and context on the grammar of the sentence.
Similarly, the application of certain grammatical formalities and the possibilities of their implementation are not of interest here (on the generation
of sentences cf. a.o. as a link between the conceptual level and language
surface structure Jacobs (PHRED 1985, KING 1987), Danlos 1987, with
respect to specific grammar formalisms Joshi 1987, Busemann 1988,
Mellish 1988, De Smedt 1990, van Noord 1990, Sigurd 1991, McKeown
& Elhadad 1991). Nor will we deal with questions which arise as a result of
a multi-modal approach, in which text, gestures, image etc. are linked
together. Instead, we shall concentrate on that phenomenon of text structure which is text-specific and plays a central role for the overall concep-

tion of a system.

What is meant by text structure is a description in which text segments are seen in definable hierarchical relation to each other. The relating process can cover single fragments of text (sentence connections, paragraphs, paragraph connections), but also the text as a whole. The theory of a text structure and determining its nature have consequences for the modularisation of a text generation system. They affect the organisation of the text content on the one hand and lexical and syntactic choices on the other. Correspondingly, this results in a threefold division of the areas of knowledge involved:

- object knowledge as knowledge of the world,
- linguistic knowledge as knowledge of lexis and grammar,
- text knowledge as knowledge of communicative standards for conveying the world through language.

Within the various disciplines, different emphasis is placed on these types of knowledge. Hence, for example, 'text structure' is considered a constitutive concept for research within the field of text linguistics, and its representations are part of text knowledge. 'Knowledge' as an organisational structure for environmental set-ups is on the other hand constitutive for cognitive schools of thought in psychology and the research of artificial intelligence. It can be observed that 'knowledge structures' have also become of interest for text linguistic research (cf. elementary treatments such as van Dijk 1977b, van Dijk & Kintsch 1983, de Beaugrande & Dressler 1981, de Beaugrande 1984). By contrast, text structures are becoming of greater interest in computer-oriented approaches, even if this process is taking place at a slower pace and on the whole with almost no contact to text linguistic research. Along with interest in the sentence, there is also increasing interest in larger units ('multi-sentence text', 'paragraph').

One clear orientation is formed by expert systems, in which interconnected sentences are produced as responses to questions put to the data base (knowledge base) (cf. examples in sub-section 3.5.2). From a linguistic point of view, this deals principally with problems such as lexicalisation, pronominalisation, ellipses, definite and indefinite nominal phrases and sentence connections. Questions arising with regard to structures and processes are to be seen above all from the problem-solving point of view. Thus the text structure is first and foremost of interest as a means for solving lexical-grammatical problems.

In the following, we will discuss some questions that have to do with the nature and significance of text structure in methods of text generation.

Here it must be stressed that on the whole this is still an uncertain field, in which general standards are just emerging (on individual questions see also Rothkegel 1990, 1992a, 1992b).

3.2 Object knowledge, linguistic knowledge, text knowledge

The concept of knowledge refers to a cognitive orientation in which arbitrary contents or information are represented in a specific form. 'Representation' refers first of all to memory models, which are intended as processing models. This kind of approach is the obvious choice for computational modelling, irrespective of whether any claim to psychological reality is made. In this sense, the representation of structures and processes is central for computer-oriented approaches and hence also for text generation processes (see also section 2.7). What, then, does this imply for the modelling of the text structure?

As is generally known, text structures are multi-dimensional. We are dealing with several text levels that are related to one another. With respect to text generation systems, it has become customary to make a rough distinction between WHAT and HOW (Thompson 1977, clear application in POPEL-WHAT and POPEL-HOW (Reithinger 1991)). The WHAT corresponds to content and text function. Their organisation is covered in a strategic component of text planning. The HOW corresponds to the linguistic realisation and is related to a tactical component. Whereas the latter characterises the initial phase of dealing with text generation, the former is becoming of increasing interest in research. It is to be foreseen that once these components have been clearly defined, the interaction of both components is also likely to play a role. However, for the time being at least, the text structure as such seems to be becoming the focus of interest. Designations such as 'text plan', 'text planning' or 'text design' are appearing here as keywords.

From the functional point of view, plan can mean a number of things. Pollack (1990) differentiates between plans as data structures and plans as mental phenomena. Agre & Chapman (1990) make a difference between plans in the sense of programs (instructions for performing effective procedures) and plans as natural language instructions. The former are considered as fixed, the latter as variable. In text generation systems, text plans are first and foremost data structures (text structures) or rules for producing such data structures. A catalogue of AI-requirements to be met by a text planning component is to be found in Paris, 1991, pp. 56f.

With respect to form we are concerned with two types: schemata and hierarchies. The former stress the sequence, the latter super- or subordination in groups. In the discussion on appropriate forms (a.o. Bateman 1991), hierarchical forms, starting from Sacerdoti's 'top-down hierarchical planner' (1977), currently seem to prevail. Treating plans as tree structures has among other things the advantage that we are able to rely on processes that are already familiar from the treatment of grammars (e.g. a context-free grammar in Scha & Polyani 1988). In our approach on the other hand, we prefer a schema-based method that also includes hierarchical considerations and takes account of the specifically sequential structure of the text as a list (see section 7.5).

Whilst – from the point of view of content – there are certain standards for the representation of WHAT and HOW (see under object knowledge and linguistic knowledge), this is by no means the case with respect to text planning. Now we might assume that only the two dimensions of the cognitive structuring of content and language (words and sentences) have their own representation level, i.e. that here there are structures that can be organised systematically. In this case, text planning principally concerns questions of sequencing prespecified units and the procedural organisation of this sequencing.

In contrast to this is a context-oriented interpretation, namely that the hierarchical and sequential structuring of the text represents a separate dimension, which is taken into account in a text representation. Seen like this, 'text' refers to a communicative structure, in which knowledge about objects, states of affairs, events etc. is embedded through linguistic means. According to this interpretation, text knowledge is first and foremost communicative knowledge that puts content into a sequence in its contextual setting and makes it available through language.

In the most recent text generation models the emphasis placed on text structure differs. This has a bearing on the representation of this structure and in general on the design of a model for text generation. Before going into the examples of this, we will outline the above-mentioned components of knowledge in their relation to one another.

'Object knowledge' is a collective term used to describe everything in the way of data, material, content, ideas etc. that goes to make up the contents of the text. With regard to computational modelling it is formally structured as 'knowledge' and organised along the lines of data processing in such a way that sections can be retrieved, added to, substituted, etc. For the structuring and organisation of object knowledge, certain standards are available, e.g. networks or frame structures. Examples of linguistic analyses of a text in the form of a semantic network are to be found in de Beaugrande & Dressler (1981) or as a referential network in Vater (1992). Formal properties of semantic networks are described in Findler ((ed.) 1979), on the formal properties of frames cf. Hayes (1980), with linguistic relevance also Engelbert & Knöpfler (1983). Applications to texts were above all worked out in Rosenberg (1980) and Tonfoni (1990).

Object knowledge falls into the area between general semantic knowledge (word meaning, sentence meaning) and domain knowledge (cf. detailed discussion in sections 5.0 and 5.1). Semantic knowledge is oriented towards the traditional subdivision of semantic relations such as generic and specific concepts, property-of, part-of. Furthermore, relations such as instance-of (type-token relation), as well as descriptive semantic categories for situations, events, actions also play a role. Whereas the former refer to units such as nouns, verbs (phrases), the latter apply to the propositional level (predicate–argument structures).

Domain knowledge refers to the structuring of a field of reference according to ordering criteria that are formally typical for that particular field of reference, or rather, meet the communicative requirements. Hence, in the representation of the object knowledge for recipes, for instance, the fact that an apple is a part of a plant (semantic relation = part-of relation) or an element in the class of fruits (generic-specific concept) is not of interest, whereas the fact that it can be peeled certainly is (possibly in contrast to a nut, which has to be shelled, cf. Koch 1991).

Whereas semantic knowledge is text-independent, domain knowledge is text-dependent in as much as it is dependent on a class of texts. If in this context we proceed from a communication-oriented definition of text types, we can say that domain knowledge is text-type-specific. The question remains as to how domain knowledge stands in relation to text structure. Are they identical? Or does something else take place in the sequential organisation of domain knowledge in the text?

'Linguistic knowledge' covers the organisation of grammatical regularities of any one language in the absence of contextual information. In text generation it provides the information required to produce individual sentences. This for instance includes the rules for producing a prepositional phrase, which might be required to indicate directions when asking the way (see below KLEIST in section 3.4). The relation between text structure and sentence structure is to be seen to the extent that the text structure has specific consequences for the lexical-grammatical level of the sentence.

Finally, 'text knowledge' includes all structural information necessary for the production of a text-specific organisation form. In this context, the concept of 'text structure' or 'discourse structure' plays a central role. In the newest approaches to text generation, there seems to be a general consensus that text structure has something to do with a communicative structure. In this sense it now remains to develop appropriate pragmatically-oriented specifications to describe the relations between communicative and linguistic structures.

The following comparisons deal with those approaches in which relations of this kind play a role for the overall coherence of the text. The theory of a communicatively determined overall text structure with linguistically interesting implications presupposes that there is such a thing as a component of 'text knowledge'. Such a component could be interpreted in the sense that it produces a communicatively-based interdependence between non-linguistic object knowledge on the one hand and linguistic, grammatical knowledge on the other. Current approaches to text generation show a certain trend in this direction.

3.3 Static and dynamic aspects

The frequently cited approach put forward by Grosz & Sidner (1986) derives its significance first and foremost from relating three text aspects to one another within the framework of a computational modelling. This must take into account:

(a) the sequential structure of utterances as a linguistic structure,
(b) the structure of purposes as an intentional structure and
(c) the respective focus of attention, which highlights objects, characteristics and relations.

These three aspects are interrelated in such a way that the 'attentional' structure governs the 'intentional' structure, and that this is reflected in the linguistic structure of the text in the form of indicators, so-called 'cue phrases'. Dynamic aspects are assigned to stative aspects, linguistic factors related to non-linguistic factors. The goal is a computer-oriented theory of text structure, which should be as simple as possible with respect to explaining what text structure is, and not unnecessarily complex for the modelling of the computer operations. On the whole, this approach can be understood as an alternative to rhetorically-oriented models (see below in section 3.5.). It claims to be both general and valid for spoken as well as written language.

The linguistic structure in this approach is based on the formation of segments within the text. What is considered problematic is defining the limits of the segments. The authors postulate that the intentional structure determines the formation of the segments and that shifts in the focus of attention are marked as segment limits. Expressions which play a role here are among others *in the first place, now, next, anyway, furthermore,* etc.

The intentional structure is explained by means of the task orientation of texts and theoretically classified in the approach of Grice (1969, 1975).

Two aspects are important:

The understanding of intention and the extension of the concept of intention to the text. Intention is equated with the 'discourse purpose'. The purpose is concerned with why the text is produced and why the particular contents are imparted in any respective case. The text is as a whole characterised by such a purpose. But each text segment also has its own 'discourse segment purpose'. The condition is that the purpose is identifiable (as compared with intentions, which may be hidden). Furthermore, the purpose is also communicative, i.e. it is related to communication partners. A classification of intentions is not aimed at. The possibilities mentioned (Grosz & Sidner, 1986, p. 179) are in fact oriented towards the text examples, but they are of a very general nature. Thus, for example, the intention behind an utterance is that

- an agent performs an action,
- an agent believes a fact,
- an agent believes that one fact supports another,
- an agent intends to identify an object,
- an agent is familiar with a property of an object.

In contrast to text structures (e.g. rhetorical structures, see under subsection 3.5.3), which place the text in an overall qualified hierarchy, the intentional structure is characterised by a number of general structural relations. The reasoning behind this approach is that the classification of superordinated intentions is in principle 'open-ended'. Thus one single utterance can at the same time inform, orientate, motivate, etc. (cf. concertina effect). Firmly established hierarchies therefore imply a severe constraint, quite apart from the fact that in natural texts it is as good as impossible to systematise the multitude of differentiation possibilities. It is therefore necessary to choose a different method of ascertaining text structure. The two fundamental relations in Grosz & Sidner's approach are those of 'dominance' and 'satisfaction precedes'.

The dominance relation presents a text construction in the form of a 'dominance hierarchy'. Sequential relations are governed by conditions of satisfaction precedes of the respective intention. What this means is that there are the kind of dependencies whereby a specific purpose presupposes the satisfaction of another purpose. Thus, for example, a hearer/reader must first of all know the necessity/significance/etc. of an action, in order for it to be possible in a subsequent step, i.e. the following text segment, to persuade him/her to perform it.

The attentional structure is an abstraction of the content structure in the course of the dynamic development of the text. It is seen as what the participants focus on during this development. One distinct point is that this is a condition of the text structure and not of the participants. The thus interpreted content structure is modelled in the form of 'focus spaces'. The shift of attention represents in each case the transition from one focus space to another ('focusing'). The section just dealt with from one of the focus spaces is known as the 'focusing structure'. Each text segment has a focus space linked to it, which covers the representations to objects, properties and relations, and at the same time includes the text segment purpose (in other words object knowledge + individual intentions). Through the manipulation of the focus spaces, information concerning intention and linguistic indicators is coordinated.

The dynamic perspective in the modelling of focus spaces and their shift also complies with the notion of an evolving text structure and the process orientation of algorithms. In this, 'focusing' is translated into operations that function as a 'stack' mechanism. Content from object knowledge is placed in a stack, from which it can later be retrieved. The process of text generation thus appears as repeated recourse to previously introduced content (from the stack) or as the introduction of new content that is added as the result of opening new focus spaces (cf. also McCoy & Cheng 1991). This type of focus-shift-mechanism makes it possible to deal with language phenomena such as the division of segments outlined above, the treatment of referential expressions (pronominalisation and use of the definite and indefinite article as a function of maintaining and shifting focus spaces) and the structure of interruptions as a function of dominances of the intentional structure. ('Interruptions' are above all discussed in approaches concerning spoken language.) Similarly, by means of linguistic indicators, this mechanism permits the recognition of the intentional structure. In this approach, text structure is taken to mean something that emerges successively as a result of the focus mechanism.

3.4 Text structure and processes of choice

KLEIST (Kohärenzbezogenes LEIstungs- und Simulationssystem zur Textgenerierung – coherence-related performance and simulation system for text generation) is a system for generating natural-language texts for giving route descriptions with specific text organisation procedures (Meier et al. 1988, Rutz 1990, Rickheit (ed.) 1991). Of interest in our context is the integration of the text structure into various sources of knowledge, which all interact with each other as components of a system (in a so-called 'constraint pool', i.e. with no integral planning component; the specifications ('constraints') are retrieved as required). In the foreground are the 'stage description types', which specify the structures of text units and refer to the description of a stage of the way. Text structure is seen here as the result of processes of choice which take place with regard to a 'cognitive map' (representation of the town map in the memory of the participants). Of significance for the description are the 'landmarks', i.e. the objects characterising the way that is to be described (here: buildings, roads, crossings). They are essential for the understanding of the description. Actions performed by an imaginary pedestrian (e.g. *turning off*) and directions are of further interest. Landmarks, actions and directions as categories for description form the conceptual basis for the text organisation. They appear as concepts such as way, direction, action, are arranged in a conceptual hierarchy and represent the link between the structure of the stages and linguistic realisation. Stages are distinguished according to initial stage, intermediate stage and destination.

Stage description plans are schemata derived from experimentally produced route descriptions on the basis of a 'model town'. As model town, subjects were given a list of town map segments and asked to generate texts giving directions with reference to an imaginary pedestrian. This material provided the basis for the stage description plans. With regard to the overall text, they form those sections that, combined together, produce the text sequence. A hierarchical structure – as is also the case in Grosz & Sidner (1986) – does not exist. There is on the other hand a close connection to components of linguistic knowledge. Hence, for example, the concepts of the stage description plans are linked to semantic knowledge, which governs the use of prepositions, and with situation-semantic schemata, which are in turn linked to syntactic knowledge. With regard to sequencing there are also discourse rules, which provide information concerning connectors, ellipses and sentence focus.

3.5 Rhetorical structures

3.5.1 Schema and hierarchy

Whilst in the approach taken by Grosz & Sidner (1986) purposes (intentional structure) and contents (attentional structure) are described as separate interrelated components, in the rhetorical approach both are considered together. Purpose orientation in this context first and foremost means addressee reference. The structuring of the content is seen from the point of view of its presentation. With regard to the structure itself, the task is to find a number of basic units or relations with which the overall structure can be established. In this context, we must make a distinction between schemata, which describe a sequence of units, and hierarchical text structures, which represent a system of relations. Whereas schemata already give the sequence as lists, in the case of hierarchical structures further information about the sequencing is needed. On the other hand, schemata are relatively inflexible, whereas tree structures can be altered at all nodes of the hierarchy. In the following, we will outline both approaches and further possibilities in an attempt to compensate for their respective shortcomings. It will be seen finally that schemata and hierarchies can be matched, or even that both organisational forms are required for text generation.

3.5.2 Text structure as schema

The idea of using schemata as the basis for the structuring of texts stems from the psychological-cognitive approach to text understanding (cf. frames and scripts in Schank & Abelson 1977, Metzing (ed.) 1980). One example of this kind of approach is given by McKeown with TEXT (1985), which can be considered the first comprehensive system of its kind.

The units that constitute the schema are known here as 'rhetorical predicates'. The notion of such predicates as text-organising relations is gleaned from modern rhetorics (here Grimes 1975). Those predicates are used that correspond to the text task. The text generation system in question (TEXT) is part of an expert system. The goal is the generation of responses referring to the description of physical objects ('ships') in text form, whereby the necessary information is taken from a relevant data base. Questions and answers are determined by the structure of the data base.

The rhetorical predicates are also closely related to the structure of the data base. IDENTIFICATION, one example of such a predicate, refers to the assignment to a generative concept (a ship is a watergoing vehicle), CONSTITUENCY to the assignment to a specific concept (modern torpedos are of 2 general types), ATTRIBUTIVE assigns properties, COMPARISON compares the object in question with another object, etc.

Sequence schemata ensue as a result of fixed combinations of such predicates, whereby recursion and repetition of individual units is possible (McKeown 1985:33):

- identification (1)
  - identification (2)
  - analogy
    - similarities (3)

- differences (4)
- particular – illustration (5)
- attributive (6)
- particular – illustration (7)

This kind of schema corresponds, for example, to the following text (McKeown, 1985, p. 33):

> (1) *A Hobie Cat is a brand of catamaran,* (2) *which is a kind of sailboat.* (3) *Catamarans have sails and a mast like other sailboats,* (4) *but they have two hulls instead of one.* (5) *That thing over there is a catamaran.* (6) *Hobie Cats have a canvas cockpit connecting the two pontoons and one or two sails.* (7) *The 16ft. Hobie Cat has a main and a jib and the 14ft. Hobie Cat has only a main.*

Schemata are relatively easy to process as a list structure. One generally recognised disadvantage is their fixed structure (cf. criticism in Hovy 1991, Bateman 1991). However, in our opinion this can be viewed from a number of angles. On the one hand it is desirable for the text structure to display a high degree of flexibility. On the other hand, there are some text types that are characterised precisely by certain communicative standards of content organisation. The goal in cases such as these is to formulate appropriate conditions. To this end, schemata are ideal. A further development (COMET system, McKeown et al. 1990) therefore attempts to combine both together. The idea is to develop more widely generalised schemata, to which more specific schemata are related in each case. Thus, for example, a general process schema can be supplemented by individual, more specific action schemata. An association with text plans results from the fact that the individual schemata can also be interpreted as sub-plans in the sense of instructions.

3.5.3 Hierarchical text structure

In the approach known as Rhetorical Structure Theory (RST, Mann & Thompson 1987, Thompson & Mann 1987) the overall structure of the text is established by setting up a hierarchy of individual rhetorical relations determined on a binary basis. This kind of rhetorical relation is included among the coherence relations. In this sense, they refer to an interrelation between different sections of the text, which develops either on the basis of the cohesion on the level of the states of affairs (e.g. temporal relations), by virtue of semantic relations (e.g. contrast) or by virtue of addressee-related association of contents (e.g. motivation, background). The structure of such relations is asymmetrical and characterised as a nucleus-satellite relation. What is meant here is that in each case a text segment (the nucleus) is central for the message of the text and that another (adjacent) segment (the satellite) supports this message.

This corresponds to the twofold argumentation schema of classical rhetorics with argumentation and reinforcement. The determining relation of dominance and subsidiarity resembles the intentional structure as described by Grosz & Sidner (1986, cf. section 3.3; cf. also the text illocution structure as put forward by Brandt & Rosengren 1991a). What they reject, namely a content specification with the acceptance of a fixed number of relation types, forms the basic framework of RST. It is successfully propagated, even though the identification of such relation types (e.g. background, elaboration, sequence, motivation, opposition, concession, purpose, etc.) cannot be definitely fixed, or rather, only when respective linguistic indicators (cue words, e.g. *in order to, for purpose*) are used. This can result in the ad-hoc introduction of relations, as, for example, when Cawsey (1990) uses precondition as being similar to, but not the same as background from Mann & Thompson's RST list (1987). The usefulness of such relations is proved above all on the sentence and sentence connection level (see example below), especially since a number of these relations correspond to traditional grammatical relations for sentence connections. What is new, however, is that they are used to construct a hierarchical text structure. The assumption is that a certain number of such defined relations is sufficient to establish the overall structure of the text by means of combination theory. Coherence is ensured by subordinating the text segments to one of the possible relations respectively.

RST finds application in a number of approaches to text generation (Cawsey 1990, Kreiß & Novak 1990, Moore & Swartout 1991, Paris 1991, Scott & de Souza 1990). Scott & de Souza develop heuristic processes, according to which rhetorical relations govern the distribution of content within the text segments and their linking together as hypo- or parataxes. One of these process rules is that one relation is assigned to one sentence respectively. The initial structure for text generating is a tree structure with branches for nucleus (n) and satellite (s) respectively. The following example stands for the relations enablement, sequence and the neutral list, whereby enablement forms the top node ('prime goal', Scott & de Souza, 1990, p. 70).

- **enablement**
    - n   *change the oil in the tank*
    - s **sequence**
        - n **list**
            - *drain the oil in the tank*

- *replace the oil filter*
- *drain the oil in the sump*
- s *refill the oil in the tank*

Result:

In order to change the oil in the tank, one must drain the tank and sump of oil, replace the oil filter, and refill the tank with oil.

Interesting from the point of view of text planning is the idea of a basic relation that can be translated into defined operations. In this way – as in a further development (Hovy 1991) – the descriptive hierarchy is transferred to an instructive hierarchy. The rhetorical relations now represent objectives that describe in what way the knowledge of the reader/hearer is to be influenced. Knowledge of the reader/hearer refers in this context to options in the knowledge base (e.g. details or generalisations). With regard to text generation, there are also further 'requirements' on the input material as well as 'growth points', to which additional linguistic material can be added on the basis of embedded plans. Both can refer either to the nucleus or the satellites. This approach, among others, also finds application in the PIT system (Presenting Information by Textplanning, Kreiß & Novak 1990), which produces responses for checking the understanding of a text (question: *what do you know about x?*).

3.6 Text planning in machine translation

In the DIOGENES system (Defrise & Nirenburg 1990), text generation forms one component within the framework of a translation system. Text production is regarded here in principle as a modularly composed process, whereby the data flow is controlled in an inter- and intramodular way. There are three components altogether:

- the restriction of the content (within the framework of a translation determined by the source text),
- the planning of the structure of the text content and
- the selection of lexical and syntactic means, as well as stipulating the word order.

The text plan is drawn up dynamically by a text planner, whereby 'rhetorical aims' (in the sense of Hovy 1988) are introduced (e.g. 'changing the level of knowledge', 'positive self-portrayal', etc.). The text plan is a list with diverse sub-tasks ('producer agenda'). The transfer into respective lexicalisations takes place with the help of so-called text planning rules.

With this, intentional specifications such as speech acts (e.g. asking, replying) and speaker attitudes (e.g. evaluation) are also used. Whereas in the approaches so far discussed the text structure represents a conceptual structure, here a text structure is established directly as a hierarchy of text segments that is represented in a frame structure (list structure). This forms the basis for the formation of sentences.

The multi-lingual Canadian approach to the production of weather reports also proceeds from a threefold division of text generation (Bourbeau et al. 1990). Here the individual phases relate to:

- determining the content,
- structuring the text and
- producing an interlingua-representation.

Whereas in the approach outlined above a predetermined content structure is taken as a basis, here a text representation is produced on the basis of the 'meaning-text theory' (Mel'cuk 1981). This concerns a lexicon-based approach to the description of the text content, which permits alternative linguistic realisations to be performed (cf. also the formation of paraphrases in text generation in Jordanskaja et al. 1991).

3.7 Text structure as structure of action

The goals of the text plan are not only speaker-related (writer-related), they can also be formulated on the content level. EPICURE (Dale 1990) is a text generation system that creates cooking recipes. The individual instructions are recorded as events, whose interdependence is represented in a hierarchical text plan. There is a prime goal, which is achieved in steps. The text structure is defined on the level of this event structure. The following structure (Dale, 1990, p. 239) shows a fragment from this kind of hierarchy (e = event,   = combined units that are not verbalised in the text):

- e: [*make butter bean soup*]
    - e1: [*prepare the ingredients*]
        - e3:   [*prepare the beans*]
            - e7: *soak the beans*
            - e8: *drain the beans*
            - e9: *rinse the beans*
        - e4: [*prepare the vegetables*]
            - e10: *prepare the onion*

- e23: *peel the onion*
  - e24: *chop the onion*
- e11: *prepare the potato*

. . .

- e5: [first stage of cooking]
  - e14: *melt the butter*
  - e15: *add the vegetables*

. . .

- e6: [second stage of cooking]
  - e19: *liquidise the soup*
  - e20: *stir in the cream*

. . .

- e2:   . . .

The resulting text reads (excerpt from Dale, 1990, p. 230):
Soak, drain and rinse the butter beans. Peel and chop the onion. Peel and chop the potato. . . . Melt the butter. Add the vegetables, etc.

As the text example shows, the grouping within the hierarchy forms the basis for the sequential arrangement. The interest with this approach lies not in the formal structure of the text (which is relatively meagre), but in the production of nominal phrases with phenomena of pronominalisation, definite phrases, anaphora and partitive nominal phrases (half of the carrots). To solve these problems, a representation of the object knowledge is referred to, which in this case is decidedly domain-specific. The relations within this domain modelling are based on contiguity (simultaneous occurrence of facts). It is also these that ensure the coherence within the text structure. Text structure in this sense means a kind of ordering of the domain knowledge that is represented in the text. The focus of interest lies on the representation of this domain knowledge. It is this knowledge that should also make it possible to create complex expressions that refer to those objects undergoing a change of state in the course of the recipe. This is the case, for example, when reference is made to individual objects (e.g. *butter, vegetables, flour,* etc.), which appear in a subsequent stage in a changed state (e.g. as a *broth* or *soup*; for these reference problems cf. also Koch 1991). Thus in the representation of object knowledge there is dynamic information as well as static information.

3.8 Summary

Although quite different with respect to preconditions and goals, the approaches outlined nevertheless show conformity as far as the relation between knowledge base and text structure is concerned. This either proceeds from predetermined knowledge representations or from domain modellings, which are derived partly from everyday or specialised knowledge, partly from structurings of the content of the text. Text plans with the status of data structures and/or instructions have the function to transfer the thus modelled object knowledge into a sequence. This may also include intentional or rhetorical aspects.

The representation of the object knowledge and its operationalisation leads to specific classifications of language knowledge. The theory of a text structure as a factual structure with separate intentional or rhetorical relations places certain emphases in this connection, which have an effect on grammatical phenomena in the sentence or sentence connections. Examples of this are anaphora, ellipses, definity of nominal phrases, sentence focus, sentence connections.

The clear orientation towards the sentence level has several reasons. On the one hand, the grammar of the sentence is still the focus of attention in computational models, even if text-relevant properties in the sentence or aspects beyond the sentence are becoming of greater interest. This is further underlined by the attempts to formulate text phenomena within the framework of existing grammatical standards (Scha & Polyani 1988, Webber 1989). A further point concerns the initial situation or motivation for text generation systems as a whole. The majority of developments are taking place within the framework of expert systems. The task here is to generate responses in the form of interconnected sentences, whereby the content and its structuring are predetermined by the data base. This also explains the total lack of text thematically-oriented approaches, in which global structures play a role. This corresponds to a tendency whereby thematic structurings tend to be related to the field of analysis or text understanding, whereas text generation refers to the processing of information within the data base with additional rhetorically motivated arrangements. If the future also sees approaches to text generation that take global text structures of a content-communicative nature into consideration, this could open up a whole new field of perspectives.

The role of text structure within the framework of current automatic text generation is above all to be seen from the point of view of modularisation. Modularisation means that there are several components with separate organisation forms, which interact within any one system. A division such as that into text knowledge, object knowledge and linguistic knowledge provides a basic pattern for such a modularisation, which indeed can be found in current approaches.

The nature of the modularisation and interaction of the components reflects the general understanding of text generation. The approaches outlined here have one thing in common, namely that the content structure in the text is related to a knowledge base (object knowledge) that exists independently of the text. According to this, generating a text means transferring concepts from the knowledge base into a sequential structure. Whereas up to now the emphasis has been on such questions that concern relating these concepts to the respective lexical-grammatical means of expression, now more and more questions that discuss the conditions of this structure and their linguistic consequences are becoming the focus of interest.

With the knowledge fields object knowledge, linguistic knowledge and text knowledge, we have already mentioned the focal points under which text generation models can be classified. If object knowledge is in the foreground (objects, states of affairs, events, etc.), then the text structure first and foremost has the function of sequencing the respective prespecified and already structured contents (cf. knowledge-based systems such as TEXT (McKeown 1985), RESEARCHER (Paris & McKeown 1987), POPEL (Reithinger 1991)). If linguistic knowledge is the focus of interest, then the function of object knowledge and text knowledge is primarily to provide parameters for the production of lexical and syntactic structures (e.g. SEMTEX (Rösner 1987), KLEIST (Meier et al. 1988)). If, finally, we are concerned with considering texts as representative structuring forms of content and purposes, then object knowledge on the one hand and linguistic knowledge on the other are functional for the modelling of text structures (possibly in PENMAN (Mann & Thompson 1987), cf. also the concept of the 'text base' in Bateman (1991)). Our approach is to be assigned to the latter. Whereas for object knowledge and linguistic knowledge standards for modelling already exist, in the field of text knowledge there is very little in this respect. Our model is to be understood as a contribution to the development of appropriate standards for text knowledge.

4 Text actions

4.0 Introduction

In chapter 2, text knowledge was explained in terms of action knowledge. It includes knowledge which is required in order to understand texts or to produce them in such a way that they are able to be understood in view of specific purposes. In this chapter, text knowledge should be understood in the narrow sense as knowledge about purpose-oriented text production. It will be explained by means of modelling text actions. The concept of text actions as text producing actions and a correspondingly formal representation scheme will be developed below. Within this framework it is shown that the treatment of text actions

- is established within the context of text production; through this a coherence is produced, which connects personal references, object knowledge, interactional knowledge and linguistic knowledge with one another; this context is the basis for the internal structure of a text action which is theoretically defined in terms of speech act theory;
- forms hierarchies and sequences which represent complex text actions; they are considered to be instructions for the formation of the text structure.

The principle of the declarative representation of procedures which is applied here makes text actions an appropriate instrument for the representation of a text plan. In computational modelling, a text plan has the job of guiding the organisation of the text according to a hierarchy of goals (e.g. the argumentative plan in Cohen (1987) or the differing between 'discourse plan' and 'domain plan' in Litman & Allen (1990)). In current text generating systems such text plans relate exclusively to the structuring of the content, so for example the structuring of action in stories (see 'story writing' in Black et al. 1982, 'narrative comprehension' in Dyer 1983) or in instructive texts such as recipes (Dale 1990, Koch 1991, cf. chapter 3). There we consider text production itself as an action, and in addition to the content level describing a level of linguistic actions, a corresponding text plan as a plan for text production can be conceived.

The connection between linguistic actions and the task of conveying information raises the question as to what is understood by linguistic action. We have set out three focal points:

- What does linguistic action mean in relation to the role of the information that is to be conveyed,
- the role of interaction between the writer and the anticipated readers which takes place with the conveying of information and
- the role of lexical and grammatical means which are used for the implementation of the linguistic actions.

4.1 Intention and change of context

As a theoretical basis for the investigation of these relationships, speech act theory seems to provide a useful device. It offers the distinction of components which are relevant for our purpose. The second point concerns information processing. Within this framework, linguistic actions are to be understood operationally. That is, structural properties are considered in relation to their function in specific procedures. Operationalisation can only take place when there are units which are capable of being isolated and differentiated, as well as steps and strategies for the organisation of these units.

But what do the units of linguistic actions look like? Linguistic actions form an object which cannot be directly observed or classified. They are valid as such in their specific dependence on utterances in particular contexts. As a basis for their determination the concept of intention plays an important role (cf. Searle 1969 (1971), 1979c, Grice 1975, 1969; cf. also the discussions of the several positions in Cole & Morgan (eds) 1975 and Cohen et al. (eds) 1990). In short, it means the following (Searle, 1969 (1971), pp. 68f.):

Speaker S makes an utterance with the intention of eliciting a reaction from the hearer H in such a way that H recognises this intention. This is possible on the basis of the conditions (situation, psychological state of S and H, language use), which are laid down in convention.

'Intention', however, is a basic term to form the delimiting line between actions and other behaviour (see von Wright 1977). On the other hand, linguistic actions may be described in the same manner as non-linguistic actions and their operationalisations. In any case, for operationalising 'intention' the term must be specified in more detail. It will be shown that a formalisation in the sense of action logic may provide such a specification. Further, for purposes of information processing this specification is re-interpreted from a cognitive point of view.

The central idea of this line is the aspect of change of context, a change which is achieved by a linguistic action. If we relate this change to the task of conveying information, then the question further arises as to what the interaction of the participants in this process looks like.

One step in the operationalisation is the specification of intention as the goal or the purpose of communication. Before we come to the computational example, we would like to develop, step by step, the underlying way of thinking. Goals or purposes can be described in terms of states. Correspondingly, the description of actions is broken down into units by means of which different states can be defined. Usually, two states are foregrounded: the state before and the state after.

In this context, Sbisà's (1987) basic observations concerning the change of context effected by speech acts are fitting. A causal, intention-related definition (principle of causation) is set against an interactional definition. In this definition there are two states and their relationship to speaker and hearer. This is not a list of features which define an action, but a description of what happens when something is viewed as an action (Sbisà, 1987, p. 258). With that state 2 is the result of an action – not the effect or the consequence – which is executed by partner 1 and which is related ('presupposes', Sbisà, 1987, p. 260) to state 1 by partner 2.

In this sense – with more regard to Austin than to Searle – she compares a specific actional perspective with a semantic one. See Sbisà (1987, p. 263): 'If they are actions merely in the sense that they are caused by (linguistic) intentions and other pro-attitudes, speech act theory turns out to be identical with a theory of speaker's meaning.' Instead speech act theory should have an object of its own: '. . . that an agent/speaker who produces an utterance may be viewed as bringing about by his/her utterance a state St2, by way of contrast to a presupposed state St1. The states that speech acts bring about are to be found (broadly speaking) in the context. Therefore, to grant that speech acts are actions is to allow for context change.' Illocutionary acts should thereby be seen, as a rule, in the context of 'a semiotic change' (not a 'physical change'). Conventionality here is assigned neither to the significance, nor to the means, but to the resulting state (Sbisà, 1987, p. 269).

In logics of action, as for example von Wright's (1977) frequently cited formulation, the assigning of states is generally valid for the description of actions. Dimter (1981, p. 53) summarises this as follows: 'An agent (A) makes use in a specific way (W) of the means (M) with the intention (I) of transferring the world from state S1 to state S2, which he considers to be more positive than state S3, which the world would find itself in without his action.' For linguistic actions this is correspondingly true (Dimter, 1981, p. 53): 'A speaker uses a declarative sentence in the way of a promise, in order to give the hearer certain knowledge regarding his future behavior. S1 and S3 are the states of uncertainty, S2 is the certainty of the hearer.'

Linguistic actions are communicative actions, that is, they always relate to a partner of interaction who should be influenced through the utterance. As this interaction is a symbolic one, the influence is to be understood as a change which takes place at the mental level of the partner. After that, the goal of a linguistic action is the influencing of the mental state of the hearer.

But the mental state is, as such, not a linguistic object. What can, on the contrary, be described linguistically, is the representation of individual units, and the relationship between them, which can be assigned to utterances. In computational linguistics, representations play a central role. They refer both to structures and algorithms and can be formulated in a declarative manner as well as in a procedural manner. Our first example is a declarative one in a predicate-logical notation which provides a speech act model embedded into a general plan of action. It is taken from a textbook on computational semantics (Allen, 1987, pp. 443ff.).

Interactional viewpoints are formed in the sense of information processing. The exchange of information is in the foreground. Exchange takes place between the knowledge base of a system and the assumed knowledge base of a user. In this model, the speech act appears as the tip of the iceberg. To analyse the speech act means to uncover the whole plan of a (physical) action which motivates the utterance in question. The example reconstructs a scene at the ticket-counter of a station, whereby the system represents the clerk and the customer is identified as the user of the system. The uttered question is *How much is a ticket on the train to Rochester?* The plan is, as follows, structured according to the several steps, whereby (7) is the uppermost goal of the overall action (slightly simplified from Allen, 1987, p. 447):

(7) TAKE-TRIP(JACK, TR, ROC)
    ↑ decomposition of
(6) BUY(JACK,CLERK,Ticket(TR))
    ↑ decomposition of
(5) GIVE(JACK,CLERK,Price(Ticket(TR)))
    ↑ enables
(4) KNOW(JACK,x,EQ(Price(Ticket(TR)),x))
    ↑ effect of

(3) INFORM(CLERK,JACK,x,EQ(Price(Ticket(TR)),x))
    ↑ enables
(2) WANT(JACK,INFORM(CLERK,JACK,x,EQ(Price(Ticket(TR)),x)))
    ↑ effect of
(1) REQUEST(JACK,CLERK,INFORM(CLERK,JACK,x,EQ(Price
    (Ticket(TR)),x)))

With respect to this:

(1) JACK formulates a speech act (REQUEST) by which he asks the clerk
to inform JACK about x,
whereby x is equal (EQ) to the price of a ticket for the train (TR).

This occurs through the expressed question *How much is a ticket on the train to Rochester?*

(2) The question in (1) is the effect of the wish of JACK (WANT)
that the clerk informs him about x.
(3) The wish in (2) permits the clerk to inform JACK about x.
(4) The informing of (3) has the effect that JACK knows x.
(5) The knowledge of the price allows JACK to pay the price to the clerk.
(6) GIVE is a semantic decomposition of BUY.
(7) BUY again is a part of the overall action, namely that JACK goes
(TAKE-TRIP) by train (TR) to Rochester (ROC) .

As a basic form for the speech act, for example INFORMING see Allen (1987, p. 445):
INFORM (speaker, hearer, proposition)
The precondition exists:
BEL (speaker, proposition)
and the effect:
BEL (hearer, proposition),
that is, the speaker and hearer both believe (BEL = BELIEVE) that the proposition contained in the utterance is true. To believe a proposition means to have the content in the respective knowledge base. After that, interaction means an interaction between two knowledge bases by which the content of the one knowledge base is transferred into the second knowledge base. On the basis of a corresponding container model, interaction takes place in the sense of information transfer. In the above example, this transfer occurs in the transition from step (3) to step (4).

The example shows a possible representation of interaction on the basis of a plan which is successively broken down into individual steps. This breaking down allows a differentiated presentation of the resulting states that are established. The change of the context in this approach is identical to the change of knowledge within a knowledge base.

The change of context can also be seen in such a way that a specific coherence between units of information is produced. Thus it does not just concern individual pieces of information which are to be transferred, but a coherent structure which is developed during the course of several utterances.

Grosz & Sidner (1986) suggest a dialogue model in which the information is indeed in the foreground, but at the same time a global structure of a text is assumed. This global structure is determined by an intentional level whereby 'intention' is identified with 'task' or 'purpose': 'A rather straightforward property of discourses, namely, that they (or, more accurately, those who participate in them) have an overall purpose, turns out to play a fundamental role in the theory of discourse structure' (Grosz & Sidner, 1986, p. 178). Three levels are distinguished: the sequence of utterances at the linguistic level, the structure of purposes at the intentional level and the state of focus of attention at the dynamic informational level.

The intentional level and the sequencing of utterances are related in such a way that a segmentation results which is considered to be the surface reflection of relationships among elements of the intentional structure. It also constrains the semantic interpretation of expressions, but this point is not of interest here. Instead the role of intentions for the segmentation and sequencing within a global discourse structure is important. The basic idea is that this global structure is built up by means of single speech acts.

The structuring effect is achieved by application of two particular relationships: 'dominance' and 'satisfaction precedes'. They are determined by 'ranges of intentions' which form a hierarchical structure. An intention can contribute to the satisfaction of another intention. Structure, in the sense of dominance, emerges in such a way that there is one dominant 'discourse purpose' (DP) which is supported by the several 'discourse segment purposes' (DSP). Each DSP specifies how this segment contributes to achieving the overall discourse purpose (Grosz & Sidner, 1986, p. 178). It is necessary that these intentions are intended to be recognized and that they are recognized during the interaction. Thus the relationship between two segments, e.g. DSP1 and DSP2, can be defined by (Grosz & Sidner, 1986, p. 179):

(a) DSP1 contributes to DSP2 or
     DSP2 dominates DSP1.

In this case DSP1 is intended to provide part of the satisfaction of DSP2.

(b) DSP1 satisfaction-precedes DSP2
whenever DSP1 must be satisfied before DSP2.

The aim of this approach is not to develop a typology of possible purposes. It is argued that such a typology is in principle not possible because there is no finite list of discourse purposes at all. Grosz and Sidner argue as follows (1986, p. 179): 'Therefore a theory of discourse structure cannot depend on choosing the DP/DSPs from a fixed list. . . . What is essential for discourse structure is that such intentions bear certain kinds of structural relationships to one another. . . . Although there is an infinite number of intentions, there are only a small number of relations relevant to discourse structure that can hold between them.'

In this approach, the intentional structure covers one of the relevant text levels. It is – as usually in AI-approaches – related to the informational level rather than to conditions of language use (Allen & Perrault 1980, Brown 1980, Ellman 1983). This perspective is more likely to be chosen in approaches to machine translation (such as in Defrise & Nirenburg 1990, also Rothkegel 1986a) or in text linguistic theories on text illocutions (cf. Brandt et al. 1983, Heinemann & Viehweger 1991). We are pursuing a view of text production in which linguistic actions are performed in order to convey information about an object by means of constructing a model of the object in question.

4.2 Text actions and text production

With the textual distribution of information which takes place in and through a text announcing the publication of a book, a variety of different processes play a role. An object is presented for a specific purpose. To this, knowledge from states of affairs, norms and beliefs is selected and organised thematically. It is fitted to the communicative function of the text, and more-or-less ordered into prespecified standards of the text type. At the same time, linguistic means from syntax and lexis are selected, and realised into a linearised form of sentence sequence according to a desired structure of content. In short, means of informing, describing, evaluating, arguing are used and simultaneously a text form is produced.

The view of text production which is represented here is that these activities should not be considered separately, but as a complex which belongs together and has internal dependencies. We are not informing on the one hand, and independently of this, organising the sequence of thematic units on the other. They are different aspects of one activity. It should be attempted to make this connection clear.

In the model which is presented here, information processes and linguistic processes are related to one another. Verbalisation and its communicative orientation are considered as belonging to one another. Therefore text production is to be seen within the context of linguistic actions.

The basic concept of explaining this connection is the text action (TA). Text actions as linguistic actions operate on several text levels. They tie together functional, thematic, text-organising and linguistic aspects, all of which are constituents of the process of text production.

The idea of seeing text production together with linguistic actions can be found in different contexts. For our purpose, those are relevant in which communicative and text-organising aspects are related to one another. So the assumption is valid that in the formulation process, apart from the text itself a thematic-functional structure is produced. This affects, for example, theories regarding text acts (Zillig 1980, Rossipal 1983), formulation actions (Antos 1982) or re-formulation actions (Gülich & Kotschi 1987, Gülich 1988). There Gülich & Kotschi (1987, p. 214) differentiate between illocutive actions and actions of text constitution such as REDUCING, STRESSING, DIFFERENTIATING, RE-CALLING, SUMMARISING, etc. As a description of communicative acts text writing is an object of the description of 'rhetorical competence' (Steinmann, 1982, p. 296) in terms of speech act theory. Here the focal point is found in principles of effectiveness of actions in relation to the impact on the reader.

Text actions, as specified in the following, have a general status. Their description aims at the connection, not the isolation of communicative and linguistic aspects. This does not rule out further differentiations of text action types, but this issue will not be discussed here. We are not interested in some ontology of linguistic actions (cf. Ballmer & Brennenstuhl 1981). Instead there are two complexes of questions to be clarified:

- What does the internal structure of text actions look like?
- In what way should complex text actions be formulated?

4.3 Structure and process of text production

One way in which we can learn something about the structure of texts is to model such processes that will lead to text structures. This attempt, in which the structure of a thing is traced to the structure forming processes, is found, above all, in the investigation of those objects whose form has developed during a specific period of time, and where the reconstruction of the development can explain relevant properties of the object in question.

In contrast to this is the goal-oriented production of technical objects, in which the formation of the structure is planned according to a goal, and carried out according to a plan. Texts appear to belong to such objects, where formation of structure is attributed as much to the principles of (free) development, as to those of plans and their realisation. This means that the modelling process should remain open for both possibilities. What is essential and applicable to both is that these processes result in a fixed structure which can be considered as a kind of trace of the process. Textualisation in this context means to determine a structure with linguistic means and to leave that text as a trace. How can this be described linguistically? We are proposing an attempt via the concept of 'context change' (see above).

What does 'change of context' mean with regard to the interaction between W and R, when bearing in mind the formation of the text structure? 'Interaction' is the mutual involvement of the communication partners participating in the change of the context ('mutual action', Sbisà, 1987, p. 253). With text production, it concerns changes of an epistemic nature, that is the level of knowledge of the participants is changed. With this, we are not assuming a transfer model, in which information is transferred from one system to another. This would mean that the actions of W would be described in such a way that they are responsible for the changes in the reader's knowledge base. Our model of text production works in such a way that the level of information of the participating communication partners, e.g. both W and R, is altered in relation to an individual, new object. Before W has an effect on R, W must first produce for him/ herself a model of the object (as a representation within the cognitive system of W). This can be described as the production of a text structure, within which this model is construed (see also Molitor-Lübbert 1989). This 'object construction' is then accessible to R as a text, so that R can in turn construct a new object. This is supported by a frame of reference which is common to the participants of the communication, i.e. to W as well as to R.

We are limiting ourselves to text actions which are performed by W. The aspect of interaction arises insofar as the text actions of W are determined by their intended effect in relation to R. Actual effects, e.g. how they are assumed as perlocutive effects, should not be considered.

    This rough connection is further specified. Subsequently the following information is conveyed:

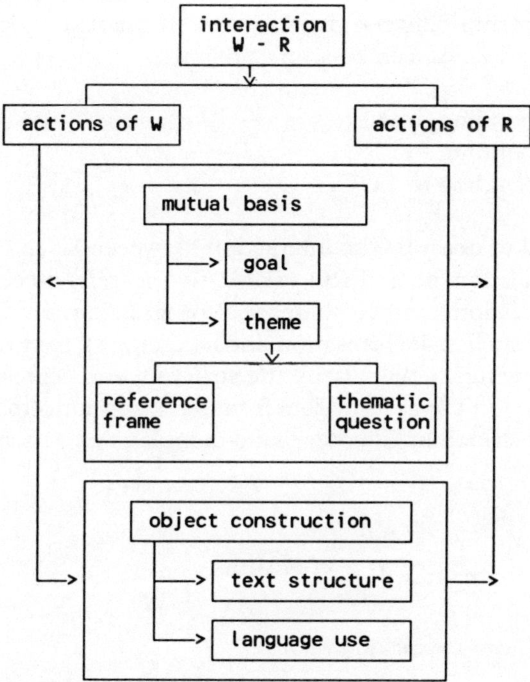

Figure 4.1 Text production within the context of interaction between writer (W) and reader (R)

(i)   -   as an interaction between W and R
       -   with the goal of conveying information
(ii)   -   about a theme
       -   on the basis of a reference frame common to W and R and
       -   specific thematic questions about the text
(iii) -   through a text (text version) which is characterised through a text structure and the use of specific lexical and syntactic inventories.

Figure 4.1 outlines this context of text production within the framework of interaction between W and R. Text actions then, are operations in which the components listed in (i) to (iii) relate to each other in a specific way. With this we go back to Searle's speech act model (1969 (1971)) and relate the three components of illocution (ILL), propositional content (PRO) and locution (LOC). Hence the basic structure of TA corresponds to

[• 1] TA: (ILL, PRO, LOC)

The relationship between the structure of the text action and the context of text production can be seen as follows:

(i)   corresponding to ILL
(ii)   corresponding to PRO
(iii)   corresponding to LOC.

ILL is used to describe the interaction betweeen W and R in relation to the communication goal. PRO relates to the reference frame, to text-thematical questions and to thematical progression. LOC relates to linguistic means such as lexicalisation and assigning syntactic structures.

In the following we will clarify the structure and representation format of text actions. On the basis of data from book announcements, simple text actions are described in Chapter 5 and complex text actions in Chapters 6 and 7.

4.4 Internal structure of text actions

4.4.1 The ILL component (illocution)

In speech-act theory, illocution is that part of an action which is explained in terms of what is understood by an utterance within the framework of communication, e.g. as a description, evaluation, instruction, regulation, etc. Illocutions are not – other than in performative use – expressed explicitly. They are implicit and must be reconstructed with understanding, or implicitly generated in production. It is possible, on the one hand, to have a top-down view of linking them to extra-linguistic phenomena of communication, and on the other hand, a bottom-up view of bringing them together with linguistic indicators. With regard to its description, illocution is a theoretical construction with very different definitions. One reason for this variety is the concept of 'intention' and its interpretations. In the present context, we are interested in it from a cognitive point of view. In such a view, the psychological state is re-formulated as a purpose. Purposes manifest themselves in the interaction model in three relationships:

(a) ILL as relation r1 between W and R (r1 indicates an interactional relationship r1(W,R))
(b) ILL as relation r2 between W and PRO (r2 indicates the involvement of W with regard to the propositional content: r2(W, PRO))
(c) ILL as relation r3 between PRO and LOC (r3 indicates an instruction for the linguistic choice of the realisation of PRO: r3(PRO, LOC)

In the function of (a), ILL relates the utterance of W to imagined or anticipated utterances of R. This aspect has to do with a conventionally fixed interest in the purpose of a text. It determines the dominance of particular text actions. In book announcements, promotional informing about an object is dominant. It implies questions of the readers concerning this object which are answered by the writers. From this global view, text actions in book announcements are answering actions. We will discuss in Chapter 5 what kind of questions and answers can be determined.

The function of (b) concerns the differentiation of ILL, which arises through the involvement of W in relation to the content. In our model, we distinguish three types of reference. The uttered states of affairs may belong to the knowledge of facts, to the knowledge of norms, or to beliefs. Facts refer to DESCRIBING, norms refer to EVALUATING, and beliefs refer to ASSERTING. The introduction of these predicates in the representation of text actions is motivated by the viewpoint of the text production context. It is the attempt to find an alternative to the 'information transfer model'. It is not necessary to interpret the carrying out of a linguistic action as a transfer of the information from W to R. We are not concerned with whether the reader knows that p is true. It does concern us that R knows that W has executed a description (or evaluation or an assertion) after which p is – for W – valid as a fact, or has a value with respect to a norm scale or as a belief of W. In how far, and in what way, R will finally assimilate p into his/her knowledge base and from that produce the construction of the object, is as much a component of the theory of text understanding as a theory of text producing (and consequently will not be discussed here). The distinctions made by Dimter (1981, pp. 62ff) of to WANT as 'being prepared to do', to EVALUATE as the assigning of a value to a positive–negative scale, and to KNOW as the assigning of a truth value, will be set out in the following in such a way that they reflect the specific interaction between the partners with regard to the content.

According to Dimter (1981, p. 54) the formal representation of INFORMING looks as follows:

INFORMING (W,L):
WANT (W, KNOW (R, TRUE (p)))
'W informs R' means:
W wants R to know that the fact of p is true.

This basic scheme creates with WANT a disposition for acting and with KNOW the epistemic area. TRUE indicates the truthfulness of the assertion, which – in the sense of information processing – clarifies the availability of information in the knowledge base of a system (human and/ or computer) (Moore & Hendrix 1982). We will modify this form using the distinctions of WANT, EVALUATE, and KNOW as introduced above. WANT shall be a signal for goal-orientation, EVALUATE is a signal for orientation towards a scale of norms and KNOW works as a signal for the insertion of a proposition into a knowledge base:

- ILL = DESCRIBING, if
  WANT (W, KNOW (R, DESCRIBE (W, TRUE (p, F))))
  W writes with the purpose that R knows
  that W makes a description
  which corresponds to the factual knowledge (F) of W.

- ILL = EVALUATING, if
  WANT (W, KNOW (R, EVALUATE (W, TRUE (p, N))))
  W writes with the purpose that R knows
  that W makes an evaluation
  which corresponds to the norms (N) of W.

- ILL = ASSERTING, if
  WANT (W, KNOW (R, ASSERT (W, TRUE (p, B))))
  W writes with the purpose that R knows
  that W makes an assertion
  which corresponds to the beliefs (B) of W.

The relation of illocution to knowledge (in various 'possible worlds') has been discussed, above all under the label of propositional attitudes or epistemic expressions (Falkenberg 1981, Doherty 1981; also Falkenberg (ed.) 1989). What is interesting for us is the re-interpretation of this logic-semantic basis from a cognitive point of view (see Bühler's discussion 1989). Proceeding from the assumption that the propositional attitude indicates a relation between the individual and the content of thought, the semantic description concerns the formulation of truth conditions on the basis of valid implications or inferences. Expressions which characterise this relation are called epistemic expressions, insofar as they relate to systems of knowledge and belief. A cognitive framework of information processing, however, concerns the relations between an individual and mental representations of a content, which can be found in the memory, or other processing device – e.g. a computer.

The epistemic expression refers to a relation which can be made explicit in terms of several types of knowledge. This is operational in the sense of information processing. With regard to this aspect, epistemic expressions designate 'operations which are realised in terms of processing mental representations' (Bühler, 1989, p. 15). Moore & Hendrix (1982) apply such a basis for a computational model of propositional attitudes. Corresponding to this is the case where *X believes that p*, if p is a part of his belief system, i.e. that p is existent in the knowledge base of X. TRUE thus means to be existent in a knowledge base.

Knowledge types interest us insofar as they supply parameters for language use. In (c)'s function (see above) ILL specifies the coupling of the components PRO and LOC. There the options for lexical choices are established. These affect lexical inventories concerning individual predicate-argument-configurations and text connectors on the level of text organisation. In this sense illocution is understood as instruction for the use of linguistic means. This idea is found in text-pragmatic approaches such as Schmidt (1973) and Große (1976) where the distinctions of types of instruction is applied to the differentiation of text types.

In our approach, the conveying of information (WANT (W, KNOW (R, p))) is dominant for the text type dealt with. The differentiation of ILL into DESCRIBING, EVALUATING, and ASSERTING allow further differentiations within the description of text-structure-forming.

The operational aspect of propositional attitudes in terms of assigning them to different manipulations in a knowledge base corresponds with the instructional aspect of the illocution, namely the instruction for selecting appropriate lexical inventories. The designations DESCRIBING, EVALUATING, ASSERTING are labels for selecting between different types of knowledge on the one hand, and, on the other hand, for choosing between different inventories of language use. Correspondingly:

W DESCRIBES p:

W combines information which belongs to his/her factual knowledge about the new object. It concerns contents which at the same time are the contents of the new book in question. There are inventories, e.g. of predicates, which reflect this relation (detailed in section 5.2):

INV(DES): { *present, introduce, . . .* }

W EVALUATES p:

W combines information about the new book with classifications which correspond to specific norms of W (of the respective discipline or the scene). In book announcements – as in advertising texts – the relevant units are valued positively:

INV(EVA): {*fascinating, the first book, . . .*}

W ASSERTS p:

W combines information about the object with his/her beliefs which may relate to the object:

INV(ASS):   {*be necessary, not to be valid, . . .* }

The interpretation of ILL as a predicate that specifies the relationship of PRO and LOC depending on the illocutionary type leads to a more precise formulation of [• 2] instead of [• 1]:

[• 2]   TA: ILL (PRO, LOC)

DESCRIBING, EVALUATING, ASSERTING are types of text action which represent in text production the three basic semiotic functions in the sense of Bühler's theory on language functions (1982/1934). DESCRIB-ING relates to the function of representation. The information about the object is in the foreground. EVALUATING relates to the writer and fulfils a symptomatic function. Values according to specific norms are in the foreground. ASSERTING relates to the reader and so fulfils the function of appeal. Beliefs of W aim at the acceptance or non-acceptance by the reader. This kind of interpretation is determined on the basis of a communicative theory and cannot be paralleled to the taxonomy of Searle (1979b), which is sentence-oriented.

4.4.2 *The PRO component (propositional content)*

The propositional content is also a constitutive part of the text action. Whilst the classic theories of speech acts do not specify the relation between illocution and the description of the propositional content, text actions are characterised by the determination of this relation. For this, it is necessary to specify PRO itself. Firstly we are assuming a predicate-argument structure, normally applied in text approaches in the line of van Dijk (1980b; for the discussion of the use of the term proposition see 1980b, p. 26). Our representation includes a predicate (PRED) and a configuration of arguments (ARGi):

[• 3]   PRO: PRED (ARG1, . . ., ARGn)

The propositional component is, in our model, the bearer of the text-thematic structure. It is in this sense that the arguments are to be specified. We assign them to thematically determined text roles (TROL), which are developed in section 5.1 by virtue of an object model and text questions. Therefore, [• 3] is modified to [• 4]:

[• 4]   PRO: PRED (TROL1, . . ., TROLn)

4.4.3 *The LOC component (locution)*

We can only speak of a linguistic action if there is a linguistic expression which indicates the action. In a linguistic view, lexicon and grammar are the domains of describing linguistic expressions. Therefore, we subsume – as opposed to Searle (1971, p. 40) – all conditions concerning lexical and syntactical choices under the label of locution. Within this framework, the component of LOC has to assume a specified function. It provides the options for lexical and/or syntactic selection. This mirrors the fact that, independent of semantic compatibility, the choice of linguistic means is dependent upon context and can be described through context parameters. On the other hand, and this can be considered trivial, there is no fixed 1:1- relationship between illocution and linguistic expressions. However, the differentiation of the illocutionary components in DESCRIBING, EVALUATING and ASSERTING allows a differentiation of language use. This is reflected in the separation of lexical inventories (INV) providing some criteria for the lexicalisation of predicates and text roles. We are primarily concerned with the selection of expressions for predicates which can be established according to the illocutionary type (TYPE) and the configuration of text roles (TROC).

[•5]   LOC: INVi/condition: (ILL=TYPE, TROC=TROLi, TROLj,. . .)

4.5 Complex text actions

Whilst in the internal structure of the text action, functional and thematical aspects of a single unit are related, in the case of complex structures of compositions of text actions we are concerned with the sequential structure of the whole text. For the description, two aspects must be separated: the formal character of the text sequence and the linearisation of the thematic-functional units.

We are assuming that the text is formed in terms of a text list (TL) consisting of a list of text units (ti):

[• 6]   TL: [t1, . . ., tn]

The thematic-functional sequence is constructed through complex text actions. They produce the coherence of the text in terms of expansions of the illocutive and thematic component (EX-ILL and EX-THEM). Thematic expansions generate the object construction as it is presented by the writer of the text. Whereas the single text action provides the selections of thematic units in terms of text roles and their configuration within a predicate-argument-structure, thematic expansions provide the composition of these propositions according to text-thematic principles such as the principle of thematic text questions. Illocutive expansions refer to the interactional aspect of the text and are reflected in the presentation mode. This mode decides whether the object construction is presented in terms of a description, a narration, an argumentation, etc. The surface markers of both illocutive and thematic expansions are the connectors (CON) which determine a specifiable connectivity structure. This structure is interpreted as the connective expansion (EX-CON). EX-ILL, EX-THEM and (EX-CON) are the three components of complex text actions (TAc), which form a structure parallel to the internal structure of simple text actions:

[• 7]   TAc: EX-ILL (EX-THEM, EX-CON)

In order to combine [• 6] and [• 7], we substitute the formal text units of the text list by the substantial units of the complex text actions in such a way that each expansion is formally constructed through a list of illocutions, propositions and connectors respectively:

[• 8] TL: [[EX-ILL: {ILL1, . . ., ILLn}],
              [EX-THEM: {(PRED (TROC))1, . . .,(PRED(TROC))n }],
              [EX-CON: {CON1, . . ., CONn}]]

The relationship between EX-ILL and the list of illocutions is a hierarchical one in the sense of a THROUGH-hierarchy, e.g.:

[• 9]   EX-ILL(DESCRIPTION)
              THROUGH {DESCRIBING1, . . ., DESCRIBINGn}
        EX-ILL(ARGUMENTATION)
              THROUGH {ASSERTING1, . . ., ASSERTINGn}

A second relationship between illocutions is that of dominance-subsidiarity (DO-SU). The dominant illocutions represent the communicative goal of the text and the subsidiary illocutions support this goal. In descriptions, for instance, DESCRIBING is dominant, whereas there may be further EVALUATINGS or ASSERTINGS which support the descriptive presentation of the object. Similarly, argumentations are characterised by the dominance of ASSERTING which is supported by EVALUATINGS and DESCRIBINGS.

[• 9'] EX-ILL(DESCRIPTION)
           DO-SU (DESCRIBING, (EVALUATING/ASSERTING))
        EX-ILL(ARGUMENTATION)
           DO-SU (ASSERTING, (EVALUATING/DESCRIBING))

Dominant illocutions are obligatory and subsidiary illocutions are facultative (marked by ' '). From that follows, for descriptions and argumentations, the specified representation of [• 10]:

[• 10] EX-ILL(DESCRIPTION)
        THROUGH {DESCRIBING1 (EVALUATING1/ASSERTING1),...,
             DESCRIBINGn (EVALUATINGn/ASSERTINGn) }
        EX-ILL(ARGUMENTATION)
        THROUGH {ASSERTING1 (EVALUATING1/DESCRIBING1),...,
             ASSERTINGn (EVALUATINGn/DESCRIBINGn) }

4.6   Text action schema (TAS)

Text actions are the instrument for the representation of text production. They represent the processes of forming text structure in an integrated view. Several text levels are tied together. The result of the application of text actions is a text representation which combines illocutive and text-thematic aspects with linguistic constraints in terms of text roles, lexical inventories for predicates and properties of the surface connectivity in texts.

For the representation of text-structure-forming processes and the resulting text representation a unique representation format is fixed. It uses the structure of attribute-value-pairs and embeds the determinations developed above in the following form:

[• 11] [TAS:[1
            [ILL1 =   TYPE]
            [PRO =
                 [PRED   =   INVi(PREDj)]
                 [TROCm   =
                      [TROL1   =   ...]

```
                        . . .
                        [TROLn      =       . . .]]
        [INVi =         . . .]
        [CON=           . . .]],
        . . .
        [n
        [ILLn =         TYPE]
        [PRO =
                [PRED         =       INVi(PREDk)]
                [TROCm    =
                        TROL1       =       . . .]
                        . . .
                        [TROLn      =       . . .]
        [INVi =         . . .]
        [CON=           . . .]]  ]
```

The various specifications of this schema are introduced and explained in the following chapters. Chapter 5 specifies the selections concerning PRO and Chapters 6 and 7 describe CON on the basis of some specified composition principles. Both kinds of specification are developed theoretically as well as empirically on the basis of authentic material.

5 Text grammar I: Selections

5.0 Overview

What do the sources of knowledge that are relevant for the compilation of a text grammar look like? This is the principal question in this chapter. Before we consider the overall organisation of the text (see compositions in Chapters 6 and 7), we would like to take a closer look at the modules that are necessary for doing so.

From a conceptual point of view, we are concerned with the selection of units that are required for building a content-functional text structure. Accordingly, we distinguish object construction and object presentation. The object construction demands semantic-thematic knowledge, the object presentation interactional knowledge. Only the two together allow the selection of linguistic units, i.e. lexicalisation within the text production. In this, we proceed from the pragmatic assumption that the use of different text action types correlates with the use of different lexical inventories of language use. Thus, for example, in order to realise the respective lexicalisations, it is important to know whether an object is being described or evaluated.

With respect to the representation of such relations, we are helped by the terms of reference of the text action schema. Correspondingly we are concerned in the following with the specifications to be developed for the component PRO as representation of the object construction, the component ILL as representation of the object presentation and the component LOC as representation for the inventories of language use.

5.1 Units of the object construction

5.1.1 Semantic representations

In the text action schema, PRO is first of all specified as predicate-argument structure. The question is now: what is it that is represented by PRO and how can it be further specified for our purposes?

In computational linguistic and AI-oriented approaches, two types of semantic representation that are relevant in our context are used for predicate-argument structures. They can be pooled as role-semantic or as knowledge-based lines of approach. This distinction roughly characterises two initial positions, proceeding from which semantic representations are introduced. Role or case-semantic approaches proceed from linguistic models and classify these in comprehensive goals (as does the present approach). Knowledge-based approaches proceed from data structures and their processing in a knowledge structure (cf. knowledge representations in expert systems), and assign these to linguistic units (words, sentences, texts). The former approach could be described as computational linguistic, the latter AI-oriented. In the various models, the respective properties can overlap. Of relevance for the representation are the relation to the syntax of the sentence and the status of the units. Syntax-oriented approaches are as a rule concerned with case roles, knowledge-based approaches on the other hand prefer concepts or simply single lexemes as units, which are related to each other in logical utterances. In this context, the choice of such concepts or lexemes is often dependent on fixed factual domains. Such determinations can also affect the definition of the argument roles in role-semantic models, which in turn, however, are more closely associated with syntax. Before going into the further possibility offered by text roles in our approach, which incorporates a text thematic level, we shall – in order to clarify the different positions – briefly discuss the sentence-semantic fundamentals of computational linguistic modellings.

Role-semantic approaches, which go back to the 1970s but are still relevant today, are concerned with conceptual deep case (Fillmore 1968, 1985), with semantic decompositions (in the sense of generative semantics as, for example, Lakoff 1972) and with mixtures of the two (e.g. Jackendoff 1983).

Deep case grammar approaches have been referred to both for the semantic analysis of sentences (e.g. Simmons as early as 1973) and for the modelling of conceptual structures of sentences (e.g. cognitive approach in Norman & Rumelhart 1975). Although the theory as such was heavily criticised for its shortcomings with respect to the definition of case roles, case roles – even in many contemporary models of text understanding and text generation – are nevertheless considered as an indispensable part of the semantic representation. The problem of role definition does not have an effect, since, for example, the emphasis is on a logical-semantic approach and only a few roles such as AGENT, INSTRUMENT, GOAL are used (cf. systems such as LILOG, in Bollinger et al. 1990, also Danlos 1987 and Palmer 1990), which are obviously ascribed a kind of universality. Alternatively, a conceptual level of the semantic representation is aimed at and the relative openness of the definition of case roles is used for domain-specific extensions or determining the role inventory (cf. text generation in SEMTEX (Rösner 1987) and AUTOKOCH (Koch 1988, 1991)).

Decompositional approaches have also been drawn on for the modelling of conceptual structures (cf. 'conceptual dependency' in Schank 1972, Schank (ed.) 1975a), but also for the treatment of procedural aspects (Winograd 1972, Charniak & Wilks (eds) 1976, Wilks 1982). The semantic representation of the sentence is based here on relations which as a 'semantic primitive' are intended to provide fundamental procedures for the connection of semantic units. Representations of this approach are further removed from the structure of the sentence (surface sentence) than deep case descriptions. In current text-oriented systems they do not play a role.

Semantic representations, which are based exclusively on knowledge representations, negate a distinction between linguistic-semantic knowledge and encyclopaedic knowledge. Consequently, knowledge base and lexicon overlap. As a representation, logical utterances composed of 'semantic predicates' describe certain relations and selected units of the knowledge base are formed (cf. Dahlgren 1988, Palmer 1990). Implemented systems as a rule deal with a very restricted domain ('miniature world'), which is hierarchically ordered through a predetermined data base or through a specific domain model. These units can be directly – as concepts or also as single lexemes – units of the representation (e.g. Dahlgren 1988). However, they can also – with closer association to the syntactic representation – be assigned to argument roles, which as a rule correspond to traditional deep case roles. In these cases the concepts of the knowledge base are the fillers of the argument slots in the sentence representation. This means that while encyclopaedic knowledge may not be distinguished from lexical-semantic knowledge, it is distinguished from sentence-semantic knowledge. Via domain-oriented classifications, context-oriented information can thus flow into the semantic representation.

Examples of such approaches are a.o. LOKI (Wachtel 1986), LILOG (Bollinger et al. 1990), KLEIST (Rickheit (ed.) 1991).

In our approach we argue in favour of a systematic separation of text and sentence level. This is substantiated above all through our text-global approach, which proceeds from a text structure and develops the representation units from this, and not from the sentence, for which separate text-oriented aspects are sought. The predicate-argument structure of the PRO component is represented by text roles and a general predicate. Both are determined by an object model and by thematic text questions. The object model specifies a domain-dependent reference frame and permits selections with respect to the integration of content in communicative contexts. Whereas case roles are of a sentence-semantic nature, text roles are of a text-semantic nature.

The question arises as to how these text roles are to be derived. They should correspond to text-specific generalisations, which make the text-constituting units independent of individual concepts or lexemes. As far as book announcement texts are concerned, it would, for example, be of no help at all if as text topic we adopted the respective main concept 'book' or the corresponding lexical designations (e.g. *volume, study, work, publication,* etc.). We could merely observe that it occurs frequently (cf. discussion on topicality in 2.3). Statements that characterise the contribution to the text structure cannot be made in this way. Rather, they require the structuring of a larger framework, within which relations of thematic fragments among themselves can be described. We put forward such a framework, which is characterised by two components:

- an object model that opens up the reference frame relevant for the text type and
- thematic text questions, which as a result of the selections from the object model in turn restrict the reference frame and establish a connection to the linguistic structure.

The introduction of text roles on the basis of the object model and the outlining of text role configurations on the basis of thematic questions is discussed in section 5.1. In section 5.2 we are concerned with the text-functional integration of thematic units. This means that a distinction can be made between propositional attitudes in which the respective content is presented. Whereas object model and thematic questions govern the object construction, the interactional model deals with the presentation mode. It is relevant for the selection of the linguistic means that can be included in respective inventories. Generally fundamental for this approach is the theory of a dialogically-founded structure of written texts. With respect to the content-thematic aspects, this structure refers to a question-answer correlation.

5.1.2 Schema knowledge and reference frame

The conveying of information as the goal of the text production requires knowledge sources. It is obvious that – in the case of a book announcement – the acquaintance with the respective book is not sufficient to structure and formulate information about this book. What is also necessary are standards for the selection of information about the respective object class.

Within the framework of a constructivist approach to text production, establishing an information structure in the text means the same as establishing an object construction. This affects the selection of information fragments in such a way that only such properties of the object in question are considered relevant as conventionally play a role in the respective communication system. The following examples illustrate what types of object structuring can be relevant:

- Classification of physical objects according to conceptual relations (generic-specific relation, property-of relation, part-of relation, instance-of relation) with the underlying question:
      what is x?
Example: ships (US Navy data base) in McKeown 1985

- Classification according to way in which objects function with the underlying question:
   how does x work?
Example: telephone, loudspeaker in Paris & McKeown 1987
   why doesn't x work?
Example: engines in Grishman 1990

- Treatment of objects by persons with the underlying question:
   what is person y doing with x?
Example: cooking instructions in Koch 1991, Dale 1990

- actions of objects with the underlying question:
   what is x doing? or
   what is x doing {still, after, because, . . .}?
Example: description of object movements such as road users in a street scene in Novak 1987; report of crime in Danlos 1987.

With respect to book announcements there are problems. They are concerned with a communicative object that is itself a text. We proceed from the assumption that there are standards for the written communication about such objects. At first we might assume that the primary text determines the content structure of the book announcement text. This, however, contradicts the different communicative functions of the two text types. Thus we cannot presume that the source text (book text) determines the content structure of book announcement texts. Rather, it is structural properties of the target text (book announcement text) that are relevant for the selections. This rules out the assumption that book announcement texts are summaries of the primary texts. This simultaneously rules out a topic model in the sense of van Dijk (1980a, 1980b), whereby the topic has the status of a summary of the text. Macrostructures characterise a hierarchically organised text structure, in which several hierarchy levels are adopted. Through successive application of the four macrorules (OMITTING, SELECTING, GENERALISING, CONSTRUCTING/INTEGRATING) van Dijk, 1980b, p. 45) to the individual propositions of the text, increasingly compressed units are supposed to emerge at the superordinated level. The uppermost level contains the formulation of the topic.

More appropriate in our opinion is a model that refers to expectation structures (cf. comments on text types in section 2.6). Expectation structures can be modelled as frames of the knowledge organisation. The concept frame has two interpretations. As a content concept it refers to schemata that are formed on the basis of stereotyped coherences of information units. They play a role in understanding to the extent that knowledge complements the respective information available. A simple demonstration example states that if someone wears shoes, we at the same time know that he/she has feet (Minsky 1990). The originally perception-psychological concept has by virtue of its generality spread successfully to various disciplines. With respect to text production, frames are above all helpful for the organisation of the 'material', which in this way already appears in a certain context. In this, it is assumed that the thematisation of a knowledge unit does not only take account of this, but also of the context in which it stands within a frame. The thematised units can thus only be considered as the 'tip of the iceberg'. Such schemata have so far been referred to primarily in connection with problems of text understanding (Lehnert & Ringle (eds) 1982, Metzing (ed.) 1980). An important role in this context is played by inference, through which text elements are related to contents not expressed in the text (Rickheit & Strohner (eds) 1985). Inferences are also considered important with respect to text production (Koch 1991). Here their role is above all to make provision for the omission of information.

The approach we pursue first and foremost requires a structuring of the 'material' for the text to be produced which provides the units for the object construction. They are to be introduced as data structures of a knowledge schema. This model considers problems that are connected with the choice of topic ('inventio' in rhetorics) and which with respect to automatic generation have so far received very little attention (cf. 'topic selection' in Hovy 1988). We dealt in detail with individual organisation structures and their relation to the text structure in the discussion of contemporary text generation systems in Chapter 3. In this chapter, we deal with questions that arise in connection with the object model.

The occupation with knowledge about objects and states of affairs ('world knowledge') in the form of structured standards has become increasingly significant, not least because of the influence of cognition-science paradigms (a.o. de Beaugrande & Dressler 1981, van Dijk 1977b, van Dijk & Kintsch 1983, Grewenig 1980, de Beaugrande 1989). In the more recent text generation systems, they play a central role as independent modules in the form of data bases (knowledge bases, cf. sub-section 3.5.2).

The relation between semantic and encyclopaedic knowledge is a subject that is permanently under discussion, whereby a separation under cognitive aspects is becoming less and less significant (cf. the approach of a 'naive semantics' in Dahlgren 1988). Whereas semantic knowledge is defined close to language as word-meaning or sentence-meaning knowledge, schema knowledge as a stereotype structuring of the world must be classified as distinctly far removed from language. As far as their structure is concerned, schemata are a system of slots, whereby each slot represents a classification with respect to a level of knowledge in a specific discourse world which can be filled by individual values ('instantiated'). What makes such schemata interesting for text production is the fact that in this system of slots a correlation is established that is typical for a class of objects or states of affairs, and which – so runs the theory – is available as knowledge of the language participants (communication partners). Seen from the content point of view, such schemata are open and can be filled at will as experience or expectation structures.

The schema concept originates in psychology (Bartlett 1932) and has been picked up in cognitive-oriented AI-approaches and further developed in the direction of programmable structures. As schemata for knowledge representations, they have been propagated under labels such as frames (Minsky 1977, Charniak 1977) or scripts (Schank 1975b, Schank & Abelson 1977). With respect to the modelling of text understanding and text production above all Minsky's frame theory plays an important role. They assume a kind of bridging function in order to explain the coherence of text fragments on the basis of knowledge about the world (cf. Metzing (ed.) 1980, Tonfoni 1990). Tonfoni (1990, pp. 17ff.) gives a list of possible relations with respect to the connection of frames and on this score develops a theory of compatibility of frames in the text, which enables statements to be made about the degree of coherence. Compatibility relations in this context principally affect the connection of individual text segments. Frames, however, can be oriented towards whole sections or the entire text. In this case, they have an influence on the thematic structure of the text. This is to be seen in such a way that they provide a superordinated context for the thematic units discussed in the text. This has among other things been examined with respect to newspaper reports (Rosenberg 1980, Zuck & Zuck 1984), contractual texts (Rothkegel 1984b), weather reports (Seelbach 1986, Kittredge et al. 1991). Knowledge schemata are of interest for the treatment of problems related to coherence building in the text in spite of their non-linguistic basis, and because of their close relationship to the text topic.

It should be noted that the structuring of a state of affairs cannot be equated with the structuring of information in the text. Frame structure is therefore not the same as text structure. A text is not the same as knowledge in the form of a sequence of sentences. It generally applies that schema knowledge is structured independently of a communication goal and a question. This is where text structure differs on the content level from schema structure. Formally, Wilks (1985) demonstrated that such schemata can indeed determine the order of parts, but can say nothing about the relation of the parts to each other, which, for example, belongs to the requirements of a text grammar. This is a point that next to the knowledge schemata demands an additional component if it is to be of any use for the linguistic modelling. Before we introduce this specifically text-thematic component as a complementary factor (in sub-section 5.1.4), we shall deal in more detail with the application of the frame theory for the modelling of the background knowledge that plays a role in book announcement texts.

Schemata as order structures also contain an ontology. For a modelling, this implies that content definitions are to be made with respect to the classification of objects and states of affairs as well as their relations. 'What's in a frame?' (Tannen 1979) reads the question, which in primarily formally-oriented approaches is in fact considered as secondary, but whose answer finally determines the actual efficiency of a system. From a linguistic viewpoint it has also been seen that word-semantic approaches are not satisfactory, but that communicative orientations are decisive for the definition of relevant units (a.o. Goffman 1974); cf. also the tests with respect to the 'pear story' relating to the selection of frames depending on the formulation of the question (Chafe (ed.) 1980). From the point of view that such schemata are employed in text generating systems for the fulfilling of specified tasks, a respective orientation of the ontology used emerges. Ontologies of this kind reappear as domain knowledge, which is particularly being discussed in the field of text generation systems being developed from the point of view of simulation.

Unlike for the structuring of semantic knowledge (word and sentence meaning), there are no general terms of reference for the structuring of discourse worlds. Here and there it is classified as 'hearer knowledge' (Dale 1990, Koch 1991), which puts the problem into a broader framework, but fails to solve it. Furthermore, we are interested in a 'writer knowledge', which decides on the object construction. If we proceed from the assumption that this knowledge forms the background from which the information in the text is to be inferrable, then the ontological units must be such that they provide 'interesting pegs' for the object construction. With respect to narrative texts, such 'salient features' have been experimentally examined for the description of events (Trabasso & Sperry 1985).

As 'probablistic features', which are understood in the sense of prototype semantics (Rosch 1975), Dahlgren in her 'naive semantics' gives examples of classifications that are assigned to objects. Thus the part-of relation is interpreted as 'if a thing is a shirt, then it probably has buttons' (Dahlgren, 1988, p. 31). Texts about an object such as 'shirt' (e.g. advertising texts), where this part-of relation is irrelevant but other features that cannot be developed in such a view of semantics play a role, are of course conceivable (e.g. prestige determined by the particular make). What we mean by this is that word or even sentence-related classifications are not sufficient, but that the communicative context is to be substituted as the governing component. In this respect, we presume that text-relevant classifications have something to do with the viewpoint from which the object is classified for certain purposes of the respective communication. Popov (1986, p. 109) expresses it thus: 'Knowledge should be organised in units convenient for interaction with man'. Within the framework of the KLEIST system, which is concerned with the production of route descriptions, 'landmarks' are referred to as the objects of a 'cognitive map', which an 'imaginary pedestrian' uses to describe the way (cf. Meier et al. 1988).

The ontologies in the knowledge base are usually constructed as hierarchies of objects, their properties, parts and individual characteristics, which begin with a neutral unit (e.g. 'object') as top node and then branch into the respective specifications (entity hierarchy). The branches are qualified, i.e. they describe certain types of relations between these specifications. To these belong the traditional relations such as 'is-a' (specific-concept-of, instance-of), 'has-a' (property), 'part-of', which determine the data structures. Knowledge representations of this kind are as a rule used for inference. Hence they have become important for text understanding systems. Palmer uses the 'pulley hierarchy' in order to produce a semantic representation of verbs such as *contact, hang* etc. with the help of inference rules. The role of the predicates is especially interesting, since they are not shown in such object-centred knowledge representations and because the typified relations between the nodes of the hierarchy have to be developed if we wish to move beyond direct substitutions such as 'is a' or 'has' (as, for example, in McKeown 1985). General problems with such ontologies of 'miniature worlds' relate to questions concerning the degree of generality, the extendibility and variability. Palmer (1990, p. 69) further includes in her requirement catalogue the role of lexical entries as well as that of syntactic, semantic and pragmatic restrictions. This means that the knowledge base would need to be augmented by linguistic knowledge or conceived with interfaces to linguistic knowledge.

The examples given refer to objects of the physical world. Book announcement texts on the other hand are concerned with the reference to communicative objects. The question is, on the basis of what criteria can 'landmarks' be defined here, or put another way: what criteria are there, according to which the data structure of a 'book world' is to be determined.

5.1.3 Object model

For book announcement texts, the topic domain is determined by the reference to the object 'book'. To this extent, the text type chosen here offers a simplification over other text types. Nevertheless, the definition of an appropriate reference frame, within which the object is discussed, raises problems. The possibility of subjects producing respective texts within an experimental framework, as was the case for route descriptions in the above-mentioned KLEIST system, does not seem to be very promising for book announcement texts by virtue of the more complex context. Since we are here also concerned with a text type that is freely available in large numbers as authentic specialised texts, it would seem obvious to have recourse to this material. In this context the question arises as to a theoretically-founded basis for corresponding empirical analyses.

With the choice of an object for description, the question arises as to what theoretical consequences result from it. Whereas it is possible with respect to physical objects as the thematic knowledge pool discussed in the text to fall back on traditional semantic classifications, for communicative objects new considerations have to be made.

A communicative object can be considered as a product that develops or is established within communication and is relevant for further communicative purposes. In this respect book announcement texts on the one hand refer to an object (book as a material object), and on the other hand to events (text as communicative action). Next to a traditional object schema with relations such as generic-specific concept, property-of, part-of, relations must also be included that refer to the coherence of events. Such relations can be seen within the framework of an action schema, whose coherence is determined by contiguity.

A general scheme for the description of events has been developed by Graesser & Clark (1985) with respect to their experiments. For an event x, a list can be compiled with questions such as (according to Dahlgren, 1985, p. 96):

What caused x?
What enabled x?
What was the goal of x?
What happened next (after x)?
What was the consequence of x?
What does x imply?
When did x happen?
Where did x happen?
How did x happen?

We are primarily interested in communicative events, which are only partly covered by the above list. For this the action description (description of linguistic actions) has paradigms that overlap with the above-mentioned questions. As action constituents, units are mentioned such as PARTICIPANT, OBJECT, GOAL, MOTIVATION, CONSEQUENCE, REALISATION (Rehbein 1977, Harras 1983). Whereas these paradigms concern general approaches that proceed from a theoretical concept of action or event, Zillig (1982b) proceeds from texts. What is of interest to us is the fact that these are also texts with a reference to the object book. He discusses descriptions and evaluations in reviews, whereby he distinguishes three kinds of conveyed information: content information (reference to book), background information and technical information. With the division into content and background information, he to some extent covers a domain as we understand it. This takes place on the basis of a structurally-oriented empirical analysis and aims at differentiating linguistic actions. The identified categories do not correspond – except the category of addressees and goal of the book – to the categories that we have established for book announcement texts. This confirms the assumption that the domain cannot be determined on the basis of the state of affairs reference alone, but that the communicative integration of the states of affairs must also be considered (cf. above Kittredge et al. 1990).

The analysis of more than 100 English texts has led to a description paradigm that is organised as a book frame. In this, we are concerned with the nominal units of the action schema. The verbal units will be dealt with within the framework of the assigned interaction model (cf. section 5.2).

For the organisation of the domain knowledge, we refer to a frame schema. This is a structure with empty slots and fillers. From the content point of view this schema corresponds to a data structure for the conceptual representation of the object book. Formally, it illustrates a dependency structure to the extent that proceeding from a dominating category (here the frame name 'book'), the slots appear in the form of attribute-value-pairs as recursively organised lists, whereby the position of an attribute can, in turn, be occupied by a dominating category, e.g. by another frame name. They are in principle extendable and variable. To illustrate this, we shall outline in the following a few fragments that are required for the decomposition of the example texts in Chapters 6 and 7.

```
('book' : (    (BOOK            =. . .)
               (AUTHOR          =. . .)
               (READER          =. . .)
               (TOPIC           =. . .)
               (INTENTION       =. . .)
               (MOTIVATION      =. . .)
               (GOAL            =. . .)
               (EFFEKT          =. . .)
               (PRESENTATION    =. . .) )   )
```

Each slot can in turn form a new frame and thus be a part of the overall reference frame. In the following, we give examples of such sub-models (which are domain-specifically extendable). The structure is organised recursively, i.e. each value can open up a new slot (with an additional value assignment). In this way, hierarchies are built that with respect to their structure are comparable to the knowledge representations outlined above. The relations between the nodes of the hierarchy refer to the remaining relations in semantic networks, which we supplement with the text-related relation of contingency (contingent-with):

'is-a' (generic-specific concept), e.g. BOOK – TYPE OF BOOK
'has-a' (property), e.g. AUTHOR – POPULARITY
'part-of' (part-of relation), e.g. TOPIC – SUB/TOPIC
'contingent-with' (contingency with), e.g. TOPIC/TREATMENT –
    TOPIC/FOCUS

In the following examples, the hierarchies are vertical and marked by insertions or brackets. We do not give any lexical fillers, but mark the open slot with '='. The book as a whole can among other things be structured with regard to its parts (*chapter, index*, etc.), to the type of book (*handbook, dictionary, monograph*, etc.), to functional and evaluation classes (*repository, classic, treasure trove*, etc.).

```
(BOOK      (is-a TYPE           =      )
           (part-of PART        =      )
           (is-a PART 1         =      )
           (is-a PART 2         =      )
           (. . .                      )
           (is-a CLASS          =      ) )
```

The author model portrays the author with respect to properties that are relevant for the book content, or quality, or for the market effectiveness. The author appears neutral (*writer, author*) or specified:

```
(AUTHOR   (has-a NAME          =      )
          (has-a PROFESSION    =      )
          (has-a COMPETENCE =        )
          (has-a POPULARITY    =      ) )
```

The reader model characterises the circle of addressees.

```
(READER   (is-a NEUTRAL          =      )
          (has-a COMPETENCE =
                 (is-an EXPERT         =     )
                 (is-a LAYMAN          =     )
                        (has-a WITH KNOWLEDGE        =     )
                        (has-a WITHOUT KNOWLEDGE =        ) ))
          (has-an EDUCATION  =
                 (is-a STUDENT         =     )
                 (is-a PUPIL           =     ) ))
```

The topic model is rather complex. Here there are structurings according to the formal structure (topic whole and part, main topics and sub-topics), according to thematic pools, according to how the topic is treated (overview, analysis, empirical method, etc.), according to temporal ordering structures (phases), etc. An assignment to the text role TOPIC is possible on the basis of the structural integration, not on the basis of semantic features (everything can be the topic). In this respect, we can only give a few examples here in which this integration is marked. We distinguish the topic-marking units and place the topic as such in square brackets:

```
(TOPIC        (is-a WHOLE                       =    )
              (part-of PART                     =
                    (is-a SUB-TOPIC 1           =    )
                    (is-a SUB-TOPIC 2           =    )
                    (. . .                           ))
              (contingent-with TREATMENT        =    )
              (contingent-with FOCUS            =    ) )
```

MOTIVATION aims at reasons why the book was written or the topic dealt with, e.g. deficit in theory and practice, out-datedness (e.g. the information), etc.:

```
(MOTIVATION      (is-a DEFICIT              =    )
                 (is-a OUT-DATEDNESS        =    ) )
```

GOAL concerns classifications that refer to the result of the changes set in motion by the motivation (a.o. updating the material, introduction of a new topic, etc.):

```
(GOAL     (contingent-with UPDATING              = )
          (contingent-with TOPIC INTRODUCTION    = ) )
```

INTENTION aims at the integration of the topic in a communication structure that characterises the position of the author (he/she wants to prove, demonstrate, criticise, introduce, legitimate x, etc.):

```
(INTENTION (contingent-with DEMONSTRATION  =    )
           (contingent-with PROOF          =    )
           (contingent-with CRITICISM      =    )
           (contingent-with INTRODUCTION   =    ) )
```

EFFECT means the envisaged effect on the readers can be different (what is supposed to change for the readers through the text: level of information, skills, sensations of pleasure, etc.):

```
(EFFECT        (is-an INFORMATION        =    )
               (is-an INSTRUCTION        =    )
               (is-an ENTERTAINMENT      =    ) )
```

Finally, the means of the content as well as the material realisation of the book also play a role. In this category belongs information concerning the linguistic or symbolic means on the one hand and information concerning the structure on the other:

```
(PRESENTATION   (has-a LANGUAGE              =
                    (is-a SINGLE LANG.          =      )
                    (is-a STYLE                 =      )
                    (is-a VOCABULARY            =      ) )
                (has-a PICTURES             =
                    (is-a PHOTO                 =      )
                    (is-a GRAPHICS              =      ) )
                (has-a STRUCTURE            =             ) )
```

This series of slots and sub-models provides possibilities that are in principle variable, both in reality through new ways of dealing with the object book and in the respective categories of the object model. In the following, we are to examine to what extent such an information structure has a linguistic effect. Whereas the slots can be relatively easily filled with corresponding nominal units, the selection of verbs raises considerable difficulties. It is not possible to translate the relations between the slots directly into verbs. Hence classifications which substitute a verb like *be* for 'is-a' would make no sense, as is done with the texts in the TEXT system (McKeown 1985; cf. *a submarine is a water-going vehicle*) in a way which is stylistically not very elegant, but which gets the message across. Sentences such as *the book is a handbook* or *the topic has several sub-topics* are not meaningful in book announcement texts. Instead several specifications are linked together (*the handbook documents the history of...*). It is this linking that is decisive for the selection of the verbs. This speaks for considering the slots with regard to their function within predicate-argument structures.

5.1.4 *Thematic text questions*

With the object model a reference frame is available for the thematic units in the text. It offers slots that are instantiated according to the frame theory by filling in individual details. This takes place when a name is chosen for AUTHOR or the designation of a state of affairs for TOPIC, etc. In our approach we are not concerned with using the frame background for the formation of nominal units (cf. generating referential expressions in Dale 1990). We are interested in the possibility of finding access to a thematic structure for the overall text and thereby also obtaining criteria for the selection of predicate units. For this, we must study the use of slots and their specific configurations with respect to such a text structure. In this respect a simple selection of individual slots is not sufficient to arrive at the construction of a text. What is needed is a system of the selected slots and a definition of the principles that determine this system. We proceed from the hypothesis that the construct of the thematic text question is suited to elucidating such principles.

Thematic text questions are a rhetorical concept (quaestio), which has recently gained importance in text-topic-oriented approaches. The concepts 'the thing in question' and 'topic' are used in Hellwig (1984) synonymously. Interesting in our context is the assumption that the text question not only concerns the structure of the overall text, but also has an effect on the structure of the sentences that lie within the scope of this question. This applies likewise for text questions whose effect was experimentally studied with the help of object descriptions, whereby the role of word order, object reference and subordination as supports for global principles of text organisation has become recognisable (Klein & von Stutterheim 1991, von Stutterheim 1992, Kohlmann et al. 1989).

From action aspects (text as a result of linguistic actions), texts can be seen as a reaction to a communicative deficit (e.g. information deficit, which it eliminates; cf. Lötscher 1987, Ehlich 1989). Accordingly, the dialogic principle in the explanation of linguistic actions (Weigand 1989) can be applied to texts insofar as they can be described as the result of response actions initiated by implicit questions (Rothkegel 1991b).

Of interest in our context is the relation of such text questions on the one hand to the object model and on the other hand to the text structure. Whereas the object model represents the reference frame for the entire theme, the text question has a restrictive function. Thematic text questions structure the selection of relevant slots from the reference frame, which in the construction of the text are filled with pertinent information. Whereas the reference frame characterises W and R's more or less mutual knowledge about the domain and the text questions lay down a canon according to which relevant and interesting fragments are focused, the result text presents an answer, in which W on the basis of these terms of reference constructs a new object. In this sense, the thematic text question characterises a dialogic situation. It can be thought of as a structuring parameter of the anticipated reader. The text is the answer of the text writer to the question. Thematic questions have to do with the mediating process between text author and text reader. The information expectations on the part of the reader can be formulated in such questions that are based on the mutual knowledge of text author and text reader. Opposed to this are the instantiations of the text author which fill the slots. This alone, however, is not sufficient. A new quality is achieved as a result of combining the fillers and placing them into a text-specific context.

Hence we are not simply concerned with 'knowledge telling' in which everything that is available as knowledge is textualised (Faigly et al., 1989, p. 28). On the contrary, selections must be organised in such a way that a re-structuring with regard to the knowledge pool can take place. This re-structuring is precisely what appears in the text as the thematic structure. It is made possible by the fact that textual-linguistic categories replace the slot categories from the knowledge base. In this way, text-composition and linguistic organisation principles can take effect. In other words, the slots take over the function of text roles, which occupy the respective argument spaces in the propositional structure of the text. What is new compared to the object model are certain text role configurations that are determined by the thematic text questions. They also have an influence on the selection of the predicate units.

5.1.5 *Text role configurations (TROC)*

What can such a text question in fact look like? It should have the form of a predicate-argument structure that we defined for the representation of the propositional component (in sub-section 4.2.2). As for the definition of the slots, here too we fall back on available authentic texts. The assumption that texts (including the book texts to be described) are the results of actions is reflected in a frequently used manner of presentation in which these actions are described. For this, we will explain the action schema introduced above. It expresses *what the book does* or *what the author does* or even *what the reader does*. This action schema has the form of a predicate-argument structure, whereby the argument slots are interpreted as text roles. They specify the propositional component PRO in the following way, whereby a general predicate class DOING is introduced:

```
[PRO [
      [PRED=DOING ]
      [TROL1=BOOK, AUTHOR, READER     ]
      [TROL2= . . .                   ]
      . . .
      [TROLn=                      ] ] ]
```

A further specification concerns the text role configuration (TROC). Text roles occur in typical configurations, e.g. in the form of

```
[TROC|i=
     [TROL1=  X ]
     [TROL2=  Y ] ]
```

This corresponds to a bivalent expansion of a text question such as: what does the book do in relation to the topic?

```
[PRO [
     [PRED=DOING ]
     [TROC|2=
            [TROL1= BOOK           ]
            [TROL2= TOPIC          ] ]]]
```

In the following, we show a number of examples which apply this description principle to authentic material. Here we sort the possible configurations according to the number of text roles involved. The principle of semantic valency is in this way applied to the description of PRO.

• The text role configuration is mono-valent: TROC|1. This results from the fact that only one text role is discussed. Grammatically, this selection is followed by the passive use of the predicate. In principle, all text roles are possible here:

```
        TROC|1:      {TOPIC, READER, BOOK, . . . }
```

[1]   [PRO [
           [PRED= *be reshaped*]
           [TROC|1=
                   [TROL1= TOPIC   ]]]]
       Text:
       The subject matter of anthropology is radically reshaped.

[2]   [PRO [
           [PRED= *intended*]
           [TROC|1=
                   [TROL1= READER *(for use . . .)*   ]]]]
       Text:
       Intended for use in a second level course (this book takes . . .)

[3]   [PRO [
           [PRED= *be included*]
           [TROC|1=

                    [TROL1= BOOK/PART (*articles*)   ]]]]
Text:
The following articles are included.

• The text role configuration is bi-valent: TROC|2; the combinations
can refer to different types of text role or to a contrast of sub-types of the
kind WHOLE/PART ([7]):

        TROC|2:   {   (BOOK/WHOLE, TOPIC/WHOLE),

                              (BOOK/PART,   TOPIC/PART   ),
                              (BOOK/WHOLE, READER   ),
                              (AUTHOR,   TOPIC   ),
                              . . .
                              (TOPIC/WHOLE, TOPIC/PART   )
                              . . .   }

[4]   [PRO [
            [PRED= *take*]
            [TROC|2=
                    [TROL1= BOOK/WHOLE (*this book*)   ]
                    [TROL2= TOPIC/WHOLE (*a . . . approach . . .*)]]]]
Text:
This book takes a 'top-down' structured approach to digital systems design.

[5]   [PRO [
            [PRED= *be applicable*]
            [TROC|2=
                    [TROL1= BOOK/WHOLE (*the material*)   ]
                    [TROL2= READER (*to both . . .*)   ]]]]
Text:
*The material is applicable to both the senior and first-year graduate level
in electrical engineering and computer science curricula.*

[6]   [PRO [
            [PRED= *focus on*]
            [TROC|2=
                    [TROL1= AUTHOR (*contributors*)   ]
                    [TROL2= TOPIC (*a . . . concern with . . . law*)]]]]
Text:
*Contributors focus on an overriding concern with contradiction in the law
and contradictions in methods of viewing the law.*

[7]   [PRO [
          [PRED= *constitute*]
          [TROC|2=
                    [TROL1= TOPIC/PART (*implications ... problems*)]
                    [TROL2= TOPIC (*major aspects of . . .*)   ]]]]
Text:
The implications and problems of the current development constitute the
major aspects of investigation.

• The text role configuration is tri-valent: TROC|3; here, too, apart
from different text roles, sub-types of a text role can also be used:

TROC|3:   {(BOOK,   READER,   TOPIC   ),
             . . .   ,
             (TOPIC/WHOLE, TOPIC/PART,   PART1,. . .)}

[8]   [PRO [
          [PRED= 0]
          [TROC|3=
                    [TROL1= BOOK/TYPE (*a reference*)   ]
                    [TROL2= READER (*for all researchers . . .*)   ]
                    [TROL3= TOPIC (*in this . . . area of engineering*)]]]]
Text:
A reference for all researchers around the world in this important area of
engineering.

[9]   [PRO [
          [PRED= *be introduced to and educated on*]
          [TROC|3=
                    [TROL1= BOOK (*in this volume*)   ]
                    [TROL2= READER (*researchers...law*)   ]
                    [TROL3= TOPIC (*the ...investigation...law*)]]]]
Text:
In this volume, researchers, students, and professors in the social sciences
and law are introduced to and educated on the empirical investigation of
phenomena in the interdisciplinary field of language and law.

[10] [PRO [
          [PRED= *come to include*]
          [TROC|3=
                    [TROL1= TOPIC (*anthropology*)   ]
                    [TROL2= TOPIC/PART (*such ...research as*)]
                    [TROL3= PART1/2/. . . (*archaeology, . . .*)]]]]

Text:
Anthropology has come to include such different fields of research as archae-ology, linguistics, ethnology, theology, human geography and human biol-ogy.

• The text role configuration is quadri-valent: TROC|4; the possibilities for expansion are here understandably restricted:

TROC|4:   {(BOOK, AUTHOR, READER, TOPIC) }

[11] [PRO [
          [PRED= *provide*]
          [TROC|4=
                    [TROL1= BOOK/TITLE *(contexts . . .)*   ]
                    [TROL2= AUTHOR/NAME *(M.B.)*   ]
                    [TROL3= READER *(the reader)*   ]
                    [TROL4= TOPIC *(with a . . . perspective . . .)*   ]]]]
     Text:
In Contexts of Competence, author Margie Berns provides the reader with a theoretical and practical perspective on the unique relationship between context and communicative competence.

With respect to the text grammar to be set up (see section 5.3), the following horizontal expansions for TROC result:

TROCi: <TROC|1, TROC|2, TROC|3, TROC|4>

Text role configurations describe the internal structure of PRO, insofar as this concerns the argument structure. In addition they determine the predicate class, insofar as it concerns the semantic assignment. Lexical assignments are only possible when the illocutionary part is also taken into consideration (see below section 5.2). As the examples show, the gram-matical filling of the individual text roles is frequently very complex. This point has to be considered in an interface to sentence production from the PRO representations (cf. also section 5.3).

The definition of the concept thematic text structure in the form of a text role structure enables us to understand the text topic as a text-grammar concept (cf. also Lötscher, 1987, p. 76). This means that proper-ties of the text structure can be understood and described with reference to this concept. In Chapter 6 it is shown how the topic model introduced here renders the presentation of sequencing strategies and their manifesta-tions in the connectivity structure of texts possible. Central to this is the idea that the constituting units are not defined in relation to words, as concepts, text referents or lexical units for example. The introduction of text-thematic roles means an addition to word or sentence-related approaches, in which the thematic structure is modelled as a reference to a homogeneous object world. In addition to the occurrence principle, here there is a functional principle. With respect to occurrence, the question is what units of the object world occur (frequently or repeatedly). From the functional viewpoint, the question is in what recurrent text functions do the units of the object world occur.

Text roles and text role configurations have the status of text-semantic units (cf. also Agricola 1979, Metzeltin & Jaksche, 1983, pp. 22–33). As constitutive units of the thematic structure they form the basis for the description of the global text structure. This is understood as the sequential expansion of text role configurations (Chapter 4). As functional units related to the sentence level, they represent a conceptual structure. As an interpretation of the propositional content (PRO) in the text action schema they are an instrument for explaining thematically-oriented selections within the framework of the object knowledge.

5.2 Interactional knowledge

5.2.1 Interaction model

The propositional content (PRO) of the text action schema is specified by the introduction of text roles (TROL) and text role configurations (TROC). These were interpreted as manifestations of the object knowledge. Interactional knowledge concerns the illocution component (ILL) and linguistic means, which are specified in inventories (INV). The aspect of interaction takes effect indirectly on the basis of the definition of illocution and illocution types. It plays a direct role in the global organisation of the text. The latter is the object of the expansion of illocutions which contribute to the building of the sequential sentence structure. We dealt with this in section 4.2. In this section, we are concerned with properties of the interactive component that affect the individual utterance.

In sub-section 4.2.2 illocutions were defined within the framework of the text action schema as propositional attitudes on the one hand and instructions on the other. As propositional attitudes they characterise the assignment of the object knowledge to various writer-oriented classifications. We oriented ourselves towards facts relating to the object, towards writer-oriented beliefs and writer-related value associations on the basis of group-specific standards. These classifications are denoted in text production by using various linguistic realisation types:

The book is   (a)   *a document about...*
                 (b)   *a repository...*
                 (c)   *necessary...*

This view differs from the likewise text-question-oriented approach as it is applied in the above-mentioned Heidelberg project (von Stutterheim 1992, Kohlmann et al. 1989). In this approach, a distinction is made between the main and the sub-structure of the text, whereby the main structure concerns the direct object description, whereas the sub-structure is characterised by additional explanations and comments on the part of the writer.

Within the framework of our action approach we differentiate on the other hand between the two text levels of the thematic and interactional component. In this context, the thematic component establishes the reference to the object knowledge independently of whether it appears as object-related in descriptions or writer-related in evaluations. This differentiation is assigned to the interactional component. A differentiation via text levels has two advantages: from the text-structural aspect it permits a flexible presentation of relations between the two text levels. From the aspect of the linguistic realisation, it opens up the possibility to establish text-type-specific lexical inventories.

Object-related realisation, what we describe with the illocution type DESCRIBE (DES), leads to utterances such as:

> *The present monography gives an historical overview of the university as a literary topic.*

For beliefs that are assigned to the illocution type ASSERT (ASS), the following utterances apply:

> *The attempt at wanting to adequately describe or succinctly define something as central and characteristic as 'Romantic irony', seems doomed to failure from the very outset.*

EVALUATE (EVAL) characterises value assignments. This is illustrated by such utterances as:

> *The clear presentation makes the book a pleasure to read. Reading this book is simply fun.*

The dialogic principle that with respect to the thematic structure is reflected as a question and answer also manifests itself as an interactional structure. The use of the various illocutions not only characterises the relation text author–text content, but at the same time accounts for various relations text author–text reader. These relations are indeed determined one-sidedly by the text author, however, they permit different reactions on the part of the reader. The choice of combination and sequence of illocution types in the text can be expressed in various presentation modes for the respective object. In our context, we are concerned with one descriptive and one argumentative text mode. This, however, does not mean that these are the only possibilities for this sort of text (cf. presentation modes such as problem solving, criticism, report, portrait, etc.). The descriptive mode primarily requires the use of DESCRIBING, the argumentative mode the illocution type ASSERTING. EVALUATING belongs to both. The presentation mode determines in what way the communication partners can be involved in the respective situation. The role of the text author is in both cases combined with the initiative. In the descriptive mode the reader is expected to accept the content conveyed. In the argumentative mode with *PRO*s and *CONTRA*s, the author is expected to take a position (on the status of initiative and reaction as dialogic principles of the linguistic action cf. Weigand 1989).

As instructions, illocutions have the function to govern lexicalisation. Not until it is known which presentation mode, i.e. which illocution type is to be realised, can the lexical units be selected for the linguistic realisation of predicate units and text roles. Since we cannot presuppose a 1:1 correspondence between pragmatic function and lexical means, we introduce lexical inventories (INV), which represent possible options as a list of lexicalisations that come into question.

At the centre of our interest are inventories for the realisation of the predicates. They are especially interesting for several reasons. Regardless of the fact that in the majority of approaches to automatic text generation that are concerned with lexicalisation the nominal units form the main focus, verbal units simultaneously point to several text-relevant properties:

• While as predicate element they combine the text roles with each other, relations to the object model also have an effect (syntagmatic properties with object reference).

• In the sequencing in the text the predicate units can form progressions which contribute to the text coherence. Such progressions denote a coherence, which is established by expanding the text question (paradigmatic and text-sequential properties).

The implication of such text properties on the use of predicate units has already been observed from various angles. Hasan (1978), for example, already points to text-specific collocation chains, which represent a typical feature of textual lexis. Tannen (1986) points out that coherence in written language is established to a greater extent via lexis than is the case in spoken language and that frames play an important role for the cohesion of lexical units. Weber (1986) has demonstrated with the help of 'propositional structures' in news texts that factual contexts are reflected in a specific sequence of verbal units. And Keseling et al. (1987) illustrate within the framework of human-text-planning that so-called frame utterances build a kind of textual framework that can already be written in even if it is not yet clear what the precise fillers for the nominal positions are to be. From this point of view the selections of the predicate units have a text-structure-forming function.

• A third aspect concerns the text type reference. Text-type-specific restrictions of language use have been discussed under the heading 'sublanguage' (Kittredge & Lehrberger (eds) 1982, Grishman & Nhan 1984). This raises the problem that it is indeed intuitively known that not every lexeme, even if the meaning matches, can be used in every sort of text, but that it is difficult on the other hand to determine criteria for these restrictions. As a rule, the discussion has been restricted to statistical solutions (occurrence frequency). A distinction according to illocution types, which distinguishes the language use depending on domain classes, text topic and writer-related classifications of domain classes, is an important step in the direction of a more precise definition of criteria.

In our context we had defined DESCRIBING, ASSERTING and EVALUATING as illocution types. Illocution types were in turn defined as differentiations with regard to the relation of PRO and LOC with respect to classifications of the knowledge that W contributes to the interaction between W (text writer) and R (text reader).

The use of the inventories can be determined by conditions. These conditions relate to co-occurrences of illocution type and text roles or text role configurations. In the following sections we give some examples of such inventories. They are intended to illustrate the approach. Approximate completeness, for which further empirical studies are required, is not aimed at.

For the representation of inventories, we employ schemata with the following parts: the inventories for predicates (INVP) have an illocutionary part (ILL), a constraint part (CONST) and a lexical list (LEXLI). It can be seen that collocations occur frequently. They are also divided among typical text role configurations:

```
[INVP         [
[ILL= TYP                     ]
[CONST= TROC|i
       [TROL1= X, . . .        ]]
[LEXLI: { v1, v2, . . ., vn }    ]] ]
```

5.2.2 DESCRIBING

DESCRIBING (DES) puts the object reference in the foreground. It is assumed that the information to be conveyed is unknown to the reader. Linguistically relevant properties of describing or descriptions have been researched experimentally and with respect to object reference in Kohlmann et al. (1989), Klein & von Stutterheim (1991).

One of the interesting problems associated with object descriptions concerns the global text structure and consists in the fact that spacial, functional or other properties and relations of an object are isolated and transferred to a sequential order. For this we had introduced the slots of the object model on the one hand and their composition and sequencing on the basis of the text questions on the other. In this section we are now interested in the effects of such divisions on lexical inventories, which differ from inventories of other interactional types. In the following, we give a few examples of verbs and collocations that are combined with certain text role configurations.

[12]   DES, TROC|1(TOPIC)

```
[INVP        [
[ILL= DES                                                        ]
[CONST= TROC|1
      [TROL1= TOPIC ]                                            ]
[LEXLI: { emphasis is placed on, proposals are made for, . . . }]] ]
```

Example:
```
[PRED=                  particular emphasis is placed on    ]
[TROL1= TOPIC           transport of . . .                  ]
```

The topic can be introduced by impersonal expressions:

```
[INVP        [
[ILL= DES                                                        ]
[CONST= TROC|1
      [TROL1= TOPIC ]                                            ]
[LEXLI: { it is shown that/how, it was found that, . . . }   ]] ]
```

Example:
```
[PRED=                  it is shown that                    ]
[TROL1= TOPIC           the development of . . .            ]
```

The topic can be explicitly designated through introductory expressions
which include designations such as *topic* etc. We assign this to the text role
TOPIC/EXPL. It permits certain lexicalisations:

         [INVP   [
         [ILL= DES   ]
         [CONST= TROC|1
              [TROL1= TOPIC/EXPL]   ]
         [LEXLI: {*be discussed, introduced, modified, reshaped, . . .* }]]]

Examples:
         [[TROL1= TOPIC/EXPL   *the subject matter*   ]
         [PRED=   *is reshaped.*   ]]

         [[TROL1= TOPIC/EXPL   *the issue of . . .*   ]
         [PRED=   *is discussed*   ]]

Topic parts can be introduced as such:

         [INVP   [
         [ILL= DES   ]
         [CONST= TROC|1
              [TROL1= TOPIC/PART]   ]
         [LEXLI: {*be included, have been worked out, . . .*   }   ]]]

Examples:
         [[TROL1= TOPIC/PART   *a . . . specification of . . .*   ]
         [PRED=   *has been worked out*   ]]

         [[TROL1= TOPIC/PART   *a design example*   ]
         [PRED=   *is included*   ]]

[13]   DES, TROC|2(AUTHOR, TOPIC)

         [INVP   [
         [ILL= DES   ]
         [CONST= TROC|2
              [TROL1= AUTHOR]
              [TROL2= TOPIC]   ]
         [LEXLI: {*to discuss, to examine, to focus (the attention) on,*

                          to give an account of, to include . . .,
                          to offer new insights into, . . .   }   ]]]

Example:
    [[TROL1= AUTHOR/NAME   *W.B.*   ]
    [PRED=   *discusses*   ]
    [TROL2= TOPIC   *new trends of . . .*   ]]

[14]   DES, TROC│2(BOOK, TOPIC)

The role AUTHOR and BOOK is in many cases interchangeable. Nevertheless, the inventories do not fully overlap.

    [INVP   [
    [ILL= DES   ]
    [CONST= TROC│2
        [TROL1= BOOK]
        [TROL2= TOPIC]   ]
    [LEXLI: {*to be based on, to contain, to deal with, to describe,*
               to go beyond, to illustrate, to show, . . .
               to lead to (new) perspectives on,
               to range from ...to . . ., . . . }   ]]]

Example:
    [[TROL1= BOOK   *this study*   ]
    [PRED=   *is based on*   ]
    [TROL2= TOPIC   *research . . .*   ]]

TROL2 can also refer to the explicit TOPIC:

    [INVP   [
    [ILL= DES   ]
    [CONST= TROC│2
        [TROL1= BOOK]
        [TROL2= TOPIC/EXPL]   ]
    [LEXLI: {*to contain, to offer an (all-encompassing) view into, . . .* }]]]

Example:
    [[TROL1= BOOK   *this collection of . . .*   ]
    [PRED=   *contains*   ]
    [TROL2= TOPIC/EXPL   *three central themes: . . .*   ]]

[15]   DES, TROC|2(TOPIC/EXPL, TOPIC)
Explicit topic can also fill the first text role:

```
[INVP       [
 [ILL= DES                                                      ]
 [CONST= TROC|2
      [TROL1= TOPIC/EXPL]
      [TROL2= TOPIC]                                            ]
  [LEXLI: {be the subject of the study, be the major focus, a wide
           range of topics shows, a wide variety of subject matter
           offers, the (fundamental) issue addressed is how...}  ]]]
```

Example:

```
[[TROL1    = TOPIC/EXPL    the subject of the study      ]
 [PRED     =               is                            ]]
 [TROL2    = TOPIC         to investigate . . .           ]
```

[16]   DES, TROC|2(BOOK, READER)

```
[INVP        [
 [ILL= DES                                                      ]
 [CONST= TROC|2
      [TROL1= BOOK]
      [TROL2= READER ]                                         ]
  [LEXLI: {to be relevant to, to be a book for, to be of (specific) interest
           to, to be a contribution to our understanding, to be intended
           for use by (teachers), to be useful to . . .        }      ]] ]
```

Examples:

```
[[TROL1    = BOOK          the book                      ]
 [PRED     =               is a contribution to          ]
 [TROL2    = READER        our understanding of . . .     ]]

[[TROL1    = BOOK/TITLE    '...'                          ]
 [PRED     =               is a book                      ]
 [TROL2    = READER        for many different people      ]]
```

[17]   DES, TROC|2(TOPIC, PURPOSE)

```
[INVP        [
 [ILL= DES                                                      ]
 [CONST= TROC|2
      [TROL1= TOPIC]
      [TROL2= PURPOSE]                                          ]
```

        [LEXLI: {*to be analyzed, to be intended as an aid to, to be intended as a*
        means of, to want to help, . . . }   ]]]

Example:

        [[TROL1   = TOPIC   *a body of ideological material*]
        [PRED   =   *is analyzed*   ]
        [TROL2   = PURPOSE   *to give an idea of . . .*   ]]

[18]   DES, TROC|2(BOOK, PURPOSE)

[INVP   [
        [ILL= DES   ]
        [CONST= TROC|2
              [TROL1= BOOK]
              [TROL2= PURPOSE]   ]
        [LEXLI: {*to be analyzed, to be intended as an aid to, to be*
                  intended as a means of, to want to help, be
                  intended to be reference guide   . . . }   ]]]

Examples:

        [[TROL1   = BOOK   *this book*   ]
        [PRED   =   *is intended as an aid*   ]
        [TROL2   = PURPOSE   *to communication . . .*   ]]

        [[TROL1   = BOOK   *the volume*   ]
        [PRED   =   *wants to help*   ]
        [TROL2   = PURPOSE   *initiating this process . . .*   ]]

Similar to the topic, the purpose of the book can also be introduced
through explicit designation:

[INVP   [
        [ILL= DES   ]
        [CONST= TROC|2
              [TROL1= PURPOSE/EXPL]
              [TROL2= PURPOSE]   ]
        [LEXLI: {*be the aim (of the study), . . .* }   ]]]

Example:

        [[TROL1= PURPOSE/EXPL *one of the main aims of the study*   ]
        [PRED =   *is*   ]
        [TROL2 = PURPOSE   *to establish . . .*   ]]

[18]   DES, TROC|3(BOOK, AUTHOR, READER)

```
[INVP        [
     [ILL= DES                                                     ]
     [CONST= TROC|3
          [TROL1= BOOK/TITLE]
          [TROL2= AUTHOR]
          [TROL3= READER]                                          ]
     [LEXLI:     {help to increase, . . . }                        ]] ]
```

Example:
```
     [[TROL1    = BOOK/TITLE   with their volume '...'     ]
     [TROL2     = AUTHOR       B.W. and G.F.               ]
     [PRED      =              to help to increase         ]
     [TROL2     = READER       our understanding of...     ]]
```

[19]   DES, TROC|3(BOOK/PART, BOOK, TOPIC)

```
[INVP        [
     [ILL= DES                                            ]
     [CONST= TROC|3
          [TROL1= BOOK/PART]
          [TROL2= BOOK]
          [TROL3= TOPIC]                                  ]
     [LEXLI:     {to teach, . . . }                       ]] ]
```

Example:
```
     [[TROL1    = BOOK/PART    in . . . chapters    ]
     [TROL2     = BOOK         this book            ]
     [PRED      =              teaches             ]
     [TROL2     = READER       how to . . .         ]]
```

5.2.3 ASSERTING

ASSERTING (ASS) refers to beliefs of W of a general nature, which are
linked to aspects of the object to be described. In this way, assertions in
connection with the object description have a special significance. This is
based on the fact that they are used for the realisation of the argumentative
presentation mode (on argumentation as speech act cf. van Eemeren &
Grootendorst 1984).

   Argumentation is a problem area that as such has been discussed in a
number of theoretical and methodical approaches. In our context, above

all the relation of the argumentative structure to the global text structure plays a role (e.g. van Dijk (1980b, advertising text), Huth (1977, newspaper report), Wonneberger (1977, New Testament, Letters of Paul), Rothkegel (1988, dialogue construction). From the point of view of the interactional definition of DESCRIBING and EVALUATING, we can see that here, too, specific inventories can be compiled. The truth value capacity, which applies simultaneously to both DESCRIBING and AS-SERTING, has no influence on this.

In book announcement texts, assertions usually occur in a sequence, in which first of all the topic as such is introduced and then the specific contribution of the respective book is described. With respect to the object model, assertions are therefore first and foremost connected to the text role TOPIC, without reference being made directly to the respective object. The integration of assertions in an argumentative structure also requires that they be capable of expressing the *PRO*s and *CONTRA*s of the argumentation. We go into this in detail in the treatment of the global text structure in Chapter 7. Here we are interested primarily in the specific lexical inventories related to this. We give some examples with typical predicate adjectives or verbs and multi-word collocations. What is striking is the fact that they contain evaluating expressions (cf. pro and contra), and yet differ from EVALUATIONS (cf. below). Statements are exclusively made about the topic. It is in the focus of the argumentation. Correspondingly, there is only one monovalent text role configuration:

[20]   ASS, TROC│1(TOPIC)

```
[INVP        [
[ILL= ASS                                                      ]
[CONST= TROC│1
        [TROL1= TOPIC ]                                        ]
[LEXLI:{ to be un(economical), to be (extremely) scarce, it should
         be clear, it is proposed that, it is claimed that, it is argued
         that, it is generally believed that, do not ( . . .), . . .} ]] ]
```

Examples:

```
    [PRED=                       it should be clear              ]
    [TROL1= TOPIC                that . . .                      ]

    [TROL1= TOPIC                '...'                           ]
    [PRED=                       is uneconomical                 ]
    [TROL1= TOPIC                ' . . . '                       ]
    [PRED=                       does not, as such, exist        ]
```

5.2.4 *EVALUATING*

Linguistically relevant studies of evaluations have each stressed different aspects. Methodical access can be viewed from a number of angles. Sandig (1979, 1991) proceeds from the linguistic expressions that are used for evaluation and then develops a pragmatically-oriented system. Similarly, they are also treated from an action-theoretical standpoint, but with a view to a typology of speech acts in Zillig (1982a, 1982b). As conceptual structures they are opposed to connotation- and emotion-oriented interpretations of lexical semantics (Fries 1991). All approaches make it clear that the diversity of the phenomena resists a simple and homogeneous description structure.

A parameter that is adopted vis-à-vis a positive or negative value for the respective state of affairs is considered constitutive for evaluations (Fries, 1991, p. 18). In the case of book announcement texts, the parameter is formed by norms, according to which all parts as well as the whole of the action schema of the topic question can be assigned such a value. In concrete terms: the predicates and text roles, as well as the overall propositions, can be assigned such a value. The basis for this assignment is a knowledge of norms on the part of W that W contributes to the interaction quasi as 'additional own information'. This knowledge of norms, which would need to be constructed as a list of expressions of the kind 'x is positive/negative, if x fulfils/does not fulfil the norm n', and likewise the assignment itself, are not the object of our model. Neither are we concerned here with a system of evaluations, but rather with the importance that evaluations have within the framework of the text structure organisation, especially with regard to defining the inventories for predicate units. Not considered are the frequent evaluations that also occur in book announcements through adjectives (*thorough, precise, reliable, brief,* etc. cf. 'scientific virtues' in Zillig, 1982b, pp. 202f.), adverbial expressions that express novelty (*for the first time*), or other constructions (e.g. relative clauses as in *Humboldt, who is considered to be one of the most important naturalists, . . .*). They can in principle be added to all text roles or propositions. In addition, it generally applies that the evaluations of interest here are linked to descriptions or assertions. What makes their differentiation relevant is the fact that the additional evaluating function leads to further inventories for the predicate units.

INVP/EVA are inventories for predicates which contain an evaluating expression (lexical marking). Evaluations through the use of evaluating predicates refer first and foremost to the text roles BOOK, TOPIC, AUTHOR, READER.

[21]   EVA, TROC│1(BOOK)

```
[INVP        [
[ILL= EVA                                                       ]
[CONST= TROC│1
        [TROL1= BOOK ]                                          ]
[LEXLI:              { to be relevant, provocative, . . .}      ]] ]
```

Example:

```
[TROL1= BOOK         the papers presented here                  ]
[PRED=               are both relevant and provocative  ]
```

[22]   EVA, TROC│1(TOPIC/EXPL)
The topic is frequently evaluated together with the explicit thematisation
of the text role:

```
[INVP         [
[ILL= EVA                                                       ]
[CONST= TROC│1
        [TROL1= TOPIC/EXPL ]                                    ]
[LEXLI:     {fascinating, . . .              }                  ]] ]
```

Example:

```
[TROL1= TOPIC        a fascinating topic                        ]
[PRED=                       0                                  ]
```

[23]   EVA, TROC│1(AUTHOR)
An indirect evaluation of the book takes place through an evaluation of the
author:

```
[INVP        [
[ILL= EVA                                                       ]
[CONST= TROC│1
        [TROL1= AUTHOR ]                                        ]
[LEXLI:{ to occupy a unique position, to imprint an indelible
         stamp on . . ., }                                      ]] ]
```

Example:

```
[TROL1= AUTHOR  I.L.                                            ]
[PRED=                  has (for many years) occupied a
                        unique position as one of the foremost
                        scholars in the fields of . . .,        ]
```

[24]   EVA, TROC|2(BOOK, BOOK/TYPE)

The book can be evaluated with respect to a particular aspect, e.g. with respect to the book type. In this way a bi-valent form emerges:

```
[INVP        [
 [ILL= EVA                                                      ]
 [CONST= TROC|2
      [TROL1= BOOK ]
      [TROL2= BOOK/TYPE]                                        ]
   [LEXLI: {to be much more than, to be the first . . .;
            to be excellent, to be/become a standard, . . .   }       ]] ]
```

Examples:

```
[TROL1= BOOK           this book                                ]
[PRED=                 is much more than                        ]
[TROL2= BOOK/TYPE      an . . . handbook                        ]


[TROL1= BOOK           this                                     ]
[PRED=                 is                                       ]
[TROL2= BOOK/TYPE      the first comprehensive textbook         ]


[TROL1= BOOK           the book                                 ]
[PRED=                 is likely to remain                      ]
[TROL2= BOOK/TYPE      a standard reference in the field        ]
```

[25]   EVA, TROC|2(BOOK, READER)

Bi-valency is also linked to the evaluation of the text role READER:

```
[INVP        [
 [ILL= EVA                                                      ]
 [CONST= TROC|2
      [TROL1= BOOK ]
      [TROL2= READER      ]                                     ]
   [LEXLI:    {to be indispensable . . . }                   ]] ]
```

Example:

```
[TROL1= BOOK           this volume                              ]
[PRED=                 is indispensable                         ]
[TROL2= BOOK/TYPE      for scientists and research workers      ]
```

[26]   EVA, TROC|2(TOPIC/PROBLEM, TOPIC/SOLUTION)
Specific verbs occur when specified roles, i.e. sub-text roles of a superordinated text role, are linked together:

```
[INVP       [
[ILL= EVA                                              ]
[CONST= TROC|2
     [TROL1= TOPIC/PROBLEM ]
     [TROL2= TOPIC/SOLUTION]                           ]
[LEXLI:        {to succeed in, . . . }           ]] ]
```

Examples:
```
[TROL1= T/PROBLEM   the model of . . .                              ]
[PRED=              succeeds                                        ]
[TROL2= T/SOLUTION  in providing a solid framework for . . .  ]
```

[27]   EVA, TROC|3(MAKE-UP, BOOK, BOOK/EXPL)
Tri-valency occurs when two slots fall to the text role BOOK:

```
[INVP       [
[ILL= EVA                                              ]
[CONST= TROC|3
     [TROL1= MAKE-UP   ]
     [TROL2= BOOK      ]
     [TROL3= BOOK/EXPL ]                               ]
[LEXLI:    {to make a (. . .) book, . . .       }    ]] ]
```

Examples:
```
[TROL1= MAKE-UP     many illustrations           ]
[PRED=              make                          ]
[TROL2= BOOK        this                          ]
[TROL3= BOOK/EXPL   a scintillating book          ]
```

5.2.5 Clusters of predicates (CLUST)

In the case of parallel repetition of the text role configuration within a text, predicates are selected from the same inventory. This leads to clusters (CLUST) as a result of preferences of an INVP:

```
[CLUST      [
[ILL= DES                                              ]
[CONST= TROC|2
```

```
            [TROL1= BOOK ]
            [TROL2= TOPIC]                                    ]
        [LEXLI: {to explore, outline, advocate, consider, discuss, . . .} ]] ]
```

Example:

[TROL1= BOOK/WHOLE	*this work*	]
[PRED=	*explores*	]
[TROL2= TOPIC/WHOLE	*the relationship between . . .*]	
[TROL1= BOOK/PART1	*chapter 1*	]
[PRED=	*outlines*	]
[TROL2= TOPIC/PART2	*arguments . . .*	]
[TROL1= BOOK/PART2	*chapter 2*	]
[PRED=	*advocates*	]
[TROL2= TOPIC/PART2	*the extension of . . .*	]
[TROL1= BOOK/PART3	*chapter 3*	]
[PRED=	*considers*	]
[TROL2= TOPIC/PART3	*the effect of . . .*	]
[TROL1= BOOK/PART4	*chapter 4*	]
[PRED=	*discusses*	]
[TROL2= TOPIC/PART4	*the implications of...*	]

5.3 Text grammar and lexicalisation

The theory of a conceptual level raises problems concerning the transition
of this level to the linguistic level. Specific for this are problems of text lexis
(Figge 1989). Our approach, as illustrated above, is illocution-oriented (c)
and in this respect can be distinguished from other, likewise context-
related approaches ((a), (b)):

(a) assignment via the description of syntactic and/or semantic roles
(b) assignment via a combination of knowledge base and role description
(c) assignment via a combination of knowledge-based text role descrip-
     tions and illocutions.

The lexicalisation of concepts can be controlled by linguistic parameters
(a). This kind of approach is, for example, pursued in text generation
systems that are grammatically oriented (e.g. Danlos 1987, de Smedt

1990). Here, conventional case frames are filled by concepts and augmented with syntactic information as required. In de Smedt (summarised from 1990, pp. 176f.) such case frames form a kind of bridge between the conceptual level and the syntactic level. They give the following form (*Otto eats an apple*):

```
(LET ((SIGN1 (A SIGN
                    (CONCEPT 'OTTO)))
      (SIGN2 (A SIGN
                    (CONCEPT (AN APPLE) )))
      (DEFINE-CASE SIGN1 'AGENT)
      (DEFINE-FEATURES SIGN1 '(DEFINITE + PLURAL –))) )
```

Lexicalisation via knowledge base and roles (b) is favoured by a word-related approach, in which the context in the structuring of the word meaning is included in the knowledge base (e.g. Dahlgren 1988, Dale 1990, Meier et al. 1988, Palmer 1990). In the knowledge base are the concepts to which linguistic utterences are assigned either directly or via a semantic representation of argument roles. The contextual structuring of the concepts permits the choice of lexical alternatives or the choice of grammatical realisations (definite/indefinite nominal phrases or pronouns; on this see above all Dale 1990).

In representations of a word meaning, all information types necessary for the linguistic realisation can thus appear combined. For the verb *buy*, Dahlgren (1988, p. 97), for example, gives the following structure:

```
buy ({what_enables(can(afford(subj,obj)))),
how(with(X) & money(X)),
where(in(Y) & store(Y)),
what_happens_next(use(subj,obj))},
{cause(need(subj,obj))},
{goal(own(subj,obj)),
consequence_of_event(own(subj,obj)),
selectional-restriction(sentient(subj)),
implies(merchandise(obj))}).
```

Such a structure contains both typified features that are oriented towards the categories of Graesser & Clark (1985) (*what . . .; how . . .*, etc. see sub-section 5.1.2), as well as roles like goal and syntactic categories like subject and object.

The specification of the illocution component (c) renders a purposive access to problems of lexicalisation in text generation possible. Whereas in both approaches (a) and (b) the factual reference is considered central for lexical selection, and language use conditional on communicative purposes is only considered implicitly through prespecified assignments to domain-specific concepts, approach (c) attempts to make both the state of affairs reference and communicative purposes as control parameters for the lexical selection explicit. The integration of all three aspects is thereby achieved through the description instrument of the simple text action. What is essential is that this integration is modelled via text roles as well as illocution types and not via concepts, which are assigned directly to certain lexical units, or via case roles, which are sentence-related. This is a consequence of an approach that does not proceed from lexical-grammatical phenomena and examine their relevance with respect to text properties, but rather which proceeds from global text properties and from there develops the lexically and grammatically effective description units.

The text action schema (cf. section 4.4) forms the basis for the representation of interactional, propositional and linguistic conditions, which are then related to one another. Proceeding from the components ILL, PRO and LOC, the following specifications emerge:

- for ILL through the respective illocution type:
  ILL: <TYPE>
  TYPE: {DESCRIBING, EVALUATING, ASSERTING}

- for the propositional component through a predicate class (PRED) that characterises the text question and through a specified configuration of certain text roles:
  PRO: < PRED, TROCi >
  TROCi: < TROC|1, . . ., TROC|n >

- for the locutive component through inventories (INV) that are defined by conditions (CONST); such conditions concern the co-occurrence of illocution type and text role configuration:
  LOC: < INVP, CONST >

In conclusion the question arises as to how the established specifications can be integrated into an operationalised text grammar. To this end, we introduce a carrier structure, which presents a formal framework for the representation of the simple text action. This is the so-called text row (TR), which is the basic unit for thematic and lexical selections. This is the case with respect to a proposition and the inventories relevant to it. In the operationalisation, a text row is produced cumulatively through representations of [PRO] and [INVP] (and possibly [CLUST]). Point of departure

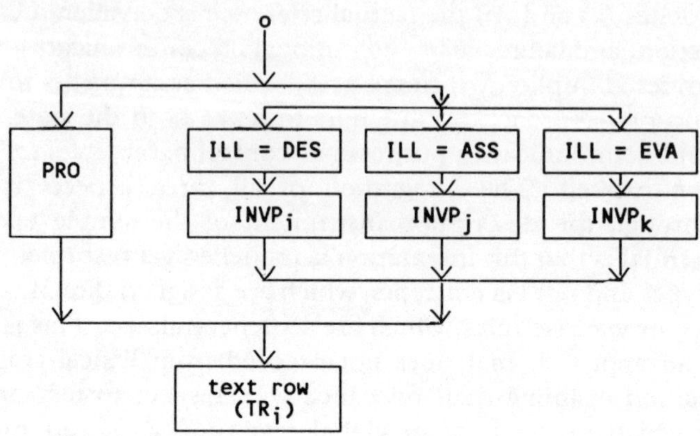

Figure 5.1 Lexical selection and production of the text row

is the designation of the text action in relation to the illocution type (Figure 5.1). The three types of inventory are specified as follows:

CONSTii: < (TROC|1 {TOPIC, TOPIC/EXPL, TOPIC/PART }),
   (TROC|2 { (AUTHOR, TOPIC), (BOOK, TOPIC),
      (BOOK, TOPIC/EXPL), (TOPIC/EXPL,
      TOPIC), (BOOK, READER), (TOPIC,
      PURPOSE), (BOOK, PURPOSE),
      (PURPOSE/EXPL, PURPOSE) }),
   (TROC/3 { (BOOK, AUTHOR, READER),
      (BOOK/PART, BOOK, TOPIC) }) >

CONSTjj < (TROC|1 {TOPIC }) >

CONSTkk < (TROC|1 { BOOK, TOPIC/EXPL, AUTHOR }),
   (TROC|2 { (BOOK, BOOK/TYPE), (BOOK, READER),
   (TOPIC(PROBLEM, SOLUTION)),
   (TROC|3 { (MAKE-UP, BOOK, BOOK/EXPL) }) >

In the following chapter we demonstrate how the integration of the illocutive, propositional and linguistic components is also effective on the global text level. This is illustrated in particular with the help of the connectivity structure, which reflects certain principles of the sequential text organisation. As in this chapter, we present the respective specification on the basis of empirical evidence.

6 Text grammar II.1: Principles of composition

6.0 Overview

We proceed from the assumption that sequentiality is the primary principle of text formation. It simply belongs to the text as a medium. Every kind of coherence – whether content, functional or formal – must be brought into a linear order. Hence from this principle we infer the specifications that are relevant within the framework of a text action grammar, and with a view to the composition processes in question.

The use of the concept 'composition' for the structural organisation in the text indicates that we are not concerned here with rigid rules of combination theory for linguistically defined units. This kind of formulation of a text grammar would not take account of the object text as a medium. On the other hand, we must also proceed from the assumption – and since 20 years of research text linguistics has done so – that texts are not a more or less coincidental conglomeration of sentences, but rather that they have something like a describable structure. The question is, in what way linguistically interesting regularities with respect to a specific structure for the medium text can be compiled. We argue in favour of doing this in such a way that general principles or text processes are formulated, proceeding from which specifications for a dynamic text grammar can be determined.

In this view, a strict separation of planning and producing phases does not seem to be suitable. They do permit a certain methodical simplification for the research of individual text processes and without doubt are also productive, as, for example, in writing research with the Flower & Hayes' (1980) division into pre-writing (planning), writing (production) and post-writing (revision), or in AI-research with the differentiation between WHAT (planning, content) and HOW (generation, linguistic form). The main disadvantage of this kind of approach is that interdependencies between the aspects cannot be ascertained and must possibly be assigned in subsequent components. This can be avoided through approaches that from the outset incorporate a greater complexity of information types. In this sense, what is meant by composition is that different levels of the consideration can be related to each other. This view is in line with text and text production research, which attempts to take precisely this complexity into account (de Beaugrande 1984, Zammuner 1988, Faigley et al. 1989, Motsch 1991). Our action approach is intended to provide a framework for the formation of structures in the text which integrates the following aspects:

- establishing coherence through expansions of illocutionary and text-thematic units,
- directionality as a dynamic principle of connectivity
- pattern formation as a structural principle of connectivity
- formal representation of the text connectivity.

The theoretically acquired specifications are demonstrated on the basis of decompositions of authentic texts. This is not concerned with a complete description of the respective text type. However, the respective specifications should make a contribution towards establishing a general paradigm for a text type description. Neither are we concerned with a complete description of a connectivity grammar. Rather, the goal is a frame in which different and individually discussed text phenomena can be organised.

6.1 Principles of sequencing

6.1.1 Coherence formation and expansions

In conformity with the basic elements of text linguistic research, we define text as a series of segments that form a coherent and cohesive structure. In this context, coherence as a structure connected with meaning and function and cohesion as a surface-related connection structure belong to the text-constitutive properties. 'Coherence' is a central concept for the consideration of the text structure (Fritz 1982). Descriptions in which coherence is understood as a connection in the text relate to relations between text units that are text-theoretically defined in different ways. In the global sense they are considered as dependent on the text topic (Hellwig 1984), or on the context of the state of affairs (Samet & Schank 1984, Tucker et al. 1986). As 'coherence relations' they characterise the linking of two text units and can be defined semantically (e.g. de Beaugrande & Dressler 1981), rhetorically (Mann & Thompson 1987) or logically (e.g. Hobbs 1979). Coherence roughly means that there is a recognisable and describable connection between the parts of the text. In our approach, we consider this connection as being explained by text-thematic and interactional aspects (see below).

Problems of text coherence are considered from many different angles in the relevant literature. With respect to the general assumptions, two viewpoints must be distinguished, which, however, are not to be seen as contrary but rather as complementary: coherence as a feature of texts or as the result of cognitive activities on the part of the reader and writer.

From the point of view of the text reference, there are again two possibilities to define coherence: as a connection at the level of the state of affairs and as a connection at the text level (van Dijk, 1980b, p. 36).

(a) In the first case, the connection at the level of the state of affairs is reproduced as the content structure of the text. This applies, for example, when in descriptions of events the order of the events determines the sequence of the text segments in the text and coherence is achieved through one partial event being the forerunner or successor of another partial event.

(b) In the second case, the connection is determined by text-specific factors. These can in turn be of a communicative and a formal nature. Communication-oriented aspects are concerned with connections that are established through the incorporation of contents in interactions (Fritz 1982, Sandig 1986, 1987, Viehweger 1991) and which in computational models are classified under the heading of 'pragmatic' and/or 'rhetorical' (e.g. Mann & Thompson 1987, Hovy 1988, 1991, Scott & de Souza 1990, Paris 1991). Text-formal aspects are concerned with connections that are established on the basis of continuity or shifts in content in the course of the text sequence (information flow) (linguistically in Chafe 1987, Hajičová 1986; computer-oriented in McKeown 1985, Grosz & Sidner 1986). The distinction between stative and dynamic aspects in the text structure description filters out various text properties (Viehweger 1987, Petöfi & Sözer 1988). Thus from a static point of view, pronominalisation in the text represents the substitution of a linear chain (Harweg 1968). From a dynamic standpoint on the other hand, the respective point in the text over which the writers and readers delay is considered. The so-called focus thus constantly shifts its position (cf. Daneš 1974a, Kallmeyer 1978, Hajičová & Sgall 1988, Fraurud & Hellman 1985, Erdmann 1990).

Implementations of dynamic models as focus mechanisms can be found in Sidner (1985), McKeown (1985), Grosz & Sidner (1986). Here, focus spaces are formed within a data base that restricts the choice of the respective focus. The linguistic realisation takes place via a focus mechanism in a stacking process: there are three stacks, one for the current focus, a second for the potential focuses and a third for the previous focus. When the previous focus becomes the focus of the new sentence, it is pronominalised. If an earlier focus is selected, it can be pronominalised, providing this does not lead to ambiguity. If a new focus is selected from the list of potential focuses, it has to be introduced by the indefinite article.

In the sense of a process-oriented, cognitive viewpoint, coherence is something that is produced in the memory of the reader and writer. This approach has above all had an effect in models concerning text understanding, which are primarily interested in the content of the text or the knowledge background. Linguistic utterances in the text are considered here as pegs for specific procedures which create a link between text and the existing knowledge of the language users. In the foreground are inferences that are derived pragmatically (van de Velde 1984, 1988), psychologically (Rickheit & Strohner (eds) 1985) or logically (Hobbs et al. 1987, Hobbs et al. 1988). Apart from these, text representations which are structured as networks also play a role (e.g. linguistically in de Beaugrande & Dressler 1981, computational-linguistically in Rollinger 1984a, 1984b, Hauenschild 1984). In such a network, coherence appears as a linking structure that is established by relating all the units of the text to one another through connections (paths of the network).

For the description of coherence it plays a role regarding what kind of units these are and what kind of connections between them are true. The units are linguistic units (e.g. words or text segments; object language level), or they are descriptions on a conceptual level (metalanguage). The connections characterise either relations between two such units, which we term local relations, or in the form of hierarchies or sequences (lists) they reflect a structure of the overall text, which we term global relations.

6.1.2 Local coherence relations

Local relations can be based on semantic relations, object-specific relations, contiguity or on rhetorical and communicative relations. Various designations for such relations are to be found in the relevant literature, whereby the concept of coherence relation seems to be establishing itself (cf. overview in Noël 1990).

Semantically valid coherence relations can be derived on the basis of word or sentence meanings. In this sense, the traditional semantic relations of generic/specific concept, property-of, part-of, instant-of, which above all are used in semantic networks and knowledge-based text approaches in Computational Linguistics and Artificial Intelligence, also apply here. Semantically valid coherence can also be produced by co-reference or partial co-reference, i.e. two adjacent sentences are considered directly connected if they have the same referent (Vater 1992).

Object-specific relations on the basis of content proximity (contiguity; with respect to thematic connections cf. Lötscher, 1987, p. 130f.) play a role above all in temporal relations (texts with series of events, cf. Moens & Steedman 1987, Dorfmüller-Karpusa 1988) and in causal relations (e.g. in explanatory texts, cf. Lang 1976). Contiguity means a connection which is established on the basis of co-occurrence of states of affairs (cf. contiguity as the greatest connection density in a semantic network in de Beaugrande & Dressler, 1981, p. 114, as 'cognitive clustering' of concepts in Koch, 1991, p. 16. The question arises as to through what means contiguity is determined as 'factual proximity'. Possibilities are data-inherent relations, task-related connections or the text production context itself. This can be a stereotype co-occurrence with typical relations (e.g. frames in Rosenberg 1980, Tonfoni 1990). Rhetorically-oriented relations refer to an addressee-related organisation of contents. They play an important role in computational modellings. Here, reference is primarily made to the model of 'Rhetorical Structure Theory' (RST, Mann & Thompson 1987, Thompson & Mann 1987), in which 24 types of relation are assumed. Rhetorical relations are a.o. PURPOSE, ELABORATION, ENABLEMENT, MOTIVATION, OPPOSITION, CONDITION. They have been worked out on the basis of empirical text analyses (over 400 texts). In Matthiessen & Thompson (1989, p. 293) two kinds are distinguished: content-oriented relations ('subject matter': e.g. ELABORATING, ENHANCING, PURPOSE, CONDITION, CIRCUM- STANCE, CONCESSION) and functionally-oriented relations ('rhetorical act': e.g. MOTIVATION, BACKGROUND, SOLUTIONHOOD, ANTITHESIS).

With respect to our approach to text production, we are interested in how far local coherence relations contribute to the formation of structures in the overall text and in this way determine the connectivity structure. Uncertain in this context is in what way sentence connections are transferrable to overall text structures, or what consequences this step has. Experiments in this direction are available for a wide variety of approaches. However, two main lines of reasoning can be distinguished: the linking of sentence sequences is based either on relations between individual words, lexemes and phrases with punctual links, or between sentences (propositions) or groups of sentences and text segments, whereby all units of the text are organised in an overall structure.

Punctual attachments via lexeme meanings had led, for example, to the early approach of isotopic chains (Greimas 1971 (1966)). The transfer of this idea to concept classes can be found in the text model of Agricola (1979). The field of reference-oriented approaches with co-reference chains or anaphoric relations and focus shifts beyond the sentence sequences, which are given considerable attention in contemporary studies on text generation, are also to be classified from this angle. McKeown (1985), Sidner (1985), Grosz & Sidner (1986), who use the focus mechanism outlined above, all belong in this category. Punctual attachment is also characteristic in referential approaches. With respect to coherence in the text, they do in fact fulfil a necessary condition, but they are not sufficient. An unlimited number of sentence sequences with co-references can be constructed without these necessarily resulting in coherent texts (Kallmeyer et al., 1986, p. 186). Altogether, word-related approaches say something about the connection of words in a text without this being equivalent to a text structure. All we know is that the text concerns x (e.g. 'about John' in McKeown, 1985, p. 63ff.), whereby this x can be followed with respect to its continuity in the text.

Word-related approaches stand in contrast to so-called rhetorical approaches, which – as already mentioned above – have gained increasing interest in current text generation models. This is concerned with the transfer of rhetorical relations (or coherence relations in general) as connections between two text units (sentences, text segments) to the overall text, which is completely covered. In this respect this is a structure which belongs to the overall text structure. Nevertheless, this raises a few problems.

Apart from the empirical problem of assigning relations to occurring text units (there are no translation rules or instructions!), a fundamental problem ensues through the transfer of a binary relation onto the overall text, whereby the latter is systematically divided into two parts, a dominant and a supporting section of text. What also remains unclear is the linguistic marking on the superordinated levels of the hierarchy, which is problematic enough with the basic relations. A third point concerns the representation as such, which operates on object-language units, thus rendering the formulation of rules more difficult, if not impossible. This is different in the AI-approach of Dahlgren (1988), in which coherence relations operate on concepts.

Noël (1990) criticises in a theoretically fundamental way the approach of using rhetorical relations as the basis for text representations. He argues that coherence relations do not correspond to what the reader understands in the text, when he/she understands a text, but rather that a text understanding must be presupposed in order to analyse coherence relations. It would be necessary to know first of all what the content context is in order to be able to judge whether a passage has the function ENABLEMENT, MOTIVATION or PURPOSE for another passage. In this respect, these are categories on the level of professional analysis, which as instructions for the text writer can indeed be useful. What on the other hand would seem to be plausible as text representation in the sense of the text user, would be schemata for content organisation which represent the message of the text. Such a schema structures the relevant content according to groups and orders these groups in a coherent sequence. What does this imply for a model of text production?

First of all it implies that a mixture of content-informative and functional categories, as takes place in RST, leads to problems. These problems not only concern the analysis, but also the production. How can we organise content units according to functional points of view, if the content itself is unorganised. Or in concrete terms: how can we assign the relation OPPOSITION, if only the text segments are available and we do not know what is in opposition. Furthermore, the question arises as to whether functional categories of local sentence connections are suitable as basic units for the description of a global text structure.

6.1.3 Global coherence relations

We proceed from the assumption that coherence relations that are developed on the basis of sentence connections and that are oriented towards these are also primarily relevant for the sentence connection level. This does not rule out the fact that for specific text types preferences can be determined with respect to the types and combinations of types. On the other hand, we consider a general transfer of the principle of sentence connection to the global text level to be wrong for reasons related to form and content. Content reasons are aimed at the fact that the global text structure is primarily to be described through globally determined categories. The text topic represents a global category in this sense.

Text topic as a separate object of research (as opposed to sentence topic) has been postulated within the framework of text linguistics (already with Agricola 1976, Bayer 1980, Brinker 1980, Brown & Yule 1984 (1983)). Lötscher (1987) gives a comprehensive overview of the various interpretations with respect to the text topic (topic as reference object, as focused object, as problem or as information core). In a global view, the text topic is closely linked with the communicative structure of a text (i.e. with the text type). It is coherence-building in the sense that it relates all the parts of the text under one another.

Thematic classifications have been undertaken from various viewpoints. Significant here have been the approaches of van Dijk (1977b, 1980a, 1980b, 1981) and van Dijk & Kintsch (1983). Here the text is understood thematically as a macro- and functionally as a superstructure in the sense of the organisation of a phrase structure grammar. The former is determined by rules (4 macrorules), which operate on propositions of the text and over several stages of the hierarchy effect a kind of summary of the content, until the topic itself as the top node completes the hierarchy. The latter is divided into constituents, which arrange the content from the functional point of view. Thus, for example, in an argumentative text the corresponding text segments are labelled as arguments *PRO* or *CONTRA*, as supports and as conclusions and arranged in a hierarchy.

A further possibility concerns the structuring of the text topic on the basis of the part-of relation as theme/whole and theme/part or as theme/main and sub-themes (Kurzon 1984, Brinker 1992). This kind of structuring can also be found in more recent text planning components of automatic text generating procedures, in which the content of an overall text is ordered in hierarchies of partial components. This is, for example, the case with the description of complex actions as they occur in instructive texts and are specified as main or sub-goals (cf. on cooking recipes Dale 1990, Koch 1991; on instructions WIP (Wahlster et al. 1989); also for route descriptions (stage description plans in KLEIST (Rickheit (ed.) 1991); see also section 3.4)).

6.1.4 Expansions of ILL and PRO

In our approach we distinguish between thematic and functional aspects ('two-layered text model', cf. Lötscher, 1987, p. 117). This method permits a flexible treatment of assignments. Correspondingly, we also distinguish between expansions that concern the thematic component and expansions that concern the interactional component. In section 5.1 description units for propositions were introduced in the form of text roles and text role configurations, which in section 5.2 were supplemented by the assignment of illocution types. The combination of both components was described as relevant with respect to the presentation of simple text actions through which the thematic and interactional information is selected. At the level of composition, however, we introduce two kinds of expansion:

- the expansion of text role configurations as a thematic development at the propositional level (EX-THEM) and
- the expansion of illocutions as a development at the interactional level (EX-ILL).

In sub-section 5.1.4 we established the dialogic integration of the object construction in the form of a thematic question (TQ). An example of such a TQ was (DOING (BOOK),. . .)?) (what does the book do . . .?). The argument roles were defined with respect to a domain-specific object model. This object model offers slots, which play a role in the respective

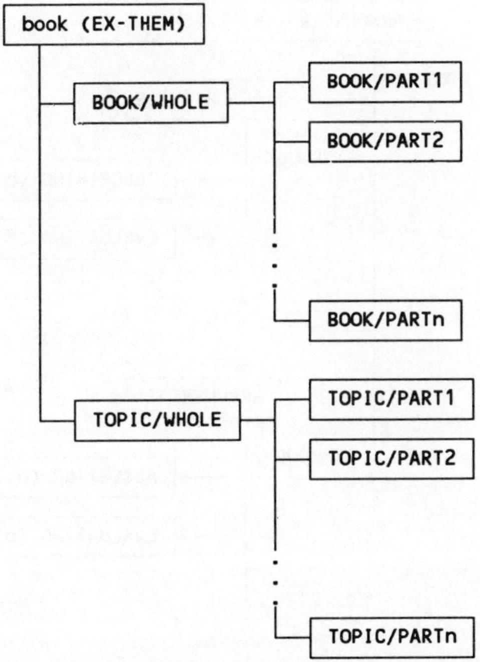

Figure 6.1 Hierarchy of the THEME-component

communication situation. Examples are BOOK, AUTHOR, READER, TOPIC, etc. In the text structure these slots appear as concept classes that characterise a certain relation within a proposition. We characterised such relations as text roles. The thematic expansion can now be defined via these text roles. They form configurations, which in the sequence are repeated, specified or changed. Correspondingly, different types of expansion can be adopted. One possibility, for example, is expansion on the basis of the part-of relation. It is used frequently in book announcements and in the case of the text role configuration TROC│2= [TROL1=BOOK, TROL2=TOPIC] can refer in parallel to the expansion of both text roles and results in a hierarchy (Figure 6.1).

Hierarchies of the illocution component occur as a result of the superordinated action ANNOUNCEMENT (main goal) being structured through sub-actions. Sub-actions are related to the main goal in the relation THROUGH, which characterises constituents (cf. section 4.3). The sub-actions are assigned to the respective propositions (p), see Figure 6.2.

Expansions of a thematic or interactional nature can be ordered according to types. Their realisation as overall expansion or composition of a number of partial expansions is determined by the kind of object construc-

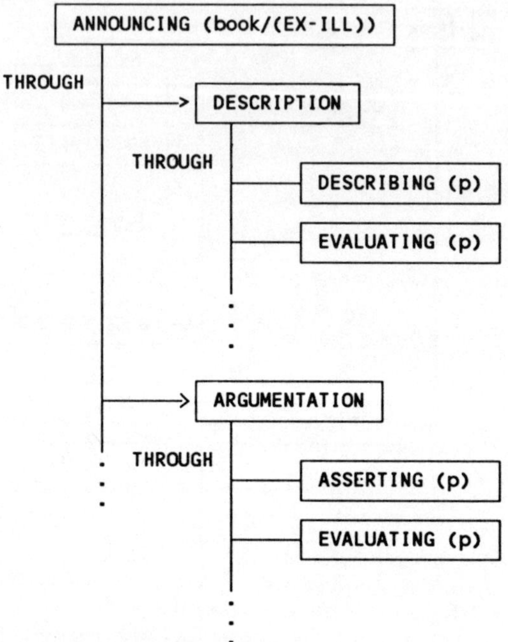

Figure 6.2 Hierarchy of the ILLOCUTION-component

tion. The connectivities related to the expansions establish the connectivity structure of the text. The dependence between expansion and connectivity forms the basis for the determination of the specifications of the text action grammar. This takes general principles of linearisation into consideration. We reconstruct such principles as global and local strategies of text production. Both have the mutual communicative goal of object presentation, which we consider in the sense of the building of a text structure.

6.2 Directionality as a dynamic principle of text forming

Composition processes are organised dynamically-progressively. In the case of the medium text two types of directionality are involved in the structure building:

- Directionality with respect to the content-functional structural organisation within the sequential order of the text
- Directionality with respect to the extension of the text in the direction of writing (in our cultural sphere from left to right).

The sequential structure is characterised by a progressive dynamism. It is considered from a socio-linguistic point of view as 'discourse dynamism' in Sinclair & Coulthard (1975), as cognitive principles of text production in de Beaugrande (1984) or with respect to grammatical categories in the Prague Functionalism (insofar as it refers to texts in Daneš 1974a ('communicative dynamism'), Hajičová & Sgall 1988, Hajičová 1991).

The dynamism can be seen both temporally and spatially (Fleischmann 1991). In psychologically-oriented research, the temporal perspective is in the foreground. Text production is seen from the standpoint of the text writer (W). The question is: what does W do in what sequence or what does W do next? The text structure is of interest to the extent that it permits the determination of the actual position of W in the writing process.

The spatial orientation is primarily directed towards the text. It is specific for linguistic approaches. Here the question: what is where in the text or what comes next in the text? is of interest (Fraurud & Hellman 1985). In the literature, the two perspectives are frequently mixed. Hence, for example, in the seven principles of linearity in de Beaugrande (1984, p. 153ff.) both temporal (e.g. 'look-back' and 'look-ahead') as well as structural (e.g. 'core and adjunct') aspects occur. The mixed reference to both spoken and written language only serves to confuse the issue further.

In our modelling we argue in favour of a methodical separation of temporal and spatial aspects. In a similar manner Brandt & Rosengren (1991b) distinguish production and sequencing. With this systematic separation we avoid a situation where one of a number of possible writing techniques is implicitly elevated to the standard, or where speech techniques are automatically transferred to writing techniques. We proceed from the assumption that a text-oriented, linguistic description can provide the basis for (psychological) tests or other writing-oriented studies. 'Spatial' in this sense means the structural after- and next-to-each-other of text elements. We assume that this text-oriented kind of directionality determines the structure of the text connectivity.

Directionality in the text has to do with the fact that the attachment of units is organised as a sequence. Sequential structures can be seen as typical for social orders of the world. In this respect, they form a second facet to hierarchical orders, which are considered as typical for orders of the physical world. In our context, the question concerning global and local connections also arises here. They reflect two kinds of directionality. Globally, this is concerned with strategies for the successive construction of the communicative goal structure. The result in each case is a schema that is determined by the sequencing of content-functional units. Locally, this involves one unit respectively, which takes on a certain position within the structural organisation.

In the following we consider the two strategies with respect to the object construction through thematic-functional expansions and the resulting connectivities. In this we distinguish between a global left–right orientation (LERI, LE –> RI) and a local right–left orientation (RILE, LE <– RI).

LERI: left–right strategies are global strategies. The idea is that the object construction is built up through successive relationing of the text segments with respect to the overall text. Global strategies refer first and foremost to two text properties. They are

- result-oriented and aim at the completing of the text,
- delimitation-oriented and aim at the delimitation of the text.

The result orientation establishes the demand for a globally determined text structure. We take account of this requirement by relating the sequential and the hierarchical structure of the text to one another. This assignment is based on the principle of reconstitutability of the hierarchical structure in the sequence (Brandt & Rosengren, 1991b, p. 14). It means that parts that form a related unit in the hierarchy may not be interrupted in the sequence. Unlike Brandt & Rosengren (1991b), who proceed from a hierarchical text structure from which the sequence is derived, we proceed simply from an assignment relation. We do not, therefore, adopt the hierarchical text structure as a kind of deep structure, which in the production is to be transferred into a sequence. Instead we presuppose that in the global, i.e. left–right-oriented organisation of the text structure, the sequence is produced as a result of the fact that on the basis of the order and kind of attachment of the parts, a hierarchical structure emerges simultaneously.

With respect to the content filling of this/these structure(s), the delimitation principle takes effect. Hierarchies, or sequences, can only emerge if it is possible to form groups. This can be determined content-thematically and/or intentionally-interactionally (Viehweger 1983). Grosz & Sidner (1986), for example, use an intentional component for content segment building in their computer-oriented text model (see also section 3.1). In McKeown (1985) and Hajičová (1986) focus sequences contribute to the thematic formation of groups in the text. Interesting in this connection is that the same principle applies, even if focus is interpreted in a completely contrary manner in the two approaches. McKeown is concerned in the psychological sense with the focus of attention, which is related to recurring units, whereas in Hajičová, focus is understood in the sense of rheme as significant information, as compared with the recurring topic (for explanation of concepts see also Hajičová 1986).

In our approach we pursue two comprehensive goals. At the level of interaction, we consider possibilities of preferential placings in the sequence that are given by the delimitation of the overall text. Thus the beginning and the ending of the text on the one hand, and the middle section on the other, provide specific possibilities for emphasis as a result of placing. This text property accounts for FRAMING in the interactional expansion. It takes account of the fact that the illocutions in the text have different functions with respect to the goal structure. They can be dominant or subsidiary. Hence, for example, DESCRIBING is dominant in object descriptions because it contributes directly to the goal structure, while EVALUATING is subsidiary and contributes only indirectly to the text goal. Illocutions used in a subsidiary role as a rule form the frame of texts. Correspondingly, evaluating text segments appear as a frame with an initial or final position in the overall text (on framing in interactional texts cf. Rothkegel 1986a). The differentiation of illocution functions in the text leads to specific hierarchical orders, which differ from the illocution hierarchies in the sense of constituent structures (Grosz & Sidner 1986, Motsch 1986, Brandt et al. 1983, Brandt & Rosengren 1991b, Viehweger 1991). It remains to be shown how these different overall structures are integrated into the sequential schema formation by means of expansions of the illocution component.

At the level of the text topic, the principles of delimitation and completing lead to groupings which in themselves correspond to delimitable units of the object model and which form chains with relation to the overall text. Correspondingly, the respective types of thematic expansion can be determined. Thus there are, for example, chains that are formed on the basis of listing parts, or constructing argumentation chains (CHAINING).

RILE: Right–left strategies are local strategies. The idea is that there is an orientation opposed to the global strategies, in which the direct delimitation of a unit to its left adjacent unit is considered. The object construction takes place here in such a way that by attaching two units, a contribution to the global structure is made in the form of PAIRING.

The fact that connections have an attachment function should be taken into account. In this context, we consider a connecting unit in relation to the connected unit. In order to avoid misunderstandings, we would like to point out here that we are not concerned with forward- or backward-oriented relations as in the distinctions between anaphoric and cataphoric constructions. In our approach both anaphoric and cataphoric relations occur as relations between connecting and connected unit (in the case of anaphora, for example, proforms are connecting, in the case of cataphora it is the respective referents). Local strategies in the above sense are based on two text properties.

They are

- repetition-oriented and are based on the text property of recurrence,
- development-oriented and are based on progression through attachment of the same or other.

Whereas in hierarchies units are ordered so that they only occur once (as a rule), sequences are, like texts, characterised by recurrence, i.e. by the repetitive occurrence of units. Recurrence refers not only to the repetition of individual referents, but to categories and all levels of the text. A clear example are text roles, whose recurrence is a prerequisite for the thematic development (section 5.1). One of the essential attachment functions consists in establishing this recurrence. This means that in the attachment unit a part or a category of the attached unit is repeated. The point cannot be that elements are merely repeated. With the repetition a further step towards the establishing of a global structure is also supposed to be realised, i.e. the repetition is specified. For this kind of specification there is a general dichotomy for the characterisation of development which can also be applied to texts: the repetition is specified as an explicit repetition ('the same again') or as an opposition to something else ('something else for a change'). It remains to be shown that with the help of this general framework, PAIRING can be represented as a local contribution to the building of global text structures. This brings a standpoint into the research discussion in which approaches on the basis of text-oriented sentence connections can be revised.

6.3 Text connectivity patterns

6.3.1 The concept of connectivity

In section 2.5 connectivity was introduced as a text constitutional feature which is responsible for linking content and functional text units and manifests itself in the text syntax in marked forms. As a complementary feature to textual reference, the conditions of textual connection have over the past 10 years become a focus of text linguistic interest (cf. collections such as Petöfi & Sözer (eds) 1983, Heydrich & Petöfi (eds) 1986, Heydrich et al. (eds) 1989, Conte et al. (eds) 1989).

Connection within the text can be seen from a global and local standpoint. From a global point of view (overall text structure), action-oriented approaches are again in the foreground (e.g. Roulet 1984, Lundquist 1989), as well as those which proceed from the syntax of the text (Grize

1989). A wide range of models stem from local approaches, in other words those in which the point of departure is sentence connection, which is integrated in a textual reference (Meyer 1975, Bajziková 1984, Warner 1985, Biasci 1986, Rudolph 1988, Haiman & Thompson (eds) 1989). In this context, dynamic text aspects relate to those of the foreground–background structure for which coordinating and subordinating linguistic means of textual connectivity are used as indicators (Givón 1987, Tomlin (ed.) 1987). Another form of text structure is concerned with discourse particles, which are understood in such a way that they trace a (hierarchical and sequential) structure of the interaction of the participants (initially in Gülich & Raible 1977, further in Levinson 1987 (1983), Schiffrin 1987, Fraser 1990, Redeker 1990, 1991, Abraham (ed.) 1991). 'Discourse markers' designate sequential relations. They have a linking function ('portion-building': what belongs together) and a limiting function ('segment-building': what does not belong together). According to Schiffrin (1987) discourse markers operate on 5 different text levels:

(a) exchange structure (conversational exchange, e.g. turn-taking)
(b) action structure (sequence of speech acts)
(c) ideation structure (relations between propositions)
(d) participation framework (relationship between speaker and hearer)
(e) information state (management of knowledge).

And in cognitive models connectors have the function of program instructions for the specified connection of semantic contents (Lang 1991, Fauconnier 1990). Lang proceeds from the assumption that the lexical meaning of a word can be described as a rule for identifying a concept. In this, conjunctions are characterised as concept-processing – in comparison to autosemantica, which are meaning-identifying: 'Conjunctions refer to operations of knowledge processing. The lexical meaning of a conjunction is not a rule for identifying an (imaginarily or really generated) concept, but rather an instruction for the mental processing of such concepts.' To such operations belong (Lang, 1991, p. 614):

(a) comparing operations
(b) ordering in sequences and bundles
(c) selection from or decision among alternatives.

In our decompositions, (b) (cf. chaining in section 7.2) and (c) (cf. contrasts in sub-section 7.3.4) will play a role. Both aspects serve here to form blocks (cf. 'composition blocks' in Schäffner et al. 1987). The operative character is expressed by considering the connections as a linguistic trace of the realisation of text actions. In computational modellings there are as yet only isolated approaches (Brée & Smit 1986, Meyer 1989, McKeown & Elhadad 1991).

In the following, connectivity (CON) is examined as types of relation which emerge as a result of left–right strategies (LERI) or right-left strategies (RILE). We mark the respective specifications with * and place them in pointed brackets:

* CON: <LERI, RILE>

According to this, sequentialisation means that connections of text units are produced that taken together can be considered as indicators for the overall structure of the text. In this sense, the text connectivity is a means of describing the text syntax. Like de Beaugrande & Dressler (1981), we not only assign the text syntax to the level of sentence connections, but also consider it as being determined by communicative strategies with which the text topic and text function in the overall text are produced.

We are interested exclusively in explicitly produced connections, which are understood as traces of text production processes. With this, we limit the area of connectivity in the text that we cover (cf. overview in Conte et al. 1989). Thus, links between text units that exist implicitly, e.g. by virtue of factual contexts, are ignored. Correspondingly, similar to Komlósi (1989), we distinguish between interpreter-bound coherence and conventionally or language-systematically determined text connectivity. Text connectivity in the sense of explicit connections which are produced by language-producers with a view to the development of content and interactional goal structures, should not, however, remain limited to conjunctions (cf. also collocation chains in the sense of Hasan (1978), the 'frame expressions' in Keseling et al. (1987), and the 'propositional sequences' in Weber (1986)).

6.3.2 Representation of connectivity

In order to represent the connectivity structure, each text segment is assigned a connectivity parameter (CON). Further differentiations of CON result from thematic-functional expansions. 'Expansion' in this sense means the extension of material that is processed on the one hand in the form of illocutions, and on the other in the form of text roles or text role configurations. Correspondingly, the text connectivity is differentiated with respect to expansions of the illocution types (EX-ILL) and expansions of the text role configurations (EX-THEM):

* CON: <CON (EX-ILL), CON (EX-THEM)>

The CON component is further structured in accordance with global and local production strategies. In the case of global linearisation, connectivity sequences (COS) emerge, in the case of local linearisation connectivity pairs (COP). Sequences are linearisations of global structures and correspond to hierarchies, pairs are linearisations of recurrences. Sequences have a left–right directionality (LERI), pairs right–left (RILE).

* CON(EX-ILL)/(EX-THEM): <COS(LERI), COP(RILE)>

Connectivity sequences (COS/LERI) characterise the transition of a text segment (ti) to the adjacent right-hand segment (ti+1). The transition is determined on the basis of the position of the respective text segment within the overall sequence of all text segments. The basis for this position is the position of the respective text segment within a list (schema), which is assigned to a hierarchical structure. In relation to the illocutions, the sequence of illocutions represents a hierarchical illocution structure, in relation to the text roles the sequence represents a hierarchical topic structure. In the former case this results in the formation of frames (COF, connectivity frame), in the latter case to the formation of chains (COC, connectivity chains).

Expansions of the illocution component (EX-ILL) lead to frames (COF), expansions of the thematic component (EX-THEM) lead to chains (COC):

* CON/LERI(EX-ILL):   <COF>
* CON/LERI(EX-THEM): <COC>

Connectivity pairs (COP/RILE) are based on recurrence schemata. Recurrence in the text means that parts of the text occur repeatedly. This is possible through direct repetition, reference, paraphrasing, contrasting, summarising, etc. We are not interested in the individual semantic relations linked to this. Of interest to us are manifestations of the connection itself. These are distinguished according to whether the text expands as a result of linking the same (sameness, SAM) or other (alterity, ALT) elements. From a strategic point of view, recurrence thus means linking to what already exists according to either the SAM or the ALT principle. SAM and ALT in this context refer to classes and not to single lexemes (see below sub-section 6.3.3). The linking strategy manifests itself in the specification of COP, which can be assigned to every segment of the

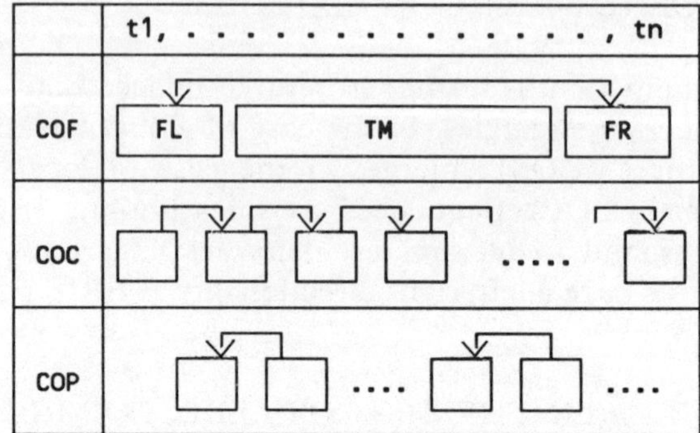

Figure 6.3 Three types of connectivity between text segments (t): COF connectivity frames, COC connectivity chains, COP connectivity pairs

respective text segment pair (Figure 6.3 illustrates a comparison of the three types of connectivity).

>   * CON/RILE: <COP>
>   * COP: <SAM, ALT>

Apart from the expansion of thematic elements (text role configurations) and interactional elements (illocutions), there is the text formal level of the expansion of the text segments themselves. Expansion of the text segments means that the text is extended in such a way that additional text segments are attached to the original unit or already adjoined text segments. This again shows a left–right orientation, corresponding to the material direction of writing. Computer-oriented approaches to text syntax attempt to view this kind of expansion as fundamental for the expansion of content aspects of the text (Webber 1989, Polanyi 1988, Scha & Polanyi 1988). These approaches attempt to process texts formally like sentences as tree structures. The left–right expansion is understood as the extension of a tree to the right (cf. 'right frontier' in Webber 1989). This affects the locally determined relations as we interpret them. Global text structures are not affected in this way. For this, a different organisation form must be used.

With respect to the structural organisation of the overall text, we proceed by adopting a text list (TL) as a formal carrier structure, which corresponds to a simple list of enumerated text segments. This carrier structure forms the basis for establishing connectivity structures that can be described in terms of LERI and RILE strategies. We subsequently distinguish the following expansion levels:

• the text segment level: this concerns the running text, which is repre-sented as a list of text segments ([-------]), enumeration (ti) and a connec-tivity parameter (CON).

```
text list (TL):       {      (t1, CON, [------]),
                             (t2, CON, [------]),
                             . . .
                             (tn, CON, [------]) }
```

• the level of globally determined relations between the text segments ('left-right'). This concerns:
•• positioning (what is where in the text) with the special connectivity form of framing with FL as the left frame and FR as the right frame.

```
CON=COF:       {(      (t1,    CON=FL,   [------]),
                      . . .
                      (tf-1, CON=FL,   [------])      ),
               (      (tf,    CON=-,     [------]),
                      . . .
                      (tg-1, CON=-,     [------])      )
               (      (tg,    CON=FR,   [------]),
                      . . .
                      (tn,    CON=FR,   [------])      )      }
```

•• order (what is sequenced how) with the special connectivity form of chaining by means of chain elements (CE).

```
CON=COC:       {      (t1,    CON=CE1, [------]),
                      (t2,    CON=CE2, [------]),
                      . . .
                      (tn,    CON=CEn, [------])      }
```

• the level of locally determined relations between the text segments ('right–left').
This concerns:
•• adjacent relations (what is attached to what and how) with the special connectivity form of pairing by means of pair elements (PE).

```
CON=COP:       {      (ti,    CON=PE1, [------]),
                      (ti+1, CON=PE2, [------])      }
```

In summary, what is valid for this approach is that various text levels that can be related to each other are comprised in the connectivity structure. The content text levels of the thematic and interactional component are set against the structural levels of the global and local text structure. Both are projected onto the basic sequential form of the text list. This entails a hierarchical organisation of the levels.

The COF component (connectivity frame) is considered to be the level of the uppermost order; incorporated in this is the connectivity chain level (COC) and in this in turn the local level of connectivity pairs (COP).

6.3.3 Connectivity scope

So far we have only discussed text segments, which are linked together. However, the connection can refer to specific parts of the text segments, which are then to be determined as the scope of connectivity. We describe the scope in accordance with the categories of our descriptive apparatus that was introduced for the description of text actions (Chapter 4). According to this, there are four types of unit that come into question as connectivity scope (CS):

- ILL   (illocutionary element)
- p   (overall proposition)
- PRED   (predicate)
- TROL   (text role as part of the role configuration)

Connectivity frames are formed through the linking of illocution types as left and right frame or through linking of text roles or whole propositions. Connectivity chains are formed through the connection of predicates and through the connection of text roles. Connectivity pairs are defined by a connection relation between corresponding units in two adjacent text segments.

6.3.4 Connectivity markers

Connectivity as an explicit connection is linguistically marked. With the help of the examples we will see that it is the text property of recurrence – the repeated occurrence of units – that favours the marked connectivity. In other words, for the formation of a sequential structure it is necessary particularly to mark the connection of text segments that are structured as repetitions of the same (SAM) and thus contribute to the completion of the text. Sequentialising that on the other hand results from attaching the 'other' (ALT), is only marked when there is a common basis for the 'other'. This observation confirms the observation of Lakoff (1972), according to which connectivity structures presuppose the existence of mutual categories.

For marked connectivity, connectors are available that can lexically and syntactically belong to different classes. The following incomplete lists of examples for classes of global and local connectors (Ci) are intended to serve as an illustration. They show that connectors in the sense of text constitution are not restricted to the word class of conjunctions:

C1 (conjunctional)	:	*{and, while, particularly since, . . .}*
C2 (attributive)	:	*{first, second, . . ., last}*
C3 (adverbial)	:	*{at first, . . ., finally}*
C4 (verbal)	:	*{begin, continue, finish, . . .}*
C5 (negative or affirmative particles)	:	*{not only – but also, not – rather, . . .}*
C6 (deictic expressions)	:	*{there, thereby, here, . . .}*

6.4 Strategies of composition

In an operational model of text production, various aspects must be related to each other. In our model, two different complexes of information are linked together: a content-interactional complex of the object construction and a formal complex of the sequential text composition. For this there are two basic elements:

- the description schema of complex text actions (Chapter 4)
- the definition of principles of composition (section 6.1).

Text actions were introduced as a descriptive instrument of text production. The action character was operationalised, so that text production processes could be described as operations. What is essential in a computational model is the way in which these are represented. To this end, a predicate-logical division of the ILL, PRO and LOC components was undertaken. The action-theoretical basis of this representation permits the linking of illocutionary, propositional and lexico-grammatical aspects. By virtue of the description of the propositional element in the form of predicate-argument structures (text role configurations), it is possible to link the text structure to be produced with linguistic units. Via the assignment of inventories, which are determined by illocutionary and propositional conditions, there are restrictions with respect to lexical preferences.

In order to describe the formation of coherence, expansions of simple text actions were introduced which allow the distinction of sequencing types both on the illocutionary and the thematic-propositional level. The

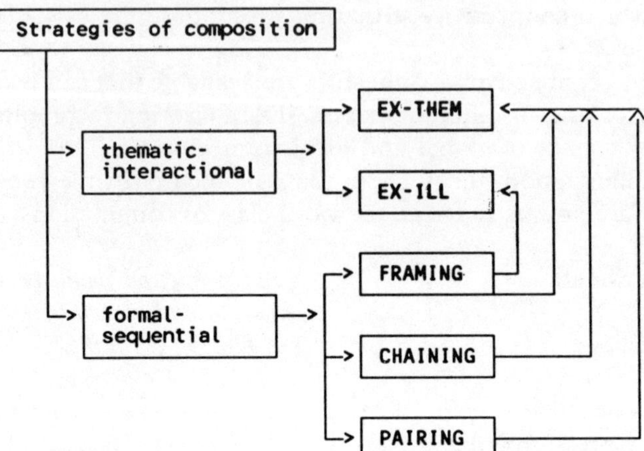

Figure 6.4 Correlation of composition strategies

former includes descriptions or argumentations, for example, the latter a.o. part-whole-schemata or problem solving schemata (see examples in Chapter 7). The development of these schemata is represented in the form of illocutionary expansions (EX-ILL) and thematic expansions (EX-THEM). Further, this information complex is to be combined with formal composition principles, which we introduce as sequence operations (SOP).

We proceed from the assumption that a few principles can be reconstructed which form the basic formal structure of texts. Since the linearisation is specific for the medium text, it is considered as the central dimension for the determination of the formal text structure. A further point is the dynamic view in which linearisation always implies sequencing: each element of the structure is determined by its position and the respective relation to a former or subsequent adjacent element.

Sequencing principles are reflected on the text surface as text connectivity. We are interested in such connections that are marked by means of linguistic indicators. These allow a systematic examination of the connectivity in the text, which is supported by lexico-grammatical regularities. Apart from the illocutionary and thematic expansions, which are defined in terms of content and interaction, further operations are to be introduced that define the sequencing from a formal point of view. We deal with three types of compositional operation: FRAMING, CHAINING, PAIRING. FRAMING refers both to the illocutionary and the thematic component. We deal with CHAINING and PAIRING in relation to the thematic component (overview in Figure 6.4).

The choice of these three operations is motivated by the fact that

Table 6.1   Text space, direction, and text profile in relation to the sequencing operations

operation	text space	direction	text profile
FRAMING	global	LERI	change
CHAINING	global	LERI	continuity
PAIRING	local	RILE	change
			continuity

together they form a relatively simple system in which a variety of text-specific phenomena can be organised. The dimension of the sequence is determined by three cardinal principles. Cardinal principles are considered as those which underline the specificity of a structure in a marked manner (see Table 6.1).

Text space refers to a supporting structure within which the sequential operations work. Brinker (1992), for example, considers the entire formal structure as a 'carrier system' for the thematic coherence. We generalise on this and assume an additional formal basic structure. This organises the linearisation in a two-dimensional line structure. In material terms this concerns the running text list comprising slots for single propositions, which can be numbered consecutively as text rows. These text list slots are an object of the processing both as overall and partial lists. Although it is only the completed text list that represents the result of text forming operations, uncompleted it still provides a structural background of possible delimitations which allow units and groups to be formed.

A text profile evolves through more or less of the same. In operational terms this means continuity or change with regard to the units used. These can of course not be single concepts or lexemes (or nominal phrases). Their continuous repetition would be absurd, their change is nothing remarkable and has no structuring force. Continuity and change must refer to units which are involved in the functional-thematic structure of the text, in other words, illocutions and text roles or text role configurations.

More of the same, i.e. the same illocution or text role (or text role configuration) leads to continuity in the text structure and from the point of view of content to a continuous (stable) object construction. All the more so, the more frequently the repetition is continued. Less of the same, i.e. change of illocution and text roles in the sequence, creates a transition to the other and leads to a non-continuous (unstable) object construction.

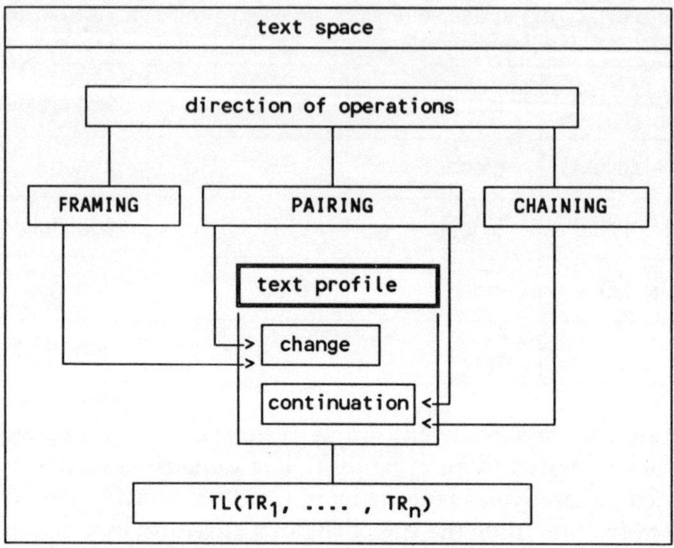

Figure 6.5 Sequencing operations and text profile within the text space

Whereas the text space is static, the profile forming is dynamic. Both are related to each other insofar as the stative text space represents a kind of basis for manoeuvre for the dynamic profile forming. The dynamism occurs as a result of the directionality of the text operations. Possible in the sequencing in the text are the directions left-right or right-left. Text space, text profile and direction are the three essential principles that determine the sequencing operations. Figure 6.5 sketches the relationship between text space and sequencing operations.

Framing concerns the overall text space (global) and sub-divides it. Groups are formed which represent independent units in themselves and at the same time are related to each other and the whole. The dynamism runs from the beginning of the text (left) to the end of the text (right). Correspondingly, a left frame (FL) and a right frame (FR) exist as frame constituents. As a result of the framing, a highlighted text middle (TM) emerges. Profile develops through a shift in the functional or thematic basic units (ILLocution and text roles). Thus frame constituents and text middle constituents differ in type.

Chaining also concerns the overall text space (global). Here, however, this is divided into several equivalent text sections, whose profile is determined by continuity. Here, too, the direction runs from beginning to end of a text or text section. Since chains are principally related to thematic expansions, the continuity concerns the continued repetition of a specific text role type in the sequence of the propositions.

Pairing concerns only parts of the text space. We restrict ourselves here to immediately adjacent units, whereby the direction right–left is fixed, i.e. contrary to the global sequencings. This follows a perspective in which the following unit is considered to be attached to the preceding unit. The profile is produced through both possibilities: either through repeating a type from the preceding unit or through contrasting another type. Here, too, we restrict ourselves to thematic information types, i.e. continuity or change always refers to text roles or text role configurations.

The sequence operations are linguistically marked. In the case of expansions of the illocution, this is shown in preferences for various lexical inventories, depending on the adherence to the illocution type and the conditions through the text role configuration. Profiling on the basis of change is thus recognisable as a change in the assigned inventories. In the case of thematic expansions, there are explicit connectors, which depending on the type of sequencing also form inventories.

7 Text grammar II.2: Sequencing operations

7.0 Overview

Having discussed individual text action types and their role in a text action grammar in Chapter 5, and presented the basic composition strategies in Chapter 6, in this chapter the two are to be related to one another in such a way that it becomes possible to describe sequences of text actions. In addition, a representation form is to be developed that allows complex text actions to be presented and operationalised in the form of a grammar. The principal sequencing operations we are concerned with are FRAMING, CHAINING and PAIRING. They refer to the thematic and interactional development of the text structure and operate within a variable text space, which provides the limitations. The complex interconnections of the various descriptive categories are analysed further from the point of view of coherence in individual forms, which can be manipulated separately. The description has been kept general and is therefore open to further extensions.

In the following, we examine a series of sequencing types with the help of authentic text examples from publishing announcements. For this, in a first description (numbered with '[ ]') we assign representation units to the running text wording that are introduced by the representation schema for complex text actions and are relevant for the respective sequencing type. In a second description (indicated by '[']') we add a generalisation, which characterises either the sequencing type or the concerned inventory of connectors with its selection conditions. The connectors in the examples are highlighted in bold type, the text roles are underlined. This refers only to the nominal core. It goes without saying that here we are dealing with complex semantic-syntactic constructions which must be considered in a separate analysis or generating step.

Completeness regarding the empirical findings is not aimed at within the framework of this analysis. This must be reserved for further research.

Rather, it is our goal here to illustrate the relations sequence of illocutionary or thematic text development on the basis of sequencing operations. The text analyses are of an exemplary nature and serve to illustrate the text-grammatical concept. This is presented subsequently in the form of connectivity forms.

7.1 Operation: FRAMING

7.1.1 Framing conditions

We proceed from the following framing conditions (see sub-section 6.1.6):

- FRAMING:
  [Dimension :   [
       [space: global   ]
       [direction: LERI   ]
       [profile: change   ]   ]]

The global dimension indicates that the linearisation principle effective here is valid for the whole text list (TL). In the ideal case, there is a threefold division, whereby a middle section (text middle, TM) is distinguished from an initial section (text beginning, TB) and a final section (text end, TE). The direction left–right (beginning –> end) thus defines the part of the text list comprised by TB as the left frame (FL), and the part of the text list comprised by TE as the right frame (FR). The profile of the structure is established through the principle of shift. This concerns the change in the information type, which results in the transition being unmarked with respect to the connectivity (CON = 0). Frames occur in the text both in the illocution structure as well as in the thematic structure. Correspondingly, we present them in our model as expansions of the components ILL (EX-ILL) and PRO (EX-PRO). Both left and right frames are facultative in text realisations.

7.1.2 Framing of illocutions (EX-FRAM/ILL)

A frame results because of functional differences in illocutions with respect to the text structure. Those illocutions which contribute first and foremost to the communicative goal of the text have a dominant function. Subsidiary are illocutions that support this goal (Brandt et al. 1983, Brandt & Rosengren 1991a, Motsch 1991; on main and co-levels cf. Klein & von Stutterheim 1991; in the computational view in Grosz & Sidner 1986). In

Chapter 5 it was argued that these differences in function are reflected in language use and can thus be differentiated as selections from different lexical inventories.

The phenomenon of framing has already been observed in various text types (business letter (Brandt & Rosengren 1991a), international agreement (Rothkegel 1986a)). Apparently it also applies to book announcement texts, as can be demonstrated through the examples given. We are concerned here primarily with illocutions such as DESCRIBING, EVALUATING and ASSERTING, which differ from each other through assignments to different types of knowledge (facts, norms, beliefs) (see section 4.2). Dominant illocutions (ILLd) form the middle section, whereas subsidiary illocutions (ILLs) occupy the initial and final sections and in this way produce a frame.

The question as to which illocutions in the text can be considered dominant depends on the type of expansion in the field of the interaction. For information-oriented texts, interactional types can in turn be described as question and answer relations. In this, the text offers the answer to implicit questions of the addressees. Such questions as *What does the book/the author do?*, *What is the author like?*, *What is the topic of the book?*, etc. underlie the descriptive presentation of the object. In the argumentative presentation, the question *what points to the fact that the book/topic is good, interesting, important* is answered. Apart from these, there are a series of additional patterns which we do not deal with here (e.g. narrative patterns). To exemplify the issue we give text analyses of authentic examples of the descriptive and argumentative presentation mode of the expansion of ILL (EX-ILL/DES or EX-ILL/ARG). In the case of the descriptive presentation, the illocution DESCRIBING is dominant. ASSERTING and EVALUATING are subsidiary. In the argumentative mode on the other hand, ASSERTING is dominant, and DESCRIBING and EVALUATING are subsidiary.

The following representation results, whereby the partial lists FL (frame left), TM (text middle), FR (frame right) of the overall text list are filled by lists of subsidiary or dominant illocutions respectively:

-    [EX-ILL
       [FL   [ILLs1, . . ., ILLsn]]
       [TM [ILLd1, . . ., ILLdn]]
       [FR   [ILLs1, . . ., ILLsn]]   ]

A simple descriptive structure with a partial frame (FL or FR) is frequently produced by placing evaluating quotations at the beginning or end of a book description. Compare the following fragment:

[1]   [EX-FRAM/ILL/DES
        [FL   [
               EVA1   *"This is a fairly documented and coolly argued book*
               EVA2   *whose moral stance and human warnings deserve the*
                       widest and most careful reading."
                       (The Year's Work in English Studies)   ]]

        [TM   [
               DES1   *This book is a critical study of the effects of information-*
                       processing technology on contemporary society.
               DES2   *There are two fundamental themes: the distribution of*
                       power in society and the responsibility of the individual.
               . . .   ]]   ]]

The corresponding rule of the text grammar includes the three partial lists, whereby the left and right frames are facultative:

[1']   [EX-ILL/DES   ->
        [(FL [EVA, . . .]), TM [DES, . . .], (FR [EVA, . . .])]]

Whilst descriptions can be facultatively complemented by evaluations (cf. above example), evaluations are obligatory for the realisation of arguments. The structure of argumentations is treated from a number of angles in the literature. In general, states of affairs-oriented and communication-oriented views are set against each other. The former concern first and foremost an argumentative relation which is derived semantically and/or logically. This view is also represented in computational modellings, where respective inferences from given knowledge bases are concerned (e.g. Cohen 1987). Communication orientation on the other hand means that *PRO* and *CONTRA* and their supports through arguments are in the foreground.

What makes this kind of presentation interesting from the text connectivity point of view is the special framing. Here it is possible for the whole text sequence to consist entirely of frames, while the actual describing element is implicit, i.e. can be drawn as inference. This observation overlaps with the analysis of argumentative text structures that was developed by van Dijk (1980b, p. 148) within the framework of a theory of the superstructure. Here, it is shown that and how the actual exhortation in an argumentative advertising text does not appear explicitly in the text, but must be inferred. In the following decomposition of an example fragment we reconstruct the argumentative development in a similar manner.

Text [2] is complicated insofar as the writer of the book announcement text integrates the arguments of the author of the book into his description of the object, and thus uses an argumentative presentation mode. The text answers the implicit question *What points to the fact that the topic is important, interesting, necessary?* The presupposition implied by this question, such as *the topic is important,* is an assertion that represents the desired result of the answer (communication goal). However, it is not made explicit in the text as an illocution, but must be ascertained from the argumentation chain. This means that the dominant illocution and hence the middle section in the text itself is missing. The arguments, *PRO* and *CONTRA*, form the left and right frames respectively.

[2]   [EX-FRAM/ILL/ARG

        [FL   [
        DES1   *The subject-matter of the present monograph is paradigmatic structure,*
        EVA2   *a not very 'à la mode' topic.*]]

        . . .   (TM: ASS topic is necessary)
        [FR   [
        DES3   *This study takes the view*
        EVA4   *that this neglect of the relationships between elements in absentia is highly unfortunate as far as word-structure is concerned.*
        DES(ASS)5 *For, it claims that among morphological theories only those are fit to uncover the principles underlying . . . in which the paradigmatic dimension of word-structure is assigned a central position.*]]]

[2']   [EX-ILL/ARG   ->
        [FL [DES/EVA, . . .], TM [0], FR [DES/EVA, . . .]]

7.1.3 Framing of thematic structure (EX-FRAM/THEM)

For the organisation of the text topic, framing means that general assignments which in themselves form a coherence that stands out from the middle section are positioned at the beginning or the end. This can be made explicit via the expansion of the text roles. Then the transitions between frame and middle section are characterised by the shift in a specific text role (TROL), e.g. TOPIC/WHOLE -> TOPIC/PART -> TOPIC/WHOLE. Here, too, the frame may be incomplete, i.e. FL and FR are facultative.

Example [3] shows an expansion of the type WHOLE-PART-WHOLE

that refers to the text role TOPIC. The left and right frames illustrate the whole topic, which is more or less repeated here, whereas the middle section gives part topics.

[3]   [EX-FRAM/THEM
            [FL   [
            TOPIC/WHOLE   *The proceedings of the fifth TRON symposium presented here cover all aspects of the TRON project, which aims at establishing <u>the new computer architecture for the 1990s.</u>]]*

            [TM   [
            TOPIC/PART1   *the papers review <u>the current status </u>of development of TRON as well as its various subprojects*
            TOPIC/PART2   *and examine <u>future trends.</u>*
            TOPIC/PART3   <u>*ITRON, BTRON, CTRON, MTRON, and TRON VLSI CPU chips *</u>*are described.]]*

            [FR   [
            TOPIC/WHOLE   *This volume gives <u>an analysis,</u> both generally and in depth, of computer <u>systems of the next decade.</u>]]   ]*

[3']   [EX-FRAM/THEM ->
        [FL [TOPIC/WHOLE1, . . .], TM [TOPIC/PART1, . . .], FR
        [TOPIC/WHOLE1, . . .]]]

Example [4] contains a problem–solution relation between FL and FR:

[4]   [EX-FRAM/THEM
            [FL   [
            PROBLEM1   <u>*Realism *</u>*is often a primary goal in the creation of computer generated imagery.*

            PROBLEM2   *A key element in creating <u>the illusion of reality </u>is displaying the object with the appropriate illumination and shading characteristics of its environment.]]*

            [TM   [
            TOPIC/WHOLE   <u>*Illumination models *</u>*are the subject of this book,*

TOPIC/PART1   *which should help the computer graphics programmer to understand the properties of light,*

TOPIC/PART2   *the problems of illumination,*

TOPIC/PART3   *and to control the visual and computational compromises inherent in the process of computer image synthesis.*]]

[FR   [

SOLUTION   *The book provides the theoretical basis and the practical guidance for generating images that are fascinatingly close to reality.*]]   ]

[4']   [EX-THEM ->
[FL [TOPIC/PROBLEM1, . . .], TM [TOPIC/PART1, . . .], FR
[TOPIC/SOLUTION1, . . .]]]

7.2 Operation: CHAINING

7.2.1 Chaining condit`ions

Chaining occurs in the global thematic expansion (EX-THEM). This concerns the linking of text role configurations according to certain sequencing schemata which have a hierarchical correspondence. In sub-section 5.1.4 we outlined an action schema (*what does the book/author do?* or DOING (BOOK/AUTHOR,. . .)?) as a fundamental structure for the topic question. This schema was structured as an object model in the form of a book frame. It forms the point of departure for the determination of the connectivity schemata presented below.

Here 'natural orders', but also text-specific orders can play a role. 'Natural orders' (cf. 'ordo naturalis' of classical rhetorics, processed as naturalness theory in Dressler 1989) are concerned with sequencings that correspond to the temporal, causal or final sequence of events (Moens & Steedman 1987, Thompson 1987, Tomlin 1987a, Dorfmüller-Karpusa 1988, Rudolph 1988, Tonfoni 1990), or can be interpreted as questions such as *what happened next* in the sense of a text-thematic progression (Hellwig, 1984, pp. 68ff.) Text-specific orders (corresponding to 'artificial orders') are independent of natural orders. As a consequence, linguistically explicit connections must be produced.

In book announcement texts there are mixtures of both principles. Thus, for example, the chapter-by-chapter enumeration – in the order that the chapters appear in the book – in a way falls under a 'natural' order. It corresponds to the structure of the object as a text in the sense of a sequence of parts. Our illustrative examples refer principally to this kind of sequencing. The organisation forms used in our model are in correlation to the relations within the object model. In the foreground is the part–whole relation, which is the basis for linkings of roles such as BOOK (subdivision) and TOPIC (topic parts). Above all those sequencings are of interest that are supported by connectivity chains. Chains are determined by the fact that all connections that exist between the individual segments are parts of one single sequencing schema, which establishes the order of the text segments.

The assignments of the chains are defined as follows:

- CHAINING:
  [dimension: [
      [space: global   ]
      [direction: LERI   ]
      [profile: continuation]   ]]

Since the profile is produced through repetition of the same, the transitions between the units are marked. Various types of connectivity can be distinguished here. In the following we illustrate a few examples of this, without aiming at a complete description.

7.2.2 Chaining through enumeration

Enumerations are realised lexically through numerals. Chains emerge whose links are fixed in order, but which can be realised according to different classes (ordinal and cardinal numbers in figures, as adjectives, etc.). Example [5] shows a simple enumeration of the chapters that fill the middle section of the text. The structure is organised as a text with a left frame, in which the overall topic (TOPIC/WHOLE) is introduced. The middle section concerns the part topics, whereby the text role TOPIC/PART is repeated.

[5] [EX-CHAIN/THEM/NUM [
      [TOPIC/WHOLE   *This theoretical work explores <u>the relationship</u> between linguistic universals and second language acquisition.*]

      [TOPIC/PART1   *Chapter **1** outlines <u>arguments</u> for UG in L1 acquisition.*]

[TOPIC/PART2	*Chapter **2** advocates <u>the extension</u> of these arguments to L2 acquisition.*]
[TOPIC/PART3	*Chapter **3** considers <u>the effects</u> of markedness.*]
[TOPIC/PART4	*Chapter **4** discusses <u>the implications</u> of cognitive modularity.*]]]

A chain with continuous cardinal numbers as connectors emerges:

[5']   CHAIN/THEM/NUM: $\{1,2,3,\ldots, n\}$.

7.2.3 Chaining through domain-specific enumeration

The enumeration character can also be achieved through the naming of parts. This is easily possible in the case of the object book, since certain sections of the book are linguistically differentiated. [6] gives an example of chaining through a sequence such as *introduction, part I, part II, part III, bibliography, glossary*. The order in the text is 'natural', i.e. it corresponds to the usual order in books. The expanded text role is the role BOOK/ WHOLE –> BOOK/PART. In this case, the connectivity scope (text role BOOK/PART) and connector overlap:

[6] [EX-CHAIN/D-NUM	[
[BOOK/WHOLE	<u>*The volume*</u> *presents – for the first time in English – the work of two major representatives of the so-called Moscow-Tartu school.*]
[BOOK/PART1	<u>***The introduction***</u> *outlines their project for a "poetics of expressiveness" against the background of the structural-semiotic movement of the '60s and '70s.*]
[BOOK/PART2	***<u>Part I</u>*** *is a systematic exposition of the theory, concentrating on the concepts of theme, expressive device, poetic world, etc.*]
[BOOK/PART3	***<u>Parts II</u> and <u>III</u>*** *apply these concepts to a structuralist portrayal of Leo Tolstoy's tales for children (. . .) and of the medieval Latin author Archpoet of Cologne (. . .).*]
[BOOK/PART4	*The volume is provided with a **<u>Bibliogra-phy</u>** of the poetics of expressiveness*]
[BOOK/PART5	*and a **<u>Glossary</u>** of its metalanguage.*]]]

The following chain results:

[6']   CHAIN/THEM/D-NUM: *{introduction, part I, part II, part III,*
                            Bibliography, Glossary }

7.2.4 Chaining through position indication

The object structure can be considered as a unit that extends in length. As possible divisions, for the most part information is used that concerns the position within the sequence of the units. [7] is an example in which the thematic organisation is made explicit corresponding to the distribution in the book. The text role TOPIC/ ORGANISATION is repeated, which proceeding from ORGANISATION/WHOLE is expanded to further parts ORGi:

[7] [EX-CHAIN/THEM/POS [
    [TOPIC/WHOLE   *The organization is clear, consistent, and logical providing flexibility to the instructor:*]
    [TOPIC/ORG1   <u>*essentials*</u> ***first,***]
    [TOPIC/ORG2   <u>*details*</u> *of more interest to the specialist in* ***later*** *sections.*]
    [TOPIC/ORG3   ***Finally,*** <u>*the principles*</u> *that are established to develop an understanding of the details of construction and operation of practical machines.*]]   ]

A variation of [7] is formed by the chain of *{first, next, finally}* instead of *{first, later, finally }*, which is applied to the text role TOPIC/PART:

[8] [EX-CHAIN/THEM/POS [
    [TOPIC/WHOLE   *This book examines* <u>*the adaptive Boundary Element Method*</u> *for applications to 2-D elastostatics.*]
    [TOPIC/PART1   *The author* ***first*** *examines several problems using a commercial BEM package* <u>*to compare it with the Finite Element Method*</u>.]
    [TOPIC/PART2   ***Next*** *the adaptive BEM is developed to obtain* <u>*accurate and reliable solutions*</u>. . . .]
    [TOPIC/PART3   ***Finally*** *an adaptive strategy* <u>*using p and h versions*</u> *is proposed.*]   ]]

The following chain results:

[8']   CHAIN/THEM/POS: { *first, next, finally* }

The connectivity markers in a chain can belong to various syntactic categories. Hence verbs that characterise positions in the sequence are also to be included (cf. *beginning* in [9] without frame). Furthermore, as a link in a chain conjunctions acquire a specific meaning that they do not have in other contexts, e.g. because of the contrast to *final, while* indicates a paragraph.

[9]   [EX-CHAIN/THEM/POS   [
      [BOOK/PART1   ***Beginning*** *at the gate level, this book builds components hierarchically.*]
      [BOOK/PART2   ***After*** *each new element is defined (. . .) its operation is explained by examining alternatives for its internal structure.*]
      [BOOK/PART3   *While the book's primary emphasis is on hardware (. . .)*]
      [BOOK/PART4   *the* ***final*** *chapter introduces those software components which are closest to the hardware interface.*]]   ]
[9']   CHAIN/THEM/POS: {*beginning, after, final* }

Of course, different connectivity types can be mixed within any one chain. The following example contains connectors of the type ordinal numbers, cardinal numbers, verb, adverb and conjunction. The following kind of chain emerges: {*first, (to) progresses, chapter 3, chapter 4 then, chapter 5, chapter 6, finally chapter 7*}. Furthermore, use is also made of the possibility to consolidate several chapters, thus interrupting the enumeration. The resumption is marked by *then* in *chapter 4 then..* Parallel to the expansion of the text role BOOK/PART runs the expansion of the text role TOPIC/PART, which we highlight in the presentation:

[10]   [EX-CHAIN/THEM   [
      [TOPIC/PART1   *The* ***first*** *chapter looks at* <u>*simple integral equations,*</u> *. . .*]
      [TOPIC/PART2   *The text* ***progresses*** *through* <u>*the theory of approximation*</u> *. . .*]
      [TOPIC/PART3   *In* ***chapter 3*** <u>*the Laplace and Poisson equations*</u> *are developed.*]
      [TOPIC/1-3   *These three chapters comprise* <u>*the course work*</u> *part of the book and . . .*]

[TOPIC/PART4 ***Chapter 4 then*** *covers* <u>*several problems*</u>
solved by BEM, . . .]
[TOPIC/PART5 ***Chapter 5*** *discusses overcoming* <u>*domain*</u>
<u>*discretization*</u> *for . . .*]
[TOPIC/PART6 ***Chapter 6*** *presenting* <u>*examples of . . .*</u>]
[TOPIC/PART7 ***Finally, Chapter*** 7 *presents a* <u>*computer*</u>
<u>*program for . . .*</u>]]]
[10'] CHAIN/THEM: { *first, progress, 3, 4 then, 5, 6, finally 7* }

7.3 Operation: PAIRING

7.3.1 Pairing conditions

Local strategies form sequences that in the left-right direction are determined by the relation of the respective text unit to the preceding unit.
Connections of two adjacent units take up a lot of space as an object of
text-related research. We are interested in relations that can be classified in
the global text structure and are thus linked to the thematic and
interactional expansions in the object construction. The text property of
recurrence is considered constitutive for this relation. 'Recurrence' means
that units in the text occur several times, whereby they form different
relations to each other. Recurrence enables structures to be formed and is
constitutive for texts. The following definition applies:

- PAIRING:
  [dimension:
  [space: local   ]
  [direction: RILE   ]
  [profile: - continuation
                 - change   ]   ]

  Pairing designates a relation that characterises the kind of attachment
between a unit and the preceding unit. Whilst the profile of the frame
develops through change and the profile of the chain through repetition,
there are two profile possibilities for the pair. The result is continuity
through repetition of the same information type or change through a shift
in the information type in comparison with the preceding unit. Continuity
or change is to be seen with respect to the construction of the object, which
can be described in the form of the thematic sepresentation units. These
encompass individual text roles, but also more extensive units such as
parts of propositions or whole propositions.

When examining connectivity in the text, those connections are of interest that are characterised by qualifying connectivity markings. According to a general composition trend, those connections are marked whose constituents belong to the same categories. In this sense, three groups can be distinguished.

Continuous object construction:

* COPYING: several kinds of repetition of a preceding unit
* SPECIFYING: several kinds of variants of a preceding unit

Non-continuous object construction:

* ALTERNATING: several kinds of what the object does not represent

The description of connectivity pairs refers to two-way expansions (EX), which are based on the recurrence of a text role or text role configuration and are characterised by the respective specific pair relation (REL). The connectors can be determined in pairs in lexical inventories (INV-CON/REL), which characterise language use and are retrieved for text production.

In addition, expansion rules are used which designate the connectivity scope in the attachment of a proposition to a preceding proposition:

* [EX-PAIR/REL [
        [TROCi= . . .,   CON1= . . .],
        [TROCi+1= . . .,   CON2= . . .]]

In our examples we give such rules and insert text sections taken from our authentic material. In the examples, we underline the part of the text that encompasses the connectivity scope (text role or text role configuration). The connectors are highlighted in bold type. In a second schema, we give the respective selection from the connectivity inventories ([']). For the selection, the respective connectivity pair is given as well as the connectivity scope as a constraint.

7.3.2 Operation: COPYING

A continuous object construction is achieved by using a text role, part of a proposition or the whole proposition of the preceding unit again in the following unit, in order to give more information about the object. We are concerned here with a variety of text reference in which the function of attachment is emphasised in contrast to the otherwise normally highlighted function of reference (for 'discourse deixis' cf. Levinson, 1987 (1983), p. 85ff., also Ehlich 1979, in a computational view Bäuerle 1988,

Webber 1989). Reference is made to text sections and not to objects of the world.

Here, the specific relation within the recurrent expansion is that of repetition. The linking is generally realised through pronominalisations or more complex anaphoric assignments. From the point of view of connectivity, pronominal adverbs and quasi pronominalisations ('quasi') are above all of interest. They are suitable for establishing the relation to text roles (TROL) or text role configurations (TROC), and thus extend the possibilities of personal pronouns which refer to concepts, lexemes or nominal phrases ('x').

Without any attempt at completeness, the following list gives several connector pairs that frequently occur for attachment in the sense of COPY:

INV-PAIR/COPY: {*(0, this)*, *(0, therefore)*, *(0, in doing so)*, *(0, this ("quasi"))*, *(this "x", it)*, *("x", this "x")*, . . . }

The text role BOOK and the filler (*this*) are repeated at the same time:

[11]   [EX-PAIR/COPY [
      [BOOK1   **This** *new textbook provides a broad introduction to mathematical methods . . .*]
      [BOOK2   ***It** is intended to provide at least a basic mathematical background ..*]]]

[11'] INV-PAIR/COPY: [
      [TROL1=BOOK, CON=*0/this*]
      [TROL2=BOOK, CON=*it*   ]   ]

The repetition can take place several times:

[12]   [EX-PAIR/COPY [
      [BOOK1   **This** *is the first comprehensive textbook on generative morphology.*]
      [BOOK2   ***It** presents the history and present status of the core concepts of morphology as a component of the generative model of grammar.*]
      [BOOK3   ***It** contains a detailed discussion of the lexicalist hypothesis, . . .*]   ]]

[12'] INV-PAIR/COPY: [
      [TROL1   =BOOK, CON= 0/this   ]
      [TROL2/3/. . .   =BOOK, CON= it]   ]

The attachment only refers to the text role, in this case the role TOPIC. This kind of linking also allows a thematic expansion TOPIC-WHOLE –> TOPIC-PART (cf. CHAINING in):

[13]   [EX-PAIR/COPY   [
        [TOPIC1   _An introduction to the theory of elasticity_ . . . _is first presented._   ]
        [TOPIC2   **_This_** _includes the treatment of some of the most common types of generalised body forces_ . . .]]]

[13']   INV-PAIR/COPY   [
        [TROL1=TOPIC, CON= 0   ]
        [TROL2=TOPIC, CON=_this_   ]]]

In the following example the whole proposition forms the connectivity scope. It is taken up again in the subsequent unit by _this_ coupled with a quasi nominalisation in which the content of the preceding unit is interpreted.

[14]   [EX-PAIR/COPY   [
        [TROC1   _This volume strips anthropology in Belgium of the colonial ties in the past._]
        [TROC2   **_This reorientation_** _of the former disciplinary and theoretical frame leads to new and refreshing perspectives._]]]

[14']   [EX-PAIR/COPY   [
        [TROC1   =   CON = 0]
        [TROC2   =   CON = _this_ (quasi)]   ]]

7.3.3 Operation: SPECIFYING

The object construction is also continuous when variants with respect to the preceding unit are attached. The respective text role or text role configuration is repeated, only the fillers are different. Three types of specification can be distinguished, which are organised parallel to the traditional semantic relations:

- super/sub-ordination (SUB)
- addition with respect to a mutual text role (ADD) and
- opposition with respect to a mutual text role (OPP).

From a syntactic point of view, many forms of sentence coordination re-emerge here. In the context of text orientation they acquire an additional function. Here, we are interested above all in those phenomena that go beyond simple sequences and mark a specific possibility for attachment.

• Expansion via SPEC/SUB as a rule adds subordinations or details to generic concepts. In [15] there is a specification about the predicate element (*be interdisciplinary*), which in the second unit in the configuration of (PRED, TROL=TOPIC) is additionally detailed (*dealing with agriculture, economics*, etc.; on additive attachment with *not only – but . . .as well* see below):

[15] [EX-PAIR/SPEC/SUB   [
        [PRED1   *The many problems arising from such a model <u>are</u>*
                  <u>interdisciplinary</u> in nature.]
        [PRED2,   **Thus**, *this work presents contributions <u>dealing</u> not*
        [TOPIC   *only <u>with agricultural questions,</u> but those <u>dealing</u>*
                  <u>with economic, sociological, geographical and</u>
                  <u>political questions</u> as well.]]]

[15'] [INV-PAIR/SPEC/SUB   [
        [PRED1t   /   CON= 0   ]
        [PRED2(TOPIC)/ CON= *thus*   ]   ]]

The subordination as such can be marked by *in particular,* in the following referring to the same text role (TROLi). In [16] it concerns the text role TOPIC:

[16] [EX-PAIR/SPEC/SUB   [
        [TOPIC1   *In this text, <u>a method</u> is outlined to obtain an*
                 accurate approximation in the domain and on the
                 boundary . . .]
        [TOPIC2 **In particular,** *<u>any derived quantity of the</u>*
                 <u>proposed approximate</u> solution can be obtained with
                 sufficient precision.]]]

[16'] [INV-PAIR/SPEC/SUB   [
        [TROLi1   /   CON = 0   ]
        [TROLi2   /   CON = *in particular*   ]]]

• In the case of additive specification, both units have the same status, i.e. are aligned within a hierarchy. This generally concerns sub-classes of a mutual text role. In the following example, the text role READER is specified so that in both occurrences a sub-class of readers is given:

[17]   [EX-PAIR/SPEC/ADD   [
     [TROL=   *The book is of specific interest <u>to social</u>*
     READER   *<u>anthropologists and politics</u> concerned with*
                 contemporary Italy,]
     [TROL=   **while** *the general argument about the different levels*
     READER   *at which political ideologies operate is relevant <u>to</u>*
                 <u>those</u> studying a wide range of societies.]]]

[17']   [EX-PAIR/SPEC/ADD   [
     [TROLi1   =   CON = 0   ]
     [TROLi2   =   CON = *while*   ]]]

[18] provides an example of a specification on the basis of the text role ORGANISATION:

[18]   [EX-PAIR/SPEC/ADD   [
                 AGA presents individual bibliographical entries
     [TROL=   *divided <u>according to topics</u>*]
     ORGANIZ
     [TROL=   *and within these topics,* **further** *arranged*
     ORGANIZ *alphabetically <u>according to authors</u>.*]   ]]

[18']   [EX-PAIR/SPEC   [
     [TROLi1   =   CON = 0   ]
     [TROLi2   =   CON = *further*]   ]]

Example [19] shows an attachment via the predicates, whereby both predicates represent a specification of the general predicate DOING (cf. text question *what does the book do?*):

[19]   [EX-PAIR/SPEC/ADD   [
                 This volume, part of a larger research project
                 on technical modernization,
     [PRED1   **not only** *reports the findings of empirical*
                 investigation,]
     [PRED2   **but** *analyzes the historical and natural*
                 components of the country, . . .]   ]]

[19']   [EX-PAIR/SPEC/ADD   [
     [PRED1   =   CON = *not only*   (. . .)]
     [PRED2   =   CON = *but*   (. . .)]   ]]

Specifications on the basis of a text role favour parallelism of the syntactic structure. The following case deals with specification of the configuration consisting of predicate and sub-roles of the text role TOPIC:

[20]   [EX-PAIR/SPEC/ADD   [
       [PRED, TROL= TOPIC/SUB-TOPIC1
          It reports regularly on studies and research work in progress in German-speaking countries]
       [PRED, TROL= TOPIC/SUB-TOPIC2
          as well as *supplying information and brief reports on projects, congresses and new publications.*]   ]]

[20']   [INV-PAIR/SPEC/ADD   [
       [PRED, SUB-THEMA1 /   CON = 0   ]
       [PRED, SUB-THEMA2 /   CON = *as well as*   ]   ]]

Additional connectivity pairs of the type SPEC/ADD are { *(O, along with)*, *(O, in addition)*, *(O, also)*, *(primarily, also)* }.

• Similar to additive specification, in the case of oppositional specifying (SPEC/OPP) sub-classes of a mutual text role or text role configuration are attached.

[21]   [EX-PAIR/SPEC/OPP   [
       [TOPIC1   ***Although most*** *of <u>the methods</u> presented are the latest developments in the field of numerical fracture mechanics,*]
       [TOPIC2   *the authors have* ***also*** *included* ***some*** *simple <u>techniques</u> which . . .*]   ]]

[21']   [INV-PAIR/SPEC/OPP   [
       [TROLi1   /   CON = *although most*]
       [TROLi2   /   CON = *also some*]]]

An opposition is frequently used with regard to the text role READER:

[22]   [EX-PAIR/SPEC/OPP   [
       [READER1 *The book is of specific interest <u>to social anthropologists and politics</u> concerned with contemporary Italy,*]
       [READER2 ***while*** *the general argument about the different levels at which political ideologies operate is relevant <u>to those</u> studying a wide range of societies.*]]]

[22']   [INV-PAIR/SPEC/OPP   [
                   |TROLi1   /   CON = 0   ]
                   [TROLi2   /   CON = *while*]   ]]

7.3.4 Operation: ALTERNATING

A non-continuous object construction is achieved when the object in question is isolated in the construction. This happens when reference is made to another (real or imaginary) object and this is compared to the object in question. Thus, for example, a book is described by saying what it is not or does not do, or does differently from usual. Hence a certain text role or text role configuration is used recurrently, whereby two different object references are available.

The text role BOOK is, for example, contrasted as follows:

[23]   [EX-PAIR/ALT   [
               [TROL =   ***Unlike most other*** *sociological and*
               BOOK   *anthropological books,*]
               [TROL =   ***these*** *publications will emphasize*
               BOOK   *the visual.*]]]

[23']   [INV-PAIR/ALT   [
               [TROL1   /   CON = *unlike most other*]
               [TROL2   /   CON = *these*]   ]]

In the case of negated forms, both alternatives are given a marking (e.g. *not – but*):

[24]   [EX-PAIR/ALT   [
               [TROL = GOAL1
                       The purpose of this study is **not** *to present facts and figures about a given settlement*]
               [TROL = GOAL2
                       but *to crystallize potential forces and to integrate them into a methodical planning process.*]]]

[24']   [INV-PAIR/ALT   [
               [TROL1   /   CON = *not*   ]
               [TROL2   /   CON = *but*   ]   ]]

In the following example, the connectivity scope refers to the whole proposition (TROCt):

[25]   [EX-REC/ALT   [
            [TROCt1   ***Instead*** *of listing the various theories of de-*
                       constructivism,]
            [TROCt2   *this volume provides an integrated overview*
                       of the current discussion on this topic.]]]

[25']   [INV-REC/ALT   [
            [TROCt1   /   CON = *instead*   ]
            [TROCt2   /   CON = 0   ]   ]]

In example [26] an alternative in a negative form is used. The affirmative contrast (*what the authors do*) is also marked:

[26]   [EX-REC/ALT   [
            [TROCt1   *The authors have* **not** *restricted themselves to*
                       traditional "printed materials".]
            [TROCt2   ***Thus****, AGA represents one of the first specialized*
                       bibliographies which provides information on the
                       news in ethnographic cinematography.]   ]]

[26']   [INV-REC/ALT   [
            [TROCt1   /   CON = *not*]
            [TROCt2   /   CON = *thus*]   ]]

7.4 Series of PAIRINGs

Repetitions can occur several times in succession, so that series of relations emerge such as { COPY(p1, p2), COPY(p2, p3), . . .}. [27] is an example of this, in which the connectivity scope encompasses the whole proposition (TROC whole):

[27]   [EX-PAIR/COPY [
            [TROC1   *In his The City of Men, a study of the ideology and*
                       sexual politics in ancient Greece, Peter Mason offers
                       an account of the mechanisms by which ideology is
                       produced within a specific social formation.]
            [TROC2   ***Thus*** *he goes beyond a Marxist account of the*
                       structure which explains and describes this
                       phenomenon, to show how one proceeds from base to
                       ideology.]
            [TROC3   ***In doing so*** *he makes extensive use of insights*
                       from psychoanalyis.]   ]]

```
[27']   [INV-PAIR/COPY [
            [TROC1      /       CON = 0     ]
            [TROC2      /       CON = thus ]

            [TROC2      /       CON = 0     ]
            [TROC3      /       CON = in doing so ] ]]
```

A combination of the three expansion types can lead to series of pairings which cover the entire text. The following example demonstrates:

- first of all repetition between TROCt1 and TROCt2, whereby the latter takes up the whole proposition of the preceding unit.
- between TROCt2 and TROCt3 there is a relation of alternative.
- TROCt4 and TROCt5 are embedded under TROCt3 and are linked in the relation of specification.
- TROCt3 and TROCt6 in turn form an attachment through repetition.

Since we are concerned in each case with twofold relations, overlappings are inevitable. We illustrate this as follows:

```
[28]    [EX-PAIR/COPY  [
            [TROCt1   Urban growth and its impact on a surrounding rural
                      life is a continuous process which brings dimensional
                      change in both areas. ]
            [TROCt2   Therefore, the presentation of a town and its ur-
                      ban development comprises more than a simple
                      description of the facts. ] ]]
        [EX-PAIR/ALT   [
            [TROCt2   . . . the presentation . . . more than . . . ]
            [TROCt3   Instead it should take the shape of a discussion of
                      sectoral and spatial interrelationships ] ]
            [EX-PAIR/SPEZ   [
                [TROCt4   in which the town is situated, ]
                [TROCt5   as well as characterize the urban notion
                          within the context of the culture. ]]]]
        [EX-PAIR/COPY  [
            [TROCt3   Instead . . . ]
            [TROCt6   J.-E. Hamesse does just this in his Sectoral and
                      Spatial Interrelations in Urban Development. ] ] ]

[28']   [INV-PAIR/COPY [
            [TROCt1     /       CON = 0             ]
            [TROCt2     /       CON = therefore     ]       ]]
```

```
[INV-PAIR/ALT    [
        [TROCt2    /        CON = more than  ]
        [TROCt3    /        CON = instead        ]        ]


[INV-PAIR/SPEZ   [
            [TROCt4    /        CON = 0    ]
            [TROCt5    /        CON = as well as   ]]


[INV-PAIR/COPY  [
        [TROCt3    /        CON = 0    ]
        [TROCt6    /        CON = this  ]        ]]
```

7.5   Connectivity forms (CONFO)

7.5.1   *General remarks*

The combination of the introduced parameters is the basis for the part of a text action grammar that combines the thematic-interactional development of the text with sequencing operations. Table 7.1 shows the parameters EX (expansion), SOP (sequencing operation), CONSTR (conditions with respect to surface-language expressions) and INV (relevant inventories for surface-language expressions) in an overview.

With reference to the text action grammar, the following correspondences present themselves: EX-ILL corresponds to the component ILL, EX-THEM corresponds to the component PRO and INV corresponds to the component LOC. The complex text action schema is now to be complemented by further sequencing parameters, i.e. by SOP and CONSTR. Altogether, the following grammar emerges. The sub-categories listed here are to be understood in an exemplary sense. For the complete presentation of the grammar further empirical studies are necessary.

```
TAc        :        < EX-ILL ( EX-THEM, INV ), SOP, CONSTR >
EX-ILL     :        < DES, ARG, . . . >
```

DESCR (description) and ARGUM (agrumentation) are two possibilities for illocution expansions. DESCR and ARGUM can in turn be characterised by different sequencings of illocution types:

```
DES        :        < DESi, SOPi , CONSTRi >
ARG        :        < ARGi, SOPi, CONSTRi >
```

Table 7.1   Expansions (EX) in relation to sequencing operations (SOP) including constraints with respect to inventories and text roles (CONSTR) and the inventory types concerned

EX	SOP	CONSTR	INV
EX-ILL	FRAMING	change/INV	INV/P
EX-THEM	FRAMING	change/INV	INV/TROL
EX-THEM	CHAINING	contin/TROL	INV/CON-C
EX-THEM	PAIRING/ COPY	contin/TROL	INV/CON-COP
EX-THEM	PAIRING/ SPEC	contin/TROL	INV/CON-SUB INV/CON-ADD INV/CON-OPP
EX-THEM	PAIRING/ ALT	change/TROL	INV/CON-ALT

The thematic expansion is characterised by sequences of text roles or text role configurations:

EX-THEM : <TROCi, SOPi, CONSTRi>

Text role configurations form a list of possible text role configurations:

TROC: { TROC1, TROC2, . . .TROCn }

Examples are (cf. section 5.1.5.):

TROC1: (TROL1=BOOK,   TROL2=TOPIC)
TROC2: (TROL1=AUTHOR, TROL2=TOPIC, TROL3=READER)

The SOP component is sub-divided as follows:

•   SOP   :   < FRAM, CHAIN, PAIR >

- FRAM   :   < FRAM/ILL, FRAM/THEM >
- FRAM/ILL   :   < FL (ILL-TYP= . . .),
                           TM   (ILL-TYP= . . .),
                           FR   (ILL-TYP= . . .) >
- FRAM/THEM: < FL (TROLj= . . .),
                           TM   (TROLk= . . .),
                           FR   (TROLl= . . .) >
- CHAIN   :   < NUM, D-NUM, POS, . . . >

- PAIR   :   < COPY, SPEC, ALT, . . . >
- SPEC   :   < SUB, ADD, OPP, . . . >

The connectivity inventories (INVC) are lists with connectors or pairs of connectors:

- INVC   :   <INVC(CHAIN/THEM), INVC(PAIR/THEM), . . . >
- INVC(CHAIN/THEM):   < INVC/NUM, INVC/POS, . . . >

  - INVC/NUM: { *(1, part I, first, . . .), (2, part II, second, . . .),*
                           . . ., (n, last part, finally, . . .) }
  - INVC/POS: { *(first, to begin, to start, . . .), (later, next,*
                           after, then, to progress, . . .), . . .
                           (finally, to end, . . .) }

- INVC(PAIR/THEM): <INVC/COPY, INVC/SUB, INVC/ADD,
                           INVC/OPP, INVC/ALT, . . . >

  - INVC/COPY: { *(0, it), (this, it), ("x", this "x"), (0, this),*
                           (0, therefore), (0, in doing so),
                           (0, this ("quasi")), . . . }
  - INVC/SUB: { *(0, thus), (0, in particular), (0, further),*
                           (primarily, also). . . }
  - INVC/ADD: { *(0, as well as), (0, as well), (0, also), (not*
                           only, but), (0, in addition), (0, along with),
                           . . . }
  - INVC/OPP: { *(0, while), (although most, also more),*
                           (many, while others), . . . }
  - INVC/ALT: { *(not, but), (not, thus), (instead, 0), (more*
                           than, instead), (unlike most other, these), . . . }

The question remains as to how this connection can be organised in an operationalisable grammar. In this context we use two structuring aids:

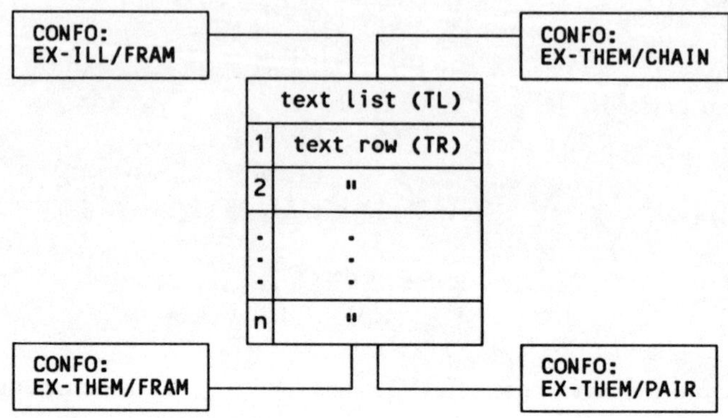

Figure 7.1 Connectivity forms (CONFO) in relation to the text list

- the notion that the different sequencing operations build up different text levels and
- the notion of text space.

In combination, the two notions lead to a concept of a text grammar, which is sub-divided into different connectivity forms (CONFO). In this context, there is one formula respectively for the combination of a content and a formal aspect of the text development through the combination of EX and SOP (see above). The linking of all forms is established through the mutual text space. We illustrate this sub-division in Figure 7.1. It shows the rough structure of the grammar. Each formula additionally has a microstructure and can be differentiated through sub-forms. The introduction of sub-forms allows the grammar to be extended at will. This applies in general for the whole system, which can be complemented by additional forms (according to the same schema) at any time. The processing of the grammar is to be seen from the point of view that each form provides a pattern for the potential development on one of the text levels dealt with. In the production of a text representation, e.g. within the framework of the text production, one of the patterns that come into question is copied into the potential text space of the new text. This happens equally for the sequencing and complex text action expansions (from Chapter 6) as well as for the realisation of the simple text actions (from Chapter 5). This is outlined in summary in Chapter 8. In the following, we would like to explain the individual connectivity forms in more detail.

Table 7.2   Example for CONFO1: Type DESCRIPTION

no	FRAM	EX-TYPE	ILL-TYPE	INV-TYPE
1	FL	DESCRIPT	EVA	INV/Pk
2	TM	DESCRIPT	DES	INV/Pk
3	TM	DESCRIPT	DES	INV/Pk
. . .	. . .	. . .	. . .	. . .
. . .	. . .	. . .	. . .	. . .
n	FR	DESCRIPT	EVA	INV/Pk

7.5.2 CONFO: EX-ILL/FRAM

Expansions of the interactional component that are indicated by connectivity means are characterised by the operation of FRAMING. Text developments without frames are of course also conceivable. In this case, there is only a text middle in the sequence in the text space. In our analyses we had dealt with description schemata and argumentation schemata. Table 7.2 shows a description including a frame and Table 7.3 shows an argumentation schema that consists entirely of frames.

Table 7.3   Example for CONFO1: Type ARGUMENTATION

no	FRAM	EX-TYPE	ILL-TYPE	INV-TYPE
1	FL	ARGUM	ASS	INV/Pj
2	FL	ARGUM	EVA	INV/Pk
3	FL	ARGUM	ASS	INV/Pj
. . .	. . .	. . .	. . .	. . .
n-1	FR	. . .	EVA	INV/Pk
n	FR	ARGUM	ASS	INV/Pj

Table 7.4 Example for CONFO2: Type THEMATIC FRAMING (WHOLE/PART) and inventories of corresponding connectors

no	FRAM	EX-TYPE	TROL-TYPE	INV-TYPE
1	FL	THEM	-/WHOLE	INV/CON-TW
2	TM	THEM	-/PART1	INV/CON-TP
3	TM	THEM	-/PART2	INV/CON-TP
. . .	. . .	. . .	. . .	. . .
n-1	. . .	. . .	-/PARTn	INV/CON-TP
n	FR	THEM	-/WHOLE	INV/CON-TW

In the case of the framed description, the left and right frame is realised as an evaluation and refers to predicate inventories that contain evaluating expressions (cf. Chapter 5). Argumentative expansion is characterised by the fact that the actual middle section is missing. This occurs because the conclusion, which contains the main statement about the object, is not explicitly expressed. The frame parts are assertions, which can be mixed with evaluations.

7.5.3 CONFO: EX-THEM/FRAM

The thematic development operates via text roles and text role configurations. The expansion type here designates the relation between frame parts and middle sections. But here, too, there are patterns for frameless development. We give a pattern with respect to the text role TOPIC. A frequently used pattern is the part-whole-relation (Table 7.4):

7.5.4 CONFO: EX-THEM/CHAIN

CHAINING is linked to conditions, e.g. to the division of the text or text section into individual parts. The connectors of the chain – different depending on the type of the chain (EX-CHAIN-TYPE) – provide this division. Compositions that do not form a chain can of course also be described. This concerns patterns of the free order of text role configurations that are developed in accordance with the representation in Chapter 5. In the sequencing they are brought into an order.

Table 7.5 Example for CONFO3: Type THEMATIC CHAINING (NUM) and inventories of corresponding connectors

no	CHAIN	EX-TYPE	TROL-TYPE	INV-TYPE
1	TM	THEM	PART1	INV/CON-C
2	TM	THEM	PART2	INV/CON-C
3	TM	THEM	PART3	INV/CON-C
. . .	. . .	. . .	. . .	. . .
n-1	. . .	. . .		INV/CON-C
n	TM	THEM	PARTn	INV/CON-C

As far as the chaining development is concerned, we are not interested in the individual development of the text role configuration (this is the subject of the text action grammar I), but the specific text role that represents the connectivity scope. It is set out as a condition under the heading CONSTR. In cases where the chaining is based on the division into individual parts, this must be a text role that contains PART as a sub-role (e.g. BOOK/PART or TOPIC/PART). The expansion type designates the kind of chaining. It is relevant for the inventories (INV) from which the respective connectors (CONi) are to be selected. Here we give just one example of the expansion NUM (enumeration with number values, see Table 7.5). Further CONFOs are to be constructed with different instances of the parameters of EX-TYPE, TROL, CONSTR and INV (see list above in sub-section 7.5.1).

7.5.5 CONFO: EX-THEM/PAIR

Connectivity forms of pairing designate only a fragment of the text space, namely two adjacent units. The expansion type (EX-TYPE) refers here to the respective sequencing operation. For every type a separate connectivity form is set up. Under PAIR the individual connectors that are selected from the inventory are given. Here, too, the conditions refer to the connectivity scope, which encompasses individual text roles or text role configurations. The following example is filled out for TROL=READER and SOP=COPY, the other expansions (e.g. SPEC with SUB, ADD and OPP or also ALT) apply by analogy (Table 7.6).

Table 7.6 Example for CONFO4: Type THEMATIC PAIRING (COPY) and inventory of corresponding connectors

no	PAIR	EX-TYPE	p/TROC/TROL	INV-TYPE
n	TM	THEM	READER	INV/CON-COP
n+1	TM	THEM	READER	INV/CON-COP

7.5.6 CONFOs and text action grammar

The CONFOs have the purpose to combine in each case a specific content aspect with a formal sequencing aspect and position the result within the text space. In this way the complexity of the relation sequence is divided into several partial representations of the text space. That means that in each case a combination of content and formal-sequential aspects forms a part of the text representation, which – placed over each other – result in the overall text representation.

At the same time there is the possibility to deal flexibly with the different information concerning the organisation of the text structure. This method is intended to be used for the text action grammar. The idea behind it is to break down the overall process of text writing into partial operations, which can be clearly integrated into the writing actions of human writers. In the last concluding chapter, we give an outlook on this possible application. It also largely determines the design of a text production system that could be employed as a support for text writing.

8 Integrated view of the text grammar

8.1 The idea of text grammar

The idea of text grammar goes back as far as the development phase of text linguistics, in which legitimations for the occupation with texts rather than sentences were in the foreground. One method in this context was to transfer principles of sentence grammar onto texts. In this sense text grammars in the form of phrase structure grammars were developed (e.g. as macro- and superstructures in van Dijk 1980a, 1980b). This approach related first of all to narrative texts (cf. 'story grammar' as a conceptual structure in Rumelhart 1975; cf. also de Beaugrande 1982). A fruitful complement to this was finally the introduction of schema concepts which could be applied to other text types (reports, scientific texts in van Dijk & Kintsch 1983, descriptions of objects and events in Schank 1975b, Schank & Abelson 1977, Chafe (ed.) 1980). The isolation of units of states of affairs or text passages as constituents of a combination theory that could be described by rules thus became a precondition for computational modelling. Meehan's 'story writing' (Meehan 1976) is one example of this. Other aspects were also considered: action relations (e.g. 'painting' in Charniak (1977), evaluation of events in Lehnert (1982), understanding of stories on the basis of a grammar of actions of the participants in Dyer (1983).

The complexity of texts soon made it clear that simple schemata can only cover a limited section of text description. Hence overall conceptions were developed in which the components of importance for the text constitution were isolated and set in relation to each other (Morgenthaler 1980, Fritz & Muckenhaupt 1981). Correspondingly, text levels were introduced (e.g. Daneš & Viehweger (eds) 1983, Heinemann & Viehweger 1991) which allow a systematic assignment of components. On the other hand, it was now also possible to concentrate on particular aspects, such as with a view to questions of text organisation (e.g. Ehrich & Koster 1983, Clyne

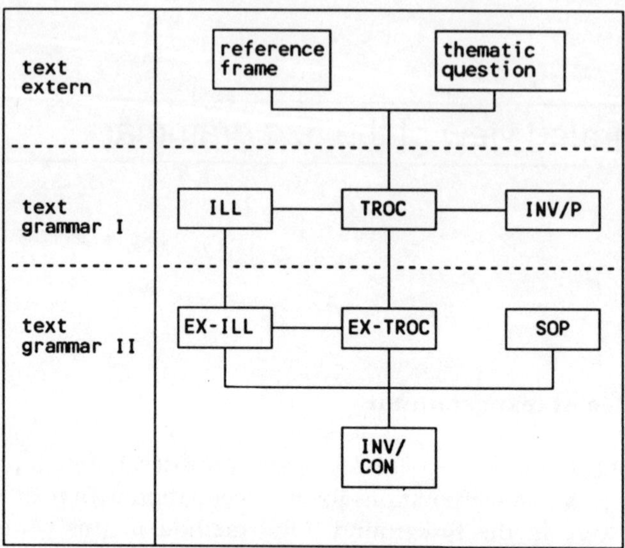

Figure 8.1 The several sources of text knowledge

1987) or on aspects concerning linguistic actions, which were considered as decisive for the text structure (Hartung 1981, Rosengren 1983, Sandig 1986, Motsch (ed.) 1986). The standpoint of grammatical orders of linguistic actions (Häfele 1979, Weigand 1989) is pursued above all in the more recent direction of dialogue grammar (Hundschnurscher & Weigand (eds) 1986, 1989, Stati et al. (1991)).

Proceeding from the assumption that written texts and their production are also parts of a communicative situation, in the present text model principles of dialogue grammar description have been applied to texts. They have been further developed in the direction of a text production grammar, which is operational and can be decomposed in partial processes. The approach to this is top-down (cf. suggestion for integrating top-down and bottom-up processes in text generation in Hovy 1991). A text planning component is conceived in such a way that a hierarchy of operations governs the selection of various text composition operations. The text structure to be formed is on the other hand not hierarchically ordered, i.e. there is no equating of text plan and text structure (cf. example in subsection 3.5.3). Instead, a text space is introduced, within which representations are produced on the basis of a carrier structure of text list and text row. There is also no transfer of sentence grammar to text grammar operations (cf. model in Scha & Polany 1988). Such punctual structural expansions (e.g. attachment, adjunction) are indeed important, but are not sufficient for a text-specific global structure production.

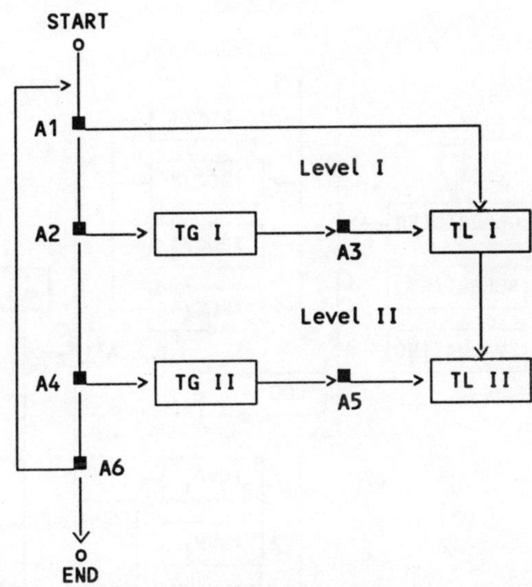

Figure 8.2 Text grammars (TG), text lists (TL) and activation points (A) within a design of text production

8.2 Design of text production

8.2.1 The several components

The developed text action grammar is conceived as the core of a computer system for supporting text production. The design of such a system is therefore strongly influenced by the text grammar approach. Insofar as this is determined on a linguistic action theory basis, the organisation of the information flow in the course of processing should also be adapted to the basic conditions of human text writing. In this section we outline the possibility of such a design.

The text knowledge sources for a text production system have been developed in the previous chapters. Figure 8.1 illustrates the relation of the several components. In the following, it is intended to show how the individual components are set in relation to one another in a processing step.

8.2.2 A two-way model: text grammar and text space

The overall framework (level 0) is formed by an organisation structure with two sub-systems (Figure 8.2). This concerns a two-way model, in which the text grammar part and the operations in the text space are

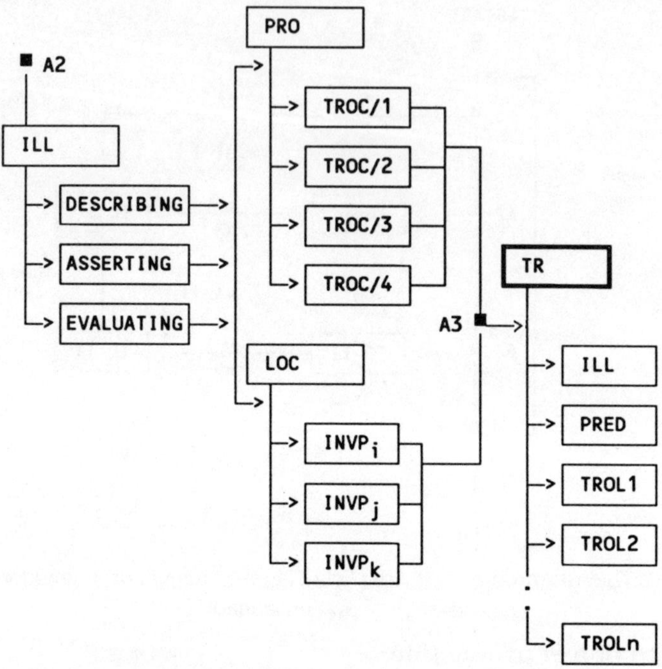

Figure 8.3 Construing the text row (TR)

constructed as separate modules. This has various advantages, among others that of independent modification and the possibility of expanding both parts. Apart from such technical advantages, this approach at the same time favours conceptual differentiations which can also be used for a text theory.

Both sub-systems in turn operate on two sub-levels. One concerns simple text actions in the field of the text grammar and manipulations in the field of text rows within the text space (level I). The other sub-level concerns complex text actions and manipulations in the field of text lists within the text space (level II). Whilst the text grammar component represents a closed system by virtue of a fixed repertoire of combination rules, the text space component is open. It contains the organisation of the input and output structure. At level 0 there are activation points, which organise operations within the components and the linking of the components. A1 links text rows and text list in the text space. A2 activates text grammar I, A3 links it with text list I. A4 activates text grammar II and A5 links this with the text list II. A6, finally, controls the continuation or the end of the processes.

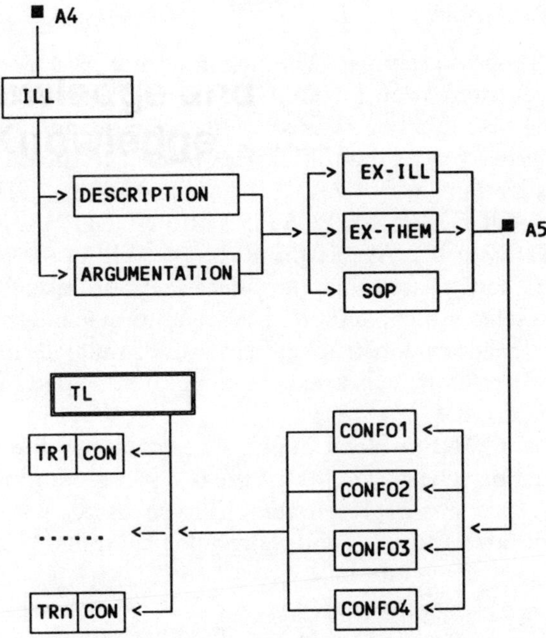

Figure 8.4 Construing the text list (TL)

8.2.3 Construing the text row (TR)

At level I the text action schema for a text unit (on the scale of a proposition) is delineated (Figure 8.3). The text grammar system provides two blocks for this. One block contains the possible text role configurations, which are ordered per block side according to the configuration type. Each block side of the second block consists in a collection of inventory lists for predicative expressions. The block sides differ on the basis of the assignment of illocution and text role configuration. A rough selection of suitable block sides is governed by the illocution type to be used. Further selections take place depending on the text roles. This corresponds to the theoretical approach that the illocution is the superordinated governing component. With respect to an implementation there are two possibilities for realisation: an automatic realisation with standard parameters (e.g. for DE-SCRIBING) or a menu organisation with options for various possibilities within the framework of an interactional system, whereby the text writer determines the individual instances. Within the field of the text space, the individual selections are filled into one text row (TR) respectively. The representation form corresponds to that of a simple text action schema.

8.2.4 Construing the text list (TL)

At level II the process is similar. The text grammar part is covered here by a block with information on the CONFOs developed in Chapter 7. Here, too, the selection is initially governed by the complex illocution (EX-ILL). There are CONFO blocks that differ with respect to the different types of sequencing operations (cf. FRAMING (ILL-FRAM, THEM-FRAM), CHAINING (NUM, DNUM, POS), PAIRING (COPYING, SPECIFY-ING (SUB, ADD, OPP), ALTERNATING)). Within the field of the text space a block is constructed that comprises the four basic CONFO types. The respective selection can either be carried out in standard form or via a menu. The instructions constructed here are formulated in the sense of a text structure formation, which can be integrated as parts in human text production (Figure 8.4).

The filled in CONFO block in the text space has the structure of a complex text action schema and forms the text representation of the text to be produced. This text representation can be used as a model for the insertion of sentence grammar and morphological units. It is the reference point for a text-sentence interface.

8.3 Summary

The study aims at a theory of text production. In this context it develops a text linguistic foundation for a computational model of text writing. In order to describe structure-forming processes, the concept of text action is introduced. The result is the formulation and formalisation of a text grammar as text action grammar. This produces text representations by means of cumulative structure forming within a text space. The model considers the following aspects:

(1) The process character of text writing is modelled. The 'higher-level' processes operative here are defined in speech-act-theory terms as text actions and represented declaratively in the form of text action schemata. By virtue of the homogeneous theoretical basis, consistency is achieved in spite of the complexity of the thematic states of affairs. The concept of text action is introduced under three considerations:

* It relates content-communicative and text organising factors to those of language use.
* The action aspect is operationalised in the sense of information processing. This is to be understood in such a way that the illocution is interpreted as a specified instruction within the framework of struc-

ture-forming text processes such as selection and composition. In this sense the illocution assumes the function of a program instruction, which locally governs the proposition forming and its linguistic realisation and globally the building of a text structure. There are simple and complex text actions correspondingly. They control the lexical selection and sequential composition.

- The text action schema provides a general representation schema for the structuring and processing of data and text grammar.

(2)   The text action grammar integrates

(a) content and communicative aspects in the sense of object construction (text semantics) and object presentation (text pragmatics). The modelling of the factual aspects is founded on frame theory. Frames, however, do not form the central structure concept. Rather, a genuine text structure is assumed, which is determined by the text topic, its expansion in the sequence in the text and its integration in communicative purposes. From this standpoint an object model is developed, which provides a frame of reference for the thematic structure of the text. Since we are concerned with book announcement texts, the object model refers to the communicative object book. A corresponding book frame, which is verified empirically on the basis of authentic texts, thus provides a grid of classificatory units, which are represented in the text structure as text roles. Text roles and their systematic linking in text role configurations form the basic units for the structure formation within the framework of the object construction.

Communicative aspects are represented as parts of the object presentation in the form of illocutions. Here, we distinguish three types of illocution (DESCRIBING, ASSERTING, EVALUATING). Their use in combination with specified text roles is considered significant for lexicalisations in the text. Correspondingly, the illocution types are provided with specific options with respect to lexical inventories, whose use is determined depending on certain role configurations. Operationalised, they are instructions for lexical selections from different inventories, which signal the assignment of the thematised states of affairs to the knowledge types such as knowledge of facts, knowledge of norms and knowledge of beliefs.

On the linguistic action level, the text structure is interpreted as dialogic. The overall sequence is considered as a quantity of response actions with respect to standard questions of the anticipated addressees (text questions), which are typical for certain communicative situations. The sequential structure is determined by compositions which with respect to content are defined by types of expansion of the text topic and the interaction. Text-thematic expansions serve the object construction, interactional expansions the object representation. The former are constructed through lists of text role configurations, the latter through sequences and hierarchies from the above-mentioned illocution types.

(b) sequential and dynamic aspects in the sense of text connectivity (text syntax). The sequencing is determined by two simple basic principles. If we proceed from a dynamic directionality of the sequential text structure, then there are two oppposing strategies that determine specific sequencing operations:

- global strategy LERI (left-right) is oriented towards the text property of delimitation and produces global connections. Two important operations are FRAMING and CHAINING.

- A local strategy RILE (right-left) is oriented towards the text property of recurrence and produces local connections through attachment to the preceding structure. This is achieved through the operation PAIRING.

The application of these strategies to illocutionary and thematic aspects is organised via CONFOs (connectivity forms). The combination of the four basic CONFOs results in the text representation for a text specimen.

(c) Text structure and text production are related against the background of a textual carrier structure with stative and dynamic aspects. Thus an abstract text list is assumed, which is composed of text rows. Text rows form the background structure for the representation of individual propositions and the lexical inventories that belong to them. The enumeration of several text rows results in the text list, insofar as additional connectivity constraints are taken into account. This process is organised dynamically within a text space and is put in concrete form through specific sequencing operations.

(3)   The relations between text grammar and operations in the text space are represented in a two-way model. They are put in concrete form on the basis of the uniform description category of text action. The output for individual text units is determined correspondingly by the schema for simple text actions, the output for the text sequence through the schema for complex text actions.

(4)   The innovative character of this approach in comparison with contemporary text description approaches as well as approaches to automatic text generation lies principally in the integrative overall perspective. The following aspects are integrated:

- integration of text-linguistic and communication-theoretical aspects with formal and operative aspects
- integrative description of several text levels (text topic, text function,

text syntax)
* linking of global and local sequential text structure in the connectivity structure
* linking of communicative-semantic aspects with those of the linguistic text surface
* linguistically represented data structures (no object language units)
* uniform representation format for all levels and data structures
* consistency of the system by virtue of a homogeneous theoretical basis.

The model permits the following applications:

* It offers theoretical-methodical terms of reference for the further research of textual sequencing structures. The assumption of only two linearisation strategies that are considered as fundamental, which – from a text linguistic point of view – have consequences for the text structure composition, provides a simple schema that is easy to verify empirically.
* Experiments concerning text production can be carried out via the methodical means of computer simulation. The simulation makes it possible to look at individual parameters or their effects in isolation. Moreover, it also opens up the possibility of a systematic compilation of a text grammar.
* Further development of software in the field of computer-aided text writing.

Open questions concern the extension of the text grammar with respect to other text types and hence from there a generalisation, the detailed implementation of the computer system and a text-sentence interface.

References

Abraham, W. (ed.), 1991, *Discourse particles. Descriptive and theoretical investigations on the logical, syntactic and pragmatic properties of discourse particles in German and English*, J. Benjamins, Amsterdam.

Agre, P. E., Chapman, D., 1990, What are plans for? *Robotics and Autonomous Systems*, (8): 17–34.

Agricola, E., 1976, *Vom Text zum Thema*. In: Daneš & Vieweger (eds), 1976: 3–27.

Agricola, E., 1979, *Textstruktur – Textanalyse – Informationskern*. VEB, Leipzig.

Airenti, G., Bara, B., Colombetti, M., 1984, *Planning and understanding speech acts by interpersonal games*. In: Bara & Guida (eds), 1984: 9–32.

Allen, J. F., 1987, *Natural Language Understanding*. The Benjamins/Cummings Publ. Comp., Menlo Park.

Allen, J. F., Perrault, C. R., 1980, Analyzing intention in utterances, *Artificial Intelligence*, 15 (3): 143–178.

Allén, St. (ed.), 1982, *Text processing. Text analysis and generation. Text typology and attribution*, Almquist & Wiksell Int., Stockholm.

Antos, G., 1982, *Grundlagen einer Theorie des Formulierens. Textherstellung in geschriebener und gesprochener Sprache*, Niemeyer, Tübingen.

Antos, G. 1984, *Textuelle Planbildung- ein Beitrag zu einer Textlinguistik zwischen Kognitionspsychologie und Handlungstheorie*, In: Rosengren (ed.), 1984: 169–205.

Antos, G., Krings, P. (eds), 1989, *Textproduktion. Ein interdisziplinärer Überblick*, Niemeyer, Tübingen.

Appelt, D. E., 1985, *Planning English sentences*, Cambridge University Press, Cambridge.

Austin, J. L., 1962 (1975), *How to do things with words*, Oxford University Press, Oxford.

Bach, E., Harms, R. I. (eds), 1968, *Universals in linguistic theory*, Holt, Rinehart and Winston, New York.

Bajziková, E., 1984, Text connectors, *Linguistica generalia*, 3: 95–100.

Ballmer, Th. T., Brennenstuhl, W., 1981, *Speech act classification*, Springer, Berlin.

Ballmer, Th., Wildgen, W. (eds), 1987, *Process Linguistics. Exploring the processual aspects of language and language use, and the methods of their description*, Niemeyer, Tübingen.

Bange, P. (ed.), 1987, *L'analyse des interactions verbales. La dame de Caluire: une consultation*, Lang, Bern.

Bara, B. G., Guida, G. (eds), 1984, *Computational models of natural language processing*, North-Holland, Amsterdam.

Bartlett, F. C., 1932, *Remembering: a study in experimental and social psychology*, Cambridge University Press, Cambridge.

Bateman, J. A., 1991, *Uncovering textual meanings: a case study involving systemic-functional resources for the generation of Japanese texts*. In: Paris et al. (eds), 1991: 125–153.

Bátori, I. S., Weber, H. J. (eds), 1986, *Neue Ansätze in Maschineller Sprachübersetzung: Wissensrepräsentation und Textbezug*, Niemeyer, Tübingen.

Bäuerle, R., 1988, Ereignisse und Repräsentationen, *LILOG-Report 43*, IBM-Deutschland, Stuttgart.

Bäuerle, R., Schwarze, C., von Stechow, A. (eds), 1983, *Meaning, use and interpretation of language*, de Gruyter, Berlin.

Bayer, J., 1980, *Diskursthemen*. In: Tschauder & Weigand (eds), 1980: 213–224.

Benson, J. D., Greaves, W. S. (eds), 1985, *Systemic perspectives on discourse*, Ablex Publ. Corp., Norwood, N.J.

Biasci, C., 1986, *Konnektive in Sätzen und Texten. Eine sprachübergreifende pragmatisch-semantische Analyse*, Buske, Hamburg.

Biber, D., 1988, *Variation across speech and writing*, Cambridge University Press, Cambridge.

Bierwisch, M., 1982, *Semantische und konzeptuelle Repräsentation lexikalischer Einheiten*. In: Motsch & Ruzička (eds), 1983: 61–100.

Binot, J. -L., Demoen, B., Hanne, K. -H., Solomon, L., Vassiliou, Y., von Hahn, W., Wachtel, T., 1988, LOKI: A logic oriented approach to data and knowledge bases supporting natural language interaction. *LOKI- report, Oct. 1988*, Universität Hamburg.

Black, J. B., Wikes-Gibbs, D., Gibbs, R. W., 1982, *What writers need to know that they don't know they need to know*. In: Nystrand (ed.), 1982: 325–343.

Bobrow, D. G., Collins, A. (eds), 1975, *Representation and Understanding. Studies in Cognitive Science*, Academic Press, New York.

Bolc, L. (ed.), 1980, *Natural Language Based Computer Systems*. Hanser etc., München.

Bollinger, T., Hedtstück, U., Rollinger, C. -R., Studer, R., 1990, *Text understanding in LILOG*. In: Schmitz et al. (eds), 1990: 21–40.

Bourbeau, L., Carcagno, D., Goldberg, E., Kittredge, R., Polguère, A., 1990, Bilingual generation of weather forecasts in an operations environment, *Proceedings of the Int. Conference on Computational Linguistics* (COLING 13), Helsinki, 1990, 318–320.

Brady, M., Berwick, R. C. (eds), 1986, *Computational models of discourse*, MIT Press, Cambridge, MA.

Brandt, M., Koch, W., Rosengren, I., Vieweger, D., 1983. *Der Einfluß der kommunikativen Strategie auf die Textstruktur, dargestellt am Beispiel des Geschäftsbriefes*. In: Rosengren (ed.), 1983: 105-135.

Brandt, M., Rosengren, I., 1991a, Handlungsstruktur und Informationsstruktur - zwei Seiten einer Münze. Sprache und Pragmatik, Arbeitsberichte, (24): 120-139, Lund.

Brandt, M., Rosengren, I., 1991b, Zur Handlungsstruktur des Textes. *Sprache und Pragmatik, Arbeitsberichte* 24: 3-46, Lund.

Brée, D. S., Smit, R.A., 1986, Linking propositions, *Proceedings of the 11th Int. Conference on Computational Linguistics* (COLING 1986), 177–180, Bonn.

Brinker, K., 1980, *Textthematik als spezifisch textlinguistischer Forschungsbereich.* In: Kühlwein & Raasch (eds), 1980, 138–141.

Brinker, K., 1992, *Linguistische Textanalyse. Eine Einführung in Grundbegriffe und Methoden,* E. Schmidt-Verlag, Berlin.

Brown, G., Yule, G., 1984, *Discourse analysis,* Cambridge University Press, Cambridge.

Brown, G. P., 1980, Characterizing indirect speech acts. *Computational Linguistics,* (6): 150–166.

Bühler, A., 1989, *Semantik kognitiver Sätze und mentale Repräsentation.* In: Falkenberg (ed.), 1989: 9–25.

Bühler, K., 1982, *Sprachtheorie. Die Darstellungsfunktion der Sprache,* (Jena 1934), Fischer, Stuttgart (English 1990, *The theory of language. The representational function of language.* J. Benjamins, Amsterdam).

Busemann, St., 1988, *Surface transformations during the generation of written German sentences.* In: McDonald & Bolc (eds), 1988: 98–165.

Cawsey, A., 1990, *Generating explanatory discourse.* In: Dale et al. (eds), 1990: 75–101.

Chafe, W. L. (ed.), 1980, *The pear stories: Cognitive, cultural, and linguistic aspects of narrative production,* Ablex, Norwood, NJ.

Chafe, W. L., 1985, *Linguistic differences produced by differences between speaking and writing.* In: Olson et al. (eds), 1985: 105–123.

Chafe, W. L., 1987, *Cognitive constraints on information flow.* In: Tomlin (ed.), 1987b: 21–51.

Charniak, E., 1977, A framed painting: the representation of a common sense fragment. *Cognitive Science,* (1) 4.

Charniak, E., Wilks, Y. (eds), 1976, *Computational semantics. An introduction to artificial intelligence and natural language comprehension.* North-Holland, Amsterdam.

Clyne, M., 1987, Cultural differences in the organization of academic texts: English and German. *Journal of Pragmatics,* (11): 211–245.

Cohen, Ph. R., Morgan, J., Pollak, M. E. (eds), 1990, *Intentions in communication,* MIT Press, Cambridge (MA).

Cohen, Ph. R., Perrault, C. R., 1979, Elements of a plan-based theory of speech acts. *Cognitive Science,* (3): 177–212.

Cohen, R., 1987, Analyzing the structure of argumentative discourse. *Computational Linguistics,* 13 (1–2): 11–24.

Cole, P., Morgan, J. L. (eds), 1975, *Syntax and semantics* (Vol.3): *speech acts.* Academic Press, New York.

Conte, M. -E., Petöfi, J. S., Sözer, E. (eds), 1989, *Text and discourse connectedness,* J. Benjamins, Amsterdam.

Dahlgren, K., 1985, The cognitive structure of social categories. *Cognitive Science,* (9): 379–398.

Dahlgren, K., 1988, *Naive semantics for natural language*, Kluwer Academic Publishers, Boston.

Dale, R., 1990, *Generating recipes: An overview of EPICURE*. In: Dale et al. (eds), 1990: 229–255.

Dale, R., Mellish, Ch., Zock, M., (eds), 1990, *Current research in natural language generation*, Academic Press, London.

Daneš, F., 1974a, *Functional sentence perspective and the organization of text*. In: Daneš (ed.) 1974b: 106–128.

Daneš, F. (ed.), 1974b, *Papers on functional sentence perspective*, Academia, Prague.

Daneš, F., Vieweger, D. (eds), 1976, *Probleme der Textgrammatik*. Studia Grammatica 11, Akademie-Verlag, Berlin.

Daneš, F., Viehweger, D. (eds), 1983, *Ebenen der Textstruktur*. (Linguistische Studien, Reihe A, Bd 112). Akademie Verlag, Berlin.

Danlos, L., 1987, *The linguistic basis of text generation*, Cambridge University Press, Cambridge.

Davey, A., 1979, *Discourse production. A computer model of some aspects of a speaker*, Edinburgh University Press, Edinburgh.

Davidson, D., Harman, G. (eds), 1972, *Semantics of Natural Language*, Reidel, Dordrecht.

de Beaugrande, R., 1984, *Text production. Toward a science of composition*, Ablex, Norwood.

de Beaugrande, R.-A., 1989, *From Linguistics to Text Linguistics to Text Production: a difficult path*. In: Antos & Krings (eds), 1989: 58–83.

de Beaugrande, R.-A., Dressler W., 1981, *Einführung in die Textlinguistik*, Niemeyer, Tübingen.

Defrise, Ch., Nirenburg, S., 1990, Meaning representation and text planning, *Proceedings of the Int. Conference on Computational Linguistics* (COLING 13), 19–224, Helsinki.

De Smedt, K. J., 1990, *IPF: An incremental parallel formulator*. In: Dale et al. (eds), 1990: 167–192.

Detering, K., Schmidt-Radefeldt, J., Sucharowski, W. (eds), 1982, *Sprache erkennen und verstehen*. Akten des 16. Linguistischen Kolloquiums, Kiel 1981, Niemeyer, Tübingen.

Dietrich, R., Graumann, C. F. (eds), 1989, *Language processing in social context*, North-Holland, Amsterdam.

Dimter, M., 1981, *Textklassenkonzepte heutiger Alltagssprache. Kommunikationssituation, Textfunktion und Textinhalt als Kategorien alltagssprachlicher Textklassifikation*, Niemeyer, Tübingen.

Doherty, M., 1981, *Grundlagen einer Theorie über sprachliche Ausdrucksmittel epistemischer Einstellungen*, Akademie-Verlag, Berlin.

Dorfmüller-Karpusa, K., 1988, *Temporal and aspectual relations as text-constitutive elements*. In: Petöfi (ed.), 1988: 134–169.

Dressler, W. (ed.), 1978, *Current trends in textlinguistics*, de Gruyter, Berlin.

Dressler, W., 1989, *Semiotische Parameter einer Natürlichkeitstheorie*, Österreichische Akademie der Wissenschaften, Wien.

Ducrot, O., 1984, Polyphonie. *Lalies*, (4).

Dyer, M., 1983, *In-depth Understanding: a computer model of integrated processing for narrative comprehension*, MIT-Press, Cambridge (MA).

Eemeren, F. H. van , Grootendorst, R., 1984, *Speech acts in argumentative discussions*, Foris Publications, Dordrecht.

Ehlich, K., 1979, *Verwendungen der Deixis beim sprachlichen Handeln*, Lang, Frankfurt.

Ehlich, K., 1989, *Zur Genese von Textformen. Prolegomena zu einer pragmatischen Texttypologie.* In: Antos & Krings (eds), 1989: 84–99.

Ellman, J., 1983, An indirect approach to types of speech acts, *Proceedings of the 8th International Conference on Artificial Intelligence*, (COLING 82): 600–602.

Endres-Niggemeyer, B. (ed.), 1988, *Das SUSO-Szenario. Materialien zur Wissensrepräsentation.* Deutsche Gesellschaft für Dokumentation 4/88. Darmstadt.

Engelberg, K. -J., Knöpfler, S., 1983, Dokumentation über Wissensrepräsentation in der KI-Forschung unter linguistischen Aspekten. *Arbeitspapier 80, SFB 99*, Universität Konstanz, Konstanz.

Engelkamp, J., Lorenz, K., Sandig, B. (eds), 1987, *Wissensrepräsentation und Wissensaustausch*, Rörig, Saarbrücken.

Erdmann, P., 1990, *Discourse and grammar: focussing and defocussing in English*, Niemeyer, Tübingen.

Faigley, L., Cherry, R. D., Jollife, D. A., Skinner, A. M., 1989, *Assessing writer's knowledge and processes of composing*, Ablex Publishing Corporation, Norwood.

Falkenberg, G., 1981, *Epistemische Operatoren und illokutionäre Kraft.* In: Hindelang & Zillig (eds), 1981: 193–203.

Falkenberg, G. (ed.), 1989, *Wissen, Wahrnehmen, Glauben. Epistemische Ausdrücke und propositionale Einstellungen*, Niemeyer, Tübingen.

Fauconnier, G., 1990, Domains and connections. *Cognitive Linguistics*, 1 (1): 151–174.

Figge, U. L., 1989, *Gedächtnis, Lexikon, Text.* In: Antos & Krings (eds), 1989: 126–145.

Fillmore, Ch., 1968, *The case for case.* In: Bach & Harms (eds), 1968: 1–88.

Fillmore, Ch., 1985, Frames and the semantics of understanding. *Quaderni di Semantica*, 6 (2): 222–254.

Findler, N. J. (ed.), 1979, *Associative networks*, Academic Press, New York.

Flower, L., Hayes, J. R., 1980, *The dynamics of composing: making plans and juggling constraints.* In: Gregg & Steinberg (eds), 1980: 31–50.

Fleischman, S., 1991, Discourse as space/discourse as time: reflections on the metalanguage of spoken and written discourse, *Journal of Pragmatics*, (16): 291–306.

Fluck, H.-R., 1988, 'Zur Analyse und Vermittlung der Textsorte 'Abstract'. In: Gnutzmann (ed.), 1988: 67–90.

Fox, B. A., 1987, *Discourse structure and anaphora. Written and conversational English*, Cambridge University Press, Cambridge.

Franke, W., 1983, *Insistieren. Eine linguistische Analyse*, Kümmerle Verlag, Göppingen.

Franke, W., 1987, Texttypen – Textsorten – Textexemplare: Ein Ansatz zu ihrer

Klassifizierung und Beschreibung, *Zeitschrift für Germanistische Linguistik*, 15: 263–281.

Fraser, B., 1990, An approach to discourse markers, *Journal of Pragmatics*, 14 (3): 383–395.

Fraurud, K., Hellman, Ch., 1985, What's next in the text. A method for investigating discourse processing, *Papers from the Institute of Linguistics*, 54, University of Stockholm.

Freedle, R. O. (ed.), 1979, *New directions in discourse processing*, Ablex, Norwood.

Fries, N. 1991, Bewertung. Linguistische und konzeptuelle Aspekte des Phänomens. *Sprache und Pragmatik, Arbeitsberichte*, 23: 1–31, Lund.

Fries, P., 1981, On the status of theme in English: arguments from discourse. *Forum Linguisticum*, 6 (1): 1–38.

Fritz, G., 1982, *Kohärenz. Grundfragen der linguistischen Kommunikationsanalyse*, Narr, Tübingen.

Fritz, G., Muckenhaupt, M., 1981, *Kommunikation und Grammatik*, Narr, Tübingen.

Garfinkel, H., 1967, *Studies in ethnomethodology*, Prentice Hall, Englewood Cliffs, NJ.

Geurts, B. (ed.), 1991, Natural language understanding in LILOG. An intermediate overview. *LILOG, IWBS Report 137*, IBM, Stuttgart.

Givón, T., 1987, *Beyond foreground and background*, In: Tomlin (ed.), 1987: 175–188.

Gnutzmann, C. (ed.), 1988, *Fachbezogener Fremdsprachenunterricht*, Narr, Tübingen.

Goffman, E., 1974, *Frame analysis*, Harper & Row, New York.

Graesser, A., Clark, L., 1985, *Structure and procedures of implicit knowledge*, Ablex, Norwood, NJ.

Gregg, L. W., Steinberg, E. R. (eds), 1980, *Cognitive processes in writing*, Erlbaum, Hillsdale, N.J.

Greimas, A. J., 1971 (1966), *Strukturale Semantik. Methodologische Untersuchungen*, Viehweg, Braunschweig.

Grewendorf, G. (ed.), 1979, *Sprechakttheorie und Semantik*, Frankfurt.

Grewenig, A., 1980, *Zur Rekonstruktion sprachlich realisierter Wissensstrukturen*, Buske, Hamburg.

Grice, H. P., 1969, Utterer's meaning and intentions. *The Philosphical Review* 78(2): 147–177.

Grice, H. P., 1975, *Logic and conversation.* In: Cole & Morgan (eds), 1975: 41- 58.

Grimes, J. E., 1975, *The thread of discourse*, Mouton Press, The Hague.

Grimes, J. E., 1982, *Reference spaces in text.* In: Allén (ed.), 1982: 381–414.

Grishman, R., 1990, *Domain modeling for language analysis.* In: Schmitz et al. (eds), 1990: 41-57.

Grishman, R., Nhan, N.T., 1984, Automated determination of sublanguage syntactic usage. *Proceedings of the Int. Conference on Computational Linguistics*, 1984: 96–98.

Grize, J.-B., 1989, *The objects of discourse: connexity and opposition.* In: Conte et al. (eds), 1989: 405-412.

Grosz, B. J., Sidner, C. L., 1986, Attention, intentions, and the structure of discourse, *Computational Linguistics*, (12): 175–204.

Große, E. U., 1976, *Text und Kommunikation. Eine linguistische Einführung in die Funktionen der Texte*, Kohlhammer, Stuttgart.

Gülich, E., 1970, *Macrosyntax der Gliederungssignale im gesprochenen Französisch*, Fink, München.

Gülich E., 1978, *Redewiedergabe im Französischen. Beschreibungsmöglichkeiten im Rahmen einer Sprechakttheorie*. In: Meyer-Hermann (ed.), 1978: 49–102.

Gülich, E., 1986, *Textsorten in der Kommunikationspraxis*. In: Kallmeyer (ed.), 1986: 15–46.

Gülich, E., 1988, Handlungsschema und Formulierungsstruktur, *Sprache und Pragmatik, Arbeitsberichte*, (8): 43–66, Lund.

Gülich, E., Kotschi, Th., 1986, *Reformulierung als Mittel der Textkonstitution. Untersuchungen zu französischen Texten aus mündlicher Kommunikation*. In: Motsch (ed.), 1986: 199–261.

Gülich, E., Kotschi, Th., 1987, *Les actes de reformulation dans la consultation "La Dame de Caluire"*. In: Bange (ed.) 1987: 15–81.

Gülich E., Raible, W., 1977, *Linguistische Textmodelle. Grundlagen, Möglichkeiten*, UTB 130, München.

Gvenzadse, M. A., 1983, Pragmatische Texttypologie. Probleme und Perspektiven, *Zeitschrift für Phonetik, Sprachwissenschaft und Kommunikationsforschung*, 36 (4): 399–405.

Habel, Ch., Herweg, M., Rehkämper, K. (eds), 1989, *Raumkonzepte in Verstehensprozessen*, Niemeyer, Tübingen.

Häfele, J., 1979, *Der Aufbau der Sprachkompetenz. Untersuchungen zur Grammatik des sprachlichen Handelns*, Niemeyer, Tübingen.

Haiman, J., Thompson, S. A. (eds), 1989, *Clause combining in discourse and grammar*, John Benjamins, Amsterdam.

Hajičová, E., 1986, Focussing – a meeting point of linguistics and artificial intelligence. *KAM series 21, Dep. of Applied Mathematics*, Charles University, Prag.

Hajičová, E., 1991, Topic-focus articulation and coreference in models of discourse production. *Journal of Pragmatics*, 16(2): 157–166.

Hajičová, E., Sgall, P., 1988, *Topic and focus of a sentence and the patterning of a text*. In: Petöfi (ed.), 1988: 70-96.

Halliday, M. A. K., 1985, *Introduction to functional grammar*, Edward Arnold, London.

Halliday, M. A. K., Hasan, R., 1976, *Cohesion in English*, Longman, London.

Hartung, W., 1981, Beobachtungen zur Organisation kommunikativer Ziele. In: Rosengren (ed.), 1981: 221–232.

Harweg, R., 1968, *Pronomina und Textkonstitution*, Fink, München.

Harweg, R., 1988, *Sentence sequences and cotextual connexity*. In: Petöfi (ed.), 1988: 26–53.

Hasan, R., 1978, *Text in the systemic-functional model*. In: Dressler (ed.), 1978: 228–246.

Hauenschild, Ch., 1984, *Entwurf eines Textmodells zur Erfassung anaphorischer Bezüge*. In: Rothkegel & Sandig (eds), 1984: 131–148.

Hayes, P. J., 1980, *The logic of frames*. In: Metzing (ed.), 1980: 46–61.

Heinemann, W., Viehweger, D., 1991. *Textlinguistik. Eine Einführung*, Niemeyer, Tübingen.

Hellwig, P., 1984, *Grundzüge einer Theorie des Textzusammenhangs*. In: Rothkegel & Sandig (eds), 1984: 51–79.

Herget, J., Kuhlen, R. (eds), *Pragmatische Aspekte beim Entwurf und Betrieb von Informationssystemen.*Universitätsverlag, Konstanz.

Herzog, O., Rollinger, C. -R. (eds), 1991, *Text understanding in LILOG*. Integrating Computational Linguistics and Artificial Intelligence. Final report on the IBM Germany LILOG-Project. Springer, Berlin.

Heydrich, W., Petöfi, J. S. (eds), 1986, *Aspekte der Konnexität und Kohärenz von Texten*, Buske, Hamburg.

Heydrich, W., Neubauer, F., Petöfi, J. S., Sözer, E. (eds), 1989, *Connexity and coherence: analysis of text and discourse*, de Gruyter, Berlin.

Hindelang, G., Zillig, W. (eds), 1981, *Sprache: Verstehen und Handeln*, Niemeyer, Tübingen.

Hobbs, J., 1979, Coherence and coreference, *Cognitive Science*, (3): 67–90.

Hobbs, J. R., Croft, W., Davies, T., 1987, Commonsense metaphysics and lexical semantics, *Computational Linguistics*, 13 (3–4): 241–250.

Hobbs, J. R., Stickel, M., Martin, P., Edwards, D., 1988, Interpretation as abduction. *Proceedings of the 26th annual meeting of the Association for Computational Linguistics*, 95–103, 1988, State University of New York, Buffalo.

Hoeppner, W., Morik, K., 1983, Das Dialogsystem HAM-ANS: Worauf basiert es, wie funktioniert es und wem antwortet es. *Linguistische Berichte*, (88): 3–37.

Horacek, H., 1990, *The architecture of a generation component.*, In: Dale et al. (eds), 1990: 193–227.

Hovy, E. H., 1988, *Generating natural language under pragmatic constraints*, Lawrence Erlbaum Ass., Hillsdale.

Hovy, E. H., 1991, *Approaches to the planning of coherent text*. In: Paris et al. (eds), 1991: 83–102.

Hundsnurscher F., Weigand, E. (eds), 1986, *Dialoganalyse I*. Referate der 1. Arbeitstagung. Münster 1986. Niemeyer, Tübingen.

Hundsnurscher, F., Weigand, E. (eds), 1989, *Dialoganalyse II*. Referate der 2. Arbeitstagung. Niemeyer, Tübingen.

Huth, L., 1977, *Zur Rolle der Argumentation im Texttyp 'Korrespondentenbericht'*. In: Schecker (ed.), 1977: 357–388.

Isenberg, H., 1984, Texttypen als Interaktionstypen. Eine Texttypologie, *Zeitschrift für Germanistik*, (3): 261–270.

Jackendoff, R. S., 1983, *Semantics and cognition*, MIT Press, Cambridge (MA).

Jacobs, P. S., 1985, PHRED: a generator for natural language interfaces, *Computational Linguistics*, (11): 219–242.

Jacobs, P. S., 1987, *KING: a knowledge-intensive natural language generator*. In: Kempen (ed.), 1987: 219–230.

Johnson-Laird, P.N., 1983, *Mental models. Towards a cognitive science of language, inference and consciousness*, Harvard University Press, Cambridge.

Johnson-Laird, P. N., Wason, P. C., (eds), 1977, *Thinking: Readings in Cognitive*

Science, Cambridge University Press, Cambridge.

Jordanskaja, L., Kittredge, R., Polguère, A., 1991, *Lexical selection and paraphrase in a meaning-text generation model*. In: Paris et al. (eds), 1991: 293–312.

Joshi, A. K., 1987, *The relevance of Tree Adjoining Grammar to generation*. In: Kempen (ed.), 1987: 233–252.

Joshi, A. K., Webber, B. L., Sag, J. A. (eds), 1981, *Elements of discourse understanding*, Cambridge University Press, Cambridge (MA).

Just, M. A., Carpenter, P. A. (eds), 1977, *Cognitive processes in comprehension*, Hillsdale.

Kallmeyer, W., 1978, *Fokuswechsel und Fokussierung als Aktivitäten der Gesprächskonstitution*. In: Meyer-Hermann (ed.), 1978: 191–241.

Kallmeyer, W. (ed.), 1986, *Kommunikationstypologie. Handlungsmuster, Textsorten, Situationstypen*, Schwann, Düsseldorf.

Kallmeyer, W., Klein, W., Meyer-Hermann, R., Netzer, K. and Siebert, H.-J., 1986 (1974, 1.Aufl.), *Lektürekolleg zur Textlinguistik*. Bd.1. Einführung. Athenäum, Frankfurt.

Kamp, H., Rohrer, Ch., 1983, *Tense in texts*. In: Bäuerle et al. (eds), 1983: 250–269.

Kasher, A. (ed.), 1989, *Cognitive aspects of language use*, North-Holland, Amsterdam.

Kempen, G. (ed.), 1987 *Natural language generation. New results in artifical intelligence, psychology and linguistics*, Martinus Nijhoff Publishers, Dordrecht.

Keseling, G., 1979, Textwissen und Gedächtniswissen als Kategorien in einer Theorie sprachlichen Handelns, *Osnabrücker Beiträge zur Sprachtheorie*, (10): 23–36.

Keseling, G., Wrobel, A., Rau, C., 1987, Globale und lokale Planung beim Schreiben. *Unterrichtswissenschaft*, (4): 349–365.

Kittredge, R., Lehrberger, J. (eds), 1982, *Sublanguage: studies of languages in restricted semantic domains*, de Gruyter, Berlin.

Kittredge, R., Koresky, T., Rambow, O., 1991, *On the need for domain communication knowledge*. Technical Report, Department of Linguistics, University of Montreal, Montreal.

Klein, W., Stutterheim, Ch. von, 1991, Text structure and referential movement. *Sprache und Pragmatik, Arbeitsberichte*, (22), Lund.

Knorr-Cetina, K., 1986, *Die Fabrikation von Erkenntnis*, Suhrkamp, Frankfurt.

Koch, W., 1988, Weltwissen, Sprachsystem und Textstruktur in einem integrierten Modell der automatischen Sprachverarbeitung. Zum Beispiel Kochrezepte. *Sprache und Pragmatik, Arbeitsberichte*, (4), Lunds universitet, Lund.

Koch, W., 1991, Automatische Generierung von Kochrezepten *Sprache und Pragmatik, Arbeitsberichte*, (21), Lund.

Kohlmann, U., Speck, A., Scharnhorst U., von Stutterheim, Ch., 1989, Textstruktur und sprachliche Form in Objektbeschreibungen. *Deutsche Sprache*, (2): 137–169.

Komlósi, L. I., 1989, *Connectedness and discourse structure: perspective semantics of predications and coherence of discourse*. In: Conte et al. (eds), 1989: 427–440.

Kreiß, J., Novak, H. -J., 1990, The textplanning component PIT of the LILOG system. *Proceedings of the Int. Conference on Computational Linguistics,* 1990: 431–433.

Krings, H. P., Antos, G. (eds), 1992, *Textproduktion. Neue Wege der Forschung,* Wissenschaftlicher Verlag, Trier.

Kühlwein, W., Raasch, A. (eds), 1980, *Sprache und Verstehen,* Narr, Tübingen.

Kuhlen, R., 1984, A knowledge-based text analysis system for the graphically supported production of cascaded text condensats. *Reihe TOPIC 9/84,* Universität Konstanz.

Kurzon, D., 1984, Themes, hyperthemes and the discourse structure of British legal texts. *TEXT,* 4 (1–3): 31–55.

Lakoff, G., 1972, *Linguistics and natural logic,* In: Davidson & Harman (eds), 1972: 545–665.

Lang, E., 1976, *Erklärungstexte.* In: Daneš & Viehweger (eds), 1976: 147–163.

Lang, E., 1991, *Koordinierende Konjunktionen.* In: von Stechow & Wunderlich (eds), 1991: 597–623.

Lehnert, W., 1982, *A narrative summarization strategy.* In: Lehnert & Ringle (eds), 1982: 375–414.

Lehnert, W., Ringle, M. H. (eds), 1982, *Strategies for natural language processing,* Erlbaum, Hillsdale/London.

Leont'ev, A. A., 1971, *Sprache, Sprechen, Sprechtätigkeit,* Kohlhammer, Stuttgart (Orig. 1969, Moskau).

Leont'ev, A. A., Leont'ev, A. N., Judin, E.G., 1984, *Grundfragen einer Theorie der sprachlichen Tätigkeit,* Hg. von D. Viehweger. Kohlhammer, Stuttgart.

Levinson, St. C., 1987 (1983), *Pragmatics,* Cambridge University Press, Cambridge.

Litman D. J., Allen, J. F., 1990, *Discourse processing and commonsense plans.* In: Cohen et al. (eds), 1990: 365–388.

Lötscher, A., 1987, *Text und Thema. Studien zur thematischen Konsistenz von Texten,* Niemeyer, Tübingen.

Lundquist, L., 1989, *Modality and text constitution.* In: Conte et al. (eds), 1989: 103–117.

Lux, F., 1981, *Text, Situation, Textsorte,* Narr, Tübingen.

McCoy, K. F., Cheng, J., 1991, *Focus of attention: constraining what can be said next.* In: Paris et al. (eds), 1991: 103–124.

McDonald, D. D., Bolc, L. (eds), 1988, *Natural language generation systems,* Springer, New York.

McKeown, K. R., 1985, *Text generation. Using discourse strategies and focus constraints to generate natural language text,* Cambridge University Press, Cambridge.

McKeown, K. R., Elhadad, M., Fukumoto, Y., Lim, J., Lombardi, C., Robin, J., Smadja, F., 1990, *Natural language generation in COMET.* In: Dale et al. (eds), 1990: 103–139.

McKeown, K. R., Elhadad, M., 1991, *A contrastive evaluation of Funktional Unification Grammar for surface language generation: a case study in choice of connectives.* In: Paris et al. (eds), 1991: 351–396.

Mandl, H., Spada, H. (eds), 1988, *Wissenspsychologie*, München.

Mann, W. C., 1985, *An introduction to the Nigel text generation grammar*. In: Benson & Greaves (eds), 1985: 84–95.

Mann, W., Thompson, S. A., 1987, *Rhetorical structure theory: description and construction of text structures*. In: Kempen (ed.), 1987: 85–95.

Matthiessen, Ch., Thompson, S. A., 1989, *The structure of discourse and 'subordination'*. In: Haiman & Thompson (eds), 1989: 275–329.

Matthiessen, C., Bateman, J., 1992, *Text generation and systemic functional linguistics*. Pinter, London.

Meehan, F., 1976, *The metanovel: writing stories by computer*, PhD., Yale University, New York.

Meier, J., Metzing D., Polzin, T., Ruhrberg, P., Rutz, H., Vollmer, M., 1988, Generierung von Wegbeschreibungen. *Kolibri, Arbeitsbericht*, (9), Forschergruppe Kohärenz, Universität Bielefeld.

Mel'cuk, I. A., 1981, Meaning-Text Models, *Annual Review of Anthropology*, (10): 27–62.

Mellish, Ch. S., 1988, Implementing systemic classification by unification. *Computational Linguistics*, 14 (1): 40–51.

Metzeltin, M., Jaksche, H., 1983, *Textsemantik. Ein Modell zur Analyse von Texten*. Narr, Tübingen.

Metzing, D. (ed.), 1980, *Frame conceptions and text understanding*, de Gruyter, Berlin.

Metzing, D. (ed.), 1981, *Dialogmuster und Dialogprozesse*, Buske, Hamburg.

Metzing, D., 1988, *Prozedurale Sprachanalyse*. In: Schnelle & Rickheit (eds), 1988: 65–79.

Meyer, P.G., 1975, *Satzverknüpfungsrelationen. Ein Interpretationsmodell für situationsunabhängige Texte*. Niemeyer, Tübingen.

Meyer, R., 1989, *Wegkonnexion*. In: Habel et al. (eds), 1989: 174–201.

Meyer-Hermann, R. (ed.), 1978, *Sprechen – Handeln – Interaktion*, Niemeyer, Tübingen.

Michel, G. (ed.) 1985, *Grundfragen der Kommunikationsbefähigung*, Bibliographisches Institut, Leipzig.

Minsky, M., 1977, *Frame System Theory*. In: Johnson-Laird & Wason (eds), 1977: 355–377.

Minsky, M., 1990, *Mentopolis*, Klett-Cotta, Stuttgart.

Moens, M., Steedman, M., 1987, Temporal ontology in natural language. *Computational Linguistics*, 14 (2): 1–7.

Molitor-Lübbert, S., 1989, *Schreiben und Kognition*, In: Antos & Krings (eds), 1989: 278–296.

Moore, J. D., Swartout, W. R., 1991, *A reactive approach to explanation: Taking the user's feedback into account*. In: Paris et al. (eds), 1991: 3–48.

Moore, R. C., Hendrix, G. C., 1982, *Computational models of belief and the semantic of belief sentences*. In: Peters & Saarinen (eds), 1982: 107–127.

Morgenthaler, E., 1980, *Kommunikationsorientierte Textgrammatik*, Schwann, Düsseldorf.

Motsch, W. (ed.), 1986, *Satz, Text, sprachliche Handlung*, Akademie-Verlag, Berlin.

Motsch, W., 1991, Anforderungen an eine modulare Textanalyse. *Sprache und Pragmatik. Arbeitsberichte* (24), 1991: 47–61, Lund.

Motsch, W., Ruzička, R. (eds), 1983, *Untersuchungen zur Semantik*, Akademie-Verlag, Berlin.

Motsch, W., Viehweger, D., 1981, *Sprachhandlung, Satz und Text*. In: Rosengren (ed.), 1981: 125–153.

Noël, D., 1990, Coherence relations and mental models. *Linguistica Antverpiensia*, No. XXIV, Universität Antwerpen.

Norman, D. A., Rumelhart, D. E., 1975, *Explorations in cognition*, Freeman, San Francisco.

Novak, H.-J., 1987, *Textgenerierung aus visuellen Daten: Beschreibungen von Straßenszenen*, Springer, Berlin.

Nystrand, M. (ed.), 1982, *What writers know. The language, process and structure of written discourse*, Academic Press, New York.

Olson, D. R., Torrance, N., Hildyard, A. (eds), 1985, *Literacy, Language, and Learning: the nature and consequences of reading and writing*, Cambridge University Press, Cambridge.

Palm, Ch., 1991, *EUROPHRAS 90*. Internationales Kolloquium für Phraseologie. Germanistisches Institut, Uppsala.

Palmer, M. St., 1990, *Semantic processing for finite domains*, Cambridge University Press, Cambridge, MA.

Paris, C. L., 1991, *Generation and explanation: building an explanation facility for the explainable expert systems framework*. In: Paris et al. (eds), 1991: 49–82.

Paris, C. L., McKeown, K. R., 1987, *Discourse strategies for describing complex physical objects*. In: Kempen (ed.), 1987: 97–115.

Paris, C. L., Swartout, W. R., Mann, W. C. (eds), 1991, *Natural language generation in artificial intelligence and computational linguistics*, Kluwer, Dordrecht.

Patten, T., 1988, *Systemic text generation as problem solving*, Cambridge University Press, Cambridge.

Peters, S., Saarinen, E. (eds), 1982, *Process, beliefs and questions*, Reidel, Dordrecht.

Petöfi, J. S. (ed.), 1979, *Text vs. sentence: basic questions of text linguistics*, I, II, Buske, Hamburg.

Petöfi, J. S. (ed.), 1988, *Text and discourse constitution: empirical aspects, theoretical approaches*, de Gruyter, Berlin, New York.

Petöfi, J.S., Sözer, E. (eds), 1983, *Micro- and macro-connexity of texts*, Buske, Hamburg.

Petöfi, J. S., Sözer, E., 1988, *Static and dynamic aspects of text constitution*. In: Petöfi (ed.), 1988: 440–477.

Polanyi, L., 1988, A formal model of the structure of discourse. *Journal of pragmatics*, 12 (5/6): 601 ff.

Popov, E. V., 1986, *Talking with computers in natural language*, Springer, Berlin (Orig. 1982, Moskau).

Redeker, G., 1990, Ideational and pragmatic markers of discourse structure. *Journal of Pragmatics*, (14): 367–381.

Redeker, G., 1991, Linguistic markers of discourse coherence. *Linguistics*, (29): 1139–1171.

Rehbein, J., 1977, *Komplexes Handeln, Elemente zur Handlungstheorie der Sprache*, Metzler, Stuttgart.

Reimer, U., Hahn U., 1987, Text condensation as knowledge base abstraction. *MIP-8723, Fakultät für Mathematik und Informatik*, Universität Passau, Passau.

Reimer, U., Hahn, U., 1990, *An overview of the text understanding system TOPIC*. In: Schmitz et al. (eds), 1990: 305–320.

Reithinger, N., 1991, *POPEL – A parallel and incremental natural language generation system*. In: Paris et al. (eds), 1991: 179–199.

Rickheit, G., (ed.), 1991, *Kohärenzprozesse. Modellierung von Sprachverarbeitung in Texten und Diskursen*, Westdeutscher Verlag, Opladen/Wiesbaden.

Rickheit, G., Strohner, H. (eds) 1985, *Inferences in text processing*, North-Holland, Amsterdam.

Rollinger, C.-R., 1984a, *Textverstehen und Textrepräsentation in SRL*. In: Rothkegel & Sandig (eds), 1984: 99–128.

Rollinger, C.-R., 1984b, *Zur Repräsentation der argumentativen Struktur von Texten*. In: Rollinger (ed.) 1984c:107–124.

Rollinger, C.-R. (ed.), 1984c, *Probleme des (Text-)Verstehens. Ansätze der Künstlichen Intelligenz*, Niemeyer, Tübingen.

Rosch, E., 1975, Cognitive representation of semantic categories, *Journal of Experimental Psychology: General*, (104): 192–233.

Rosenberg, St. J., 1980, *Frame-based text processing*. In: Metzing (ed.), 1980: 96–119.

Rosengren, I. (ed.), 1981, *Sprache und Pragmatik*, Lunder Symposium 1980. Glerup, Lund.

Rosengren, I. (ed.), 1983, *Sprache und Pragmatik*, Lunder Symposium 1982. Almquist & Wiksell Int., Stockholm.

Rosengren, I., 1983, *Die Realisierung der Illokutionsstruktur auf der Vertextungsebene*. In: Daneš & Viehweger (eds), 1983: 133–151.

Rosengren, I. (ed.), 1984, *Sprache und Pragmatik*, Lunder Symposium 1984. Almqvist & Wiksell International, Stockholm.

Rosengren, I. (ed.), 1986, *Sprache und Pragmatik*, Lunder Symposium 1986. Almqvist & Wiksell International, Stockholm.

Rösner, D., 1987, *The automated news agency: SEMTEX – a text generator for German*. In: Kempen (ed.), 1987: 133–148.

Rossipal, H., 1983, *Argumentationswert und Interaktionswert von Sprechakten und Textakten*. In: Rosengren (ed.), 1983: 373–420.

Rothkegel, A., 1984a, *Sprachhandlungstypen in interaktionsregelnden Texten*. In: Rosengren (ed.), 1984: 255–278.

Rothkegel, A., 1984b, *Frames und Textstruktur*. In: Rothkegel & Sandig (eds), 1984: 238–261.

Rothkegel, A., 1986a, TEXAN. Eine semantisch-pragmatische Textanalyse. *Arbeitsbericht des Projekts A3*, TEMA, Nr. 1 (Textstrukturen und maschinelle Übersetzung), SFB 100, Universität Saarbrücken.

Rothkegel, A., 1986b, Pragmatics in Machine Translation. *Proceedings of the International Conference on Computational Linguistics*, (COLING 86), 335–337, Bonn.

Rothkegel, A., 1986c, *Spiele und Verträge. Formen des Dialogs auf einem PC*. In:

Hundsnurscher & Weigand (eds), 1986: 387–398.

Rothkegel, A., 1988, *Argumentationshandlungen im SUSO-Szenario*. In: Endres-Niggemeyer (ed.), 1988: 78–91.

Rothkegel, A., 1989a, Textualisierung von Wissen. Einige Forschungsfragen zum Umgang mit Wissen im Rahmen computerorientierter Textproduktion. *LDV–Forum*, 6 (1): 3–13.

Rothkegel, A., 1990, *Knowledge representation and text processing*. In: Schmitz et al. (eds), 1990: 331–352.

Rothkegel, A., 1991a, Wissen und Informationsstruktur im Text. *Folia Linguistica*, XXV (1–2): 189–217, Wien.

Rothkegel, A., 1991b, *The dialogical basis of text production*. In: Stati et al. (eds), 1991: 393–403.

Rothkegel, A., 1992a, *Textstruktur und Computermodelle der Textgenerierung*. In: Krings & Antos (eds), 1992: 339–353.

Rothkegel, A., 1992b, *Text pragmatics and computational modelling*. In: Stein (ed.), 1992: 665–683.

Rothkegel, A., Sandig, B. (eds), 1984, *Text, Textsorten, Semantik. Linguistische Modelle und maschinelle Verfahren*, Buske, Hamburg.

Roulet, E., 1984, Speech acts, discourse structure and pragmatic connectives. *Journal of pragmatics*, 8 (1): 31–47.

Rudolph, E., 1988, *Connective relations – connective expressions – connective structures*. In: Petöfi (ed.), 1988: 96–133.

Rumelhart, D., 1975, *Notes on a schema for stories*. In: Bobrow & Collins (eds), 1975: 211–236.

Rutz, H., 1990, Aspekte der Generierung von Wegbeschreibungen: Lokale und globale Kohärenz. *Kolibri, Arbeitsbericht*, (1): 51–62, Bielefeld.

Sacerdoti, E., 1977, *A structure for plans and behavior*, American Elsevier North-Holland, New York.

Samet, R., Schank, R .C., 1984, Coherence and connectivity. *Linguistics and Philosophy*, 7 (1): 57–82.

Sandig, B., 1979, Ausdrucksmöglichkeiten des Bewertens, *Deutsche Sprache*, (7): 137–159.

Sandig, B., 1986, *Stilistik der deutschen Sprache*, de Gruyter, Berlin.

Sandig, B., 1987, *Textwissen. Beschreibungsmöglichkeiten und Realisierungen von Textmustern am Beispiel der Richtigstellung*. In: Engelkamp et al. (eds), 1987: 115–155.

Sandig, B., 1991, *Formeln des Bewertens*. In: Palm (ed.), 1991: 225–252.

Sbisà, M., 1987, *Speech acts and context change*. In: Ballmer & Wildgen (eds), 1987: 252–280.

Scha, R., Polanyi, L., 1988, An augmented context free grammar for discourse. *Proceedings of the 12th International Conference on Computational Linguistics*, (COLING 88), 573–577, Budapest.

Schäffner, Ch., Shreve G. M., Wiesemann U., 1987, A procedural analysis of argumentative political texts. *Zeitschrift für Anglistik und Amerikanistik*, (2): 105–117, Leipzig.

Schank, R. C., 1972, Conceptual dependency: a theory of natural language understanding, *Cognitive Psychology*, (3): 552–631.

Schank, R. C. (ed.), 1975a, *Conceptual information processing*, North-Holland, Amsterdam.

Schank, R. C., 1975b, *The structure of episodes in memory*. In: Bobrow & Collins (eds), 1975: 237–272.

Schank, R. C., Abelson, R. P., 1977, *Scripts, plans, goals and understanding*, Erlbaum, Hillsdale.

Schank, R. C., Colby, K. (eds), 1973, *Computer models of thought and language*, Freeman, New York.

Schecker, M. (ed.), 1977, *Theorie der Argumentation*, Narr, Tübingen.

Scherner, M., 1984, *Sprache als Text. Ansätze zu einer sprachwissenschaftlich begründeten Theorie des Textverstehens*, Narr, Tübingen.

Schiffrin, D., 1987, *Discourse markers*, Cambridge University Press, Cambridge.

Schmidt, S. J., 1973, *Texttheorie. Probleme einer Linguistik der sprachlichen Kommunikation*, Fink, München.

Schmidt, W. (ed.), 1981, *Funktional-kommunikative Sprachbeschreibung. Theoretisch-methodische Grundlegung*, Bibliographisches Institut, Leipzig.

Schmitz, U., Schütz, R., Kunz, A. (eds), 1990, *Linguistic approaches to artificial intelligence*, Lang, Frankfurt usw.

Schnelle, H., Rickheit, G. (eds), 1988, *Sprache in Mensch und Computer*, Westdeutscher Verlag, Opladen.

Schnotz, W., 1988, *Textverstehen als Aufbau mentaler Modelle*. In: Mandl & Spada (eds), 1988: 299–330.

Schwarz, M., 1992, *Einführung in die Kognitive Linguistik*. UTB/Francke, Tübingen.

Scott, D. R., de Souza, C. S., 1990, *Getting the message across in RST-based text generation*. In: Dale et al. (eds), 1990: 47–73.

Searle, J. R., 1969, *Speech acts*, Cambridge University Press, Cambridge (German 1971, Suhrkamp, Frankfurt).

Searle, J. R., 1979a, *Expression and meaning. Studies in the theory of speech acts*, Cambridge University Press, Cambridge.

Searle, J. R., 1979b, *A taxonomy of illocutionary acts*. In: Searle 1979a: 1–29.

Searle, J. R., 1979c, *Intentionalität und der Gebrauch der Sprache*. In: Grewendorf (ed.), 1979: 149–171.

Seelbach, D., 1986, Zum propositionalen und textuellem Wissen für das Verstehen französischer Wetterberichte. *LDV-Forum*, 4 (1): 46–62.

Sidner, C., 1986, *Focusing in the comprehension of definite anaphora*. In: Brady & Berwick (eds), 1986: 267–330.

Sigurd, B., 1991, *Referent Grammar in text generation*. In: Paris et al. (eds), 1991: 313–327.

Simmons, R. F., 1973, *Semantic networks: their computation and the use for understanding English sentences*. In: Schank & Colby (eds), 1973: 63–113.

Sinclair, J.M., Coulthard, R.M., 1975, *Towards an analysis of discourse: the English used by teachers and pupils*. Oxford University Press, London

Sitter, St., Stein, A., 1990, Dialoge zur Informationsgewinnung: ein Modell ihrer Pragmatik. In: Herget & Kuhlen (eds), 1990: 339–354.

Sperber, D., Wilson, D., 1986, *Relevance. Communication and cognition*, Blackwell, Oxford.

Stati, S., Weigand, E., Hundsnurscher, F. (eds), 1991, *Dialoganalyse III*, Referate der 3. Arbeitstagung, Bologna 1990. Niemeyer, Tübingen.

von Stechow, A., Wunderlich, D. (eds), 1991, *Semantik / Semantics. Ein internationales Handbuch der zeitgenössischen Forschung*, de Gruyter, Berlin usw.

Stein, D. (ed.), 1992, *Cooperating with written texts. The pragmatics and comprehension of written texts*, Mouton de Gruyter, Berlin, New York.

Steiner, E., 1991, *A functional perspective on language, action, and interpretation*, Mouton de Gruyter, Berlin.

Steiner, E., Veltman, R. (eds), 1988, *Pragmatics, discourse text: some systemically inspired approaches*, Pinter, London.

Steinmann, M., 1982, *Speech-Act Theory and Writing*, In: Nystrand (ed.), 1982: 291–323.

Tannen, D., 1979, *What's in a frame? Surface evidence for underlying expectations.* In: Freedle (ed.), 1979: 137–181.

Tannen, D., 1986a, *Spoken and written narrative in English and Greek.* In: Tannen (ed.), 1986b: 21–41.

Tannen, D. (ed.), 1986b, *Coherence in spoken and written discourse*, Ablex Publ. Comp., Norwood, N.J.

Thompson, H., 1977, Strategy and tactics in language production. In: Beach, W.A., Fox, S.E., Philosoph, S. (eds), *Papers from the 13th regional meeting of the Chicago Linguistics Society*, Chicago.

Thompson, S. A., 1987, *Subordination and narrative event structure.* In: Tomlin (ed.), 1987: 435–454.

Thompson, S. A., Mann, W. C., 1987, Rhetorical structure theory: a framework for the analysis of texts. *Papers in Pragmatics*, 1, (1): 79–105.

Tomlin, R. S., 1987a. *Linguistic reflections of cognitive events.* In: Tomlin (ed.), 1987b: 455–479.

Tomlin, R. S. (ed.), 1987b, *Coherence and grounding in discourse*, J. Benjamins Publ. Comp., Amsterdam.

Tonfoni, G., 1990, *Text representation systems*, Eurographica, Helsinki.

Trabasso, T., Sperry, L.L., 1985. Causal relatedness and importance of story events. *Journal of memory and language*, 24 (1): 595–611.

Tschauder, G., Weigand, E. (eds), 1980, *Perspektive: textintern*, Tübingen.

Tucker, A., Nirenburg, S., Raskin, V., 1986, Discourse and cohesion in expository text. *Proceedings of the Int. Conference on Computational Linguistics* (COLING 86), 1986: 181–183.

Uszkoreit, H., 1991, Strategies for adding control information to declarative grammars, *Proceedings of the 1991 Annual Meeting of the Association of Computational Linguistics*, June 1991, Berkeley, CA.

Vachek, J. (ed.), 1989, *Written language revisited*, J. Benjamins, Amsterdam.

van de Velde, R. S., 1988, *Inferences as (de)compositional principles.* In: Petöfi (ed.), 1988: 283–314.

van de Velde, R. S., 1984, *Prolegomena to inferential discourse processing*, J. Benjamins, Amsterdam.

van Dijk, T. A., 1972, Foundations for typologies of texts. *Semiotica*, (6): 297–323.

van Dijk, T. A., 1977a, *Connectives in text grammar and text logic.* In: van Dijk & Petöfi (eds), 1977: 11–63.

van Dijk, T. A., 1977b, *Semantic macro-structure and knowledge frames in discourse comprehension.* In: Just & Carpenter (eds), 1977: 3–32.

van Dijk, T. A., 1980a, *Macrostructures. An interdisciplinary study of global structures in discourse, interaction and cognition,* Erlbaum, Hillsdale.

van Dijk, T. A., 1980b, *Textwissenschaft. Eine interdisziplinäre Einführung,* dtv, München.

van Dijk, T. A., 1981, *Studies in the pragmatics of discourse,* Mouton, The Hague.

van Dijk, T. A., Petöfi, J.S. (eds), 1977, *Grammars and descriptions,* de Gruyter, Berlin.

van Dijk, T. A., Kintsch, W., 1983, *Strategies of discourse comprehension and production.* Academic Press, New York.

van Noord, G., 1990, *An overview of head-driven bottom-up generation.* In: Dale et al. (eds), 1990: 141–165.

Vater, H., 1992, *Einführung in die Textlinguistik,* UTB/Fink, München.

Viehweger, D., 1983, *Sequenzierung von Sprachhandlungen und Prinzipien der Einheitenbildung im Text.* In: Motsch & Ružička (eds), 1983: 369–394.

Viehweger, D., 1987, Grundpositionen dynamischer Textmodelle, *Linguistische Studien 164,* Reihe A, 1 ff, Berlin.

Viehweger, D., 1991, Illokutionsstrukturen und Subsidiaritätsrelationen. *Sprache und Pragmatik, Arbeitsberichte,* (24): 62–76, Lund.

von Hahn, W., 1990, *Analysis and generation of discourse.* In: Schmitz et al. (eds), 1990: 59–70.

von Hahn, W., Hoeppner, W., Jameson, A., Wahlster, W., 1980, *The anatomy of the natural language dialogue system HAM-RPM.* In: Bolc (ed.), 1980:119–253.

von Stutterheim, Ch. 1992, *Quaestio und Textstruktur.* In: Krings & Antos (eds), 1992: 159–171.

Wahlster, W., André, E., Hecking, M., Rist, T., 1989, WIP: Knowledge-based presentation of information. *Report WIP-1,* Deutsches Forschungszentrum für Künstliche Intelligenz, Saarbrücken.

Wachtel, T., 1986, Pragmatic sensitivity in natural language interfaces and the structure of conversation. *Proceedings of the 11th Int. Conference on Computational Linguistics* (COLING 86), 1986: 35–41.

Warner, R. G., 1985, *Discourse connectives in English,* Garland Publishing, New York.

Webber, B. L., 1989, Deictic reference and discourse structure, *Paper no. MS-CIS-89-55, Department of Computer and Information Science,* University of Pennsylvania (PA).

Weber, H. J., 1986, *Faktoren einer textbezogenen maschinellen Übersetzung: Satzstrukturen, Kohärenz- und Koreferenzrelationen, Textorganisation.* In: Bátori & Weber (eds), 1986: 229–261.

Weigand, E., 1989, *Sprache als Dialog. Sprechakttaxonomie und kommunikative Grammatik,* Niemeyer, Tübingen.

Wiegand, H. E., 1983, Nachdenken über wissenschaftliche Rezensionen.

Anregungen zur linguistischen Erforschung einer wenig erforschten Textsorte, *Deutsche Sprache*, (11): 122–137.

Wilks, Y., 1982, *Some thought on procedural semantics*. In: Lehnert & Ringle (eds), 1982: 495–516.

Wilks, Y., 1985, Text structures and knowledge structures, *Quaderni di semantica*, 6 (2): 335–344.

Winograd, T., 1972, *Understanding natural language*, Academic Press, New York.

Winograd, T. and Flores, F., 1986, *Understanding computers and cognition. A new foundation for design*, Addison-Wesley Publishing Company, Reading.

Wonneberger, R., 1977, *Überlegungen zur Argumentation bei Paulus*. In: Schecker (ed.), 1977: 243–310.

von Wright, G. H., 1968, *An essay in deontic logic and the general theory of action*, North Holland, Amsterdam.

von Wright, G. H., 1977, *Handlung, Norm und Intention. Untersuchungen zur deontischen Logik*, de Gruyter, Berlin, New York.

Wunderlich, D., 1981, *Ein Sequenzmuster für Ratschläge. Analyse eines Beispiels*. In: Metzing (ed.), 1981: 1–30.

Wygotski, L. S., 1972, *Denken und Sprechen*, Fischer, Stuttgart (Orig. 1934, Moskau).

Zammuner, V. L., 1988, *Discourse planning and production: an outline of the process and some variables*. In: Zock & Sabah (eds), Vol II, 1988: 144–160.

Zillig, W., 1980, *Textakte*. In: Tschauder & Weigand (eds), 1980: 189–200.

Zillig, W., 1982a, *Bewerten. Sprechakttypen der bewertenden Rede*, Niemeyer, Tübingen.

Zillig, W., 1982b, *Textsorte 'Rezension'*. In: Detering et al. (eds), Band 2, 1982: 197–208.

Zock, M., Sabah, G. (eds), 1988, *Advances in natural language generation. An interdisciplinary perspective*. Vol. I, II, Pinter, London.

Zuck, J. G., Zuck, L. V., 1984, Scripts: an example from newspaper texts, *Reading in a foreign language*, 21 (1): 147–155.

Index

action 6, 19, 22, 23, 52, 54, 62, 118, 170
  action structure 9, 48
  action theory 22, 29, 66
  language as action 1, 59
  linguistic action 3, 9, 23, 53, 54, 55, 67
    see speech act, text action
addressees 15, 43, 171
  see reader
alterity 27, 127, 128, 130
ALTERNATING 154
argumentation 46, 101f, 118, 123
ASSERTING 6, 22, 24, 63, 64f, 69, 93, 94, 95, 101ff, 138, 171
attribute-value-pairs 69
AUTOKOCH 19, 30, 73

case role 22, 72f, 108
CHAINING 5, 7, 123, 132, 142ff, 162
change 124, 133, 134, 137, 147
cognition 6, 13, 44, 79
  social cognition 1, 34
coherence 10, 13, 14, 18, 25, 26, 40, 46, 78, 94, 112ff
collocation 95
  collocation chains 11, 94, 126
communication 1, 3, 8, 9, 18, 20, 29, 39, 62, 78, 139
  communicative action 34, 55, 59, 81
  communicative knowledge 38
  communicative strategies 10, 12
  communicative structure 38, 171
complexity 33, 112
composition 4, 5, 13, 15, 25, 67, 119, 171
  composition blocks 125

compositional principles 70
compositional strategies 10, 12, 131f
connectivity 11, 18, 25f, 112, 124ff, 148, 172
  connectivity chain (COC) 28, 128
  connectivity form (CONFO) 28, 157ff, 160ff, 172
  connectivity frame (COF) 28, 128
  connectivity marker 130f, 146, 148
  connectivity pair (COP) 28, 128
  connectivity scope 130, 144, 155
  connectivity structure 14, 18, 68, 127f, 173
connector 68, 125, 148, 149
construction
  in computational modeling 33
  object construction 2, 20, 60, 72, 77, 133, 147, 150, 154, 171
context change 53f, 57, 60
contiguity 49, 82
continuity 133, 147
CONTRA 16
COPYING 148ff

DESCRIBING 6, 21, 24, 63, 64f, 69, 93, 94, 95, 96ff, 123, 138, 171
directionality 112, 120
discourse
  discourse marker 26, 125
  discourse structure 39
  see text structure
dominance 41, 57
dynamic aspects 16, 30, 40, 49, 50ff

ellipses 36
enumeration 143, 144, 146

EPICURE 16, 30, 48
EVALUATING 6, 22, 24, 63, 64f, 69, 93, 94, 95, 103ff, 123, 138, 171
expansion 5, 68, 118, 119, 122, 132, 140, 171
expectation structure 18, 76f

focus 16, 27, 113, 122
    focus of attention 40
    focus spaces 42
frame 76, 78, 139
    book frame 82ff
    frame theory 20, 78
    frame properties 38f
    reference frame 19, 20, 61, 74, 75, 86
FRAMING 5,7, 123, 132, 137ff, 161
functionality 33f

illocution 4, 54, 61ff, 92f, 118, 120, 123, 127, 133, 137
inference 15, 16, 76
information flow 17
information processing 33f, 53, 55, 64
intention 40, 41, 48, 53ff, 57
interaction 2, 20, 21, 25, 30, 53, 55, 56, 60, 92ff, 113
inventories 61, 67, 94, 95, 103, 135, 148, 171

KING 12, 35
KLEIST 16, 19, 30, 39, 42, 51, 74, 80
knowledge
    domain knowledge 18, 39, 49, 82
    knowledge base (data base) 15, 18, 44, 50, 55, 64, 72, 107
    knowledge representation 80, 82
    knowledge structure 36
    knowledge telling 87
    knowledge types 9, 38, 42, 77, 171
    linguistic knowledge 39, 51
    semantic knowledge 38, 79
    text knowledge 8ff, 36, 40, 51

landmark 43
language use 32, 58, 71, 114, 170
left–right (LE-RI) 3, 27, 122f, 126, 127, 129, 137, 147, 172
lexicalisation 4, 20, 36, 67, 71, 94, 107, 108, 170

LILOG 12, 73, 74
linearisation 1, 20, 25, 26f, 67, 137
locution 4, 61f, 67
LOKI 12, 74

macrostructure 17
modularity 33, 50

NAOS 13, 30
naturalness 142, 143

object
    communicative object 30, 76, 80
    object in action 30, 36
    object knowledge 30, 38, 49, 79, 93
    object model 21, 80
    physical object 44, 75

PAIRING 5, 7, 123, 124, 132, 147ff, 155f, 163
PAULINE 15,
PENMAN 12, 24, 28, 29, 51
PHRED 12, 35
plan 37, 38, 47, 48, 52
    see text planning
POPEL 13, 51
position indication 145
pragmatic perspective 2, 23, 29, 39
presentation 2, 4, 19, 21, 43, 68
production process 2, 32, 127
profile 134
pronominalisation 36, 49, 113, 149
proposition 4, 5, 12, 17, 27, 64, 87, 119, 147, 169
    propositional attitude 64f, 74
    propositional content 4, 61f, 66, 88, 92, 118
PROTEUS 19, 30

reader 14, 96
recurrence 124, 127, 147, 149
reference 15, 18, 49
    co-reference 115
    referential network 38
representation 33, 37, 48, 108, 126, 136, 172, 173
    in computational modeling 3, 19, 33
    representation schema 34
        see semantic representation, text representation

RESEARCHER 13, 30, 51
rhetorical structure 24, 43, 45f, 115, 116
right attachment 28
right frontier 28
right–left (RI–LE) 3, 27, 123f, 126, 128, 129, 147, 172
role
    see case role, text role
sameness 27, 127, 128, 130, 143
schema 43f, 46, 76, 77, 81, 121
selection 3f, 13, 23, 71ff, 75, 85, 125
semantic knowledge 15, 39, 43, 77
semantic network 16, 38
semantic representation 72f
SEMTEX 12, 27, 30, 51, 73
sentence connection 36, 46
sentence generation 12
sentence orientation 16, 17, 50, 74, 109
sequence operations 132, 133, 135, 136ff, 157, 158
sequencing strategies 3, 91, 125, 127
sequentiality 112, 122
sign functions 21, 24
SPECIFYING 150ff
speech act
    computational modelling of speech acts 14, 23, 52, 55f
    speech act theory 23, 52f, 170
sublanguage 30
systemic grammar 8, 22

target text 32, 76
TEXT 13, 27, 30, 44f, 51
text action 3, 24, 52f, 58f, 67f , 110, 118, 170
    text action grammar 111, 165ff, 171
    text action schema 72, 109, 169, 170
text generation 13, 35ff, 94

text generation systems 30, 35, 37, 46, 77, 79, 107
    vs. text analysis 33
text grammar 10, 26, 71, 107, 109, 111, 165
text list 38, 133, 170
text organisation 5, 10, 36, 44, 165
text planning 13, 37, 47, 118
text production 2, 3, 11ff, 28, 52, 58, 60, 71, 75, 76, 121
text purpose 41, 57
text question
    see thematic question
text representation 11, 13, 38, 69, 117
text role 27, 67, 74, 83f, 103, 118, 130, 133, 171
    text role configuration 87, 91, 92, 135, 154, 169
text segment 21, 40, 41, 57, 115, 129
text space 133, 134, 160, 172
text structure 8, 23, 37, 39, 48, 92
text topic 14ff, 17, 20, 30, 91, 117, 123, 140, 171
text type 18, 21, 29f, 32, 95
text understanding 12, 47, 77
text writing 3, 34
textualisation 60
thematic progression 17
thematic question 18, 19, 61, 74, 85f, 140
topic 16, 17, 18, 27, 77
    see text topic
TOPIC 16, 17,
translation 12, 13, 47
    machine translation 47, 59

WIP 13, 30
WISBER 13,
writing 3, 10, 32, 76, 111, 120, 121, 173

thematic text question. Like this, the text topic and its sequential expansion can be specified with regard to the communicative task. These expansions are the object of text grammar rules, which produce the text thematic structure.

Three focus points emerge for the concretisation:

- How is the domain structured as a reference frame?
  What problems result from the type of object and the type of target text?
  What does an object model 'book' that is suitable for the task of book announcements look like?
  To what extent does the frame theory propose a suitable basis for the development of an object model? (see section 5.1)

- How is the reference frame related to the thematic text question in question?
  How does this relation affect the semantic structure of the sentences (predicate-argument structure)?
  Can a text-oriented structure of recurrent argument roles be produced in this way?
  What role does a thus-derived semantic role structure play for lexical choice?
  Are there specific criteria for the selection of verbs (which are not accorded to reference-oriented approaches)? (see section 5.2)

- In what ways can text sequencing be presented on the basis of the expansion of the text question?
  What restrictions are there with the interactional assignment?
  What are the combined effects with the text-specific information strategies? (see Chapters 6 and 7)

2.4 Text function
(functional relations: text pragmatics)

We consider a communicative text communication community which is not geographically demarcated on the one hand, but interactionally demarcated on the other.
Dialogue is bound to interaction and refers to the question-answer exchange. It is characterized by an expectation structure in the form of the conversational expectation. Moreover, the text itself means a certain textual structure. The structured type of the sequence together with the communicative intent is coordinated.